The Social Aesthetics of Human Environments

Also available from Bloomsbury:

Aesthetics and Nature, by Glenn Parsons
Aesthetics of Care, by Yuriko Saito
Andean Aesthetics and Anticolonial Resistance, by Omar Rivera
Human Beings and their Images, by Christoph Wulf

The Social Aesthetics of Human Environments

Critical Themes

Arnold Berleant

BLOOMSBURY ACADEMIC
LONDON • NEW YORK • OXFORD • NEW DELHI • SYDNEY

BLOOMSBURY ACADEMIC
Bloomsbury Publishing Plc
50 Bedford Square, London, WC1B 3DP, UK
1385 Broadway, New York, NY 10018, USA
29 Earlsfort Terrace, Dublin 2, Ireland

BLOOMSBURY, BLOOMSBURY ACADEMIC and the Diana logo are trademarks of Bloomsbury Publishing Plc

First published in Great Britain 2023
This paperback edition published 2025

Copyright © Arnold Berleant, 2023

Arnold Berleant has asserted his right under the Copyright, Designs and Patents Act, 1988, to be identified as Author of this work.

For legal purposes the Acknowledgments on p. x constitute an extension of this copyright page.

Cover image: YAY Media AS/Alamy Stock Photo

All rights reserved. No part of this publication may be reproduced or transmitted in any form or by any means, electronic or mechanical, including photocopying, recording, or any information storage or retrieval system, without prior permission in writing from the publishers.

Bloomsbury Publishing Plc does not have any control over, or responsibility for, any third-party websites referred to or in this book. All internet addresses given in this book were correct at the time of going to press. The author and publisher regret any inconvenience caused if addresses have changed or sites have ceased to exist, but can accept no responsibility for any such changes.

A catalogue record for this book is available from the British Library.

A catalog record for this book is available from the Library of Congress.

ISBN: HB: 978-1-3503-4932-2
PB: 978-1-3503-4936-0
ePDF: 978-1-3503-4933-9
eBook: 978-1-3503-4934-6

Typeset by Deanta Global Publishing Services, Chennai, India

To find out more about our authors and books visit www.bloomsbury.com and sign up for our newsletters.

Contents

List of Figures	vii
Preface	viii
Acknowledgments	x
Permissions	xii

Part I Wherefore Aesthetics?

1	Questioning Aesthetics	3
2	The Transformations of Aesthetics	8

Part II The Complicit Participant

3	Objects into Persons: The Way to Social Aesthetics	21
4	Duchampian Reflections on Descartes	33

Part III Environment as Cultural

5	The Cultural Aesthetics of Environment	45
6	Some Questions for Ecological Aesthetics	56

Part IV Aesthetic Exploitation

7	A Critical Aesthetics of Disney World	71
8	The Subversion of Beauty	83

Part V Negative Aesthetics

9	Art, Terrorism, and the Negative Sublime	95
10	Reflections on the Aesthetics of Violence	107

Part VI Aesthetics as Cultural Critique

11	The Sublime Troubles of Postmodernism	119

Part VII Aesthetic Community

12	Getting along Beautifully: Ideas for a Social Aesthetics	129
13	Aesthetics and Community	145

Appendix: Publications in Social and Political Aesthetics by
   Arnold Berleant   163
Notes   170
Bibliography   190
Index   197

Figures

1	Johannes Vermeer (1632–75), "Girl with Pearl Earring" (1665)	21
2	Rembrandt (1606–69), "Self-Portrait" (1655)	22
3	Amedeo Modigliani (1884–1920), "Nu couché" (1917)	23
4	Édouard Manet (1832–83), "Dejeuner sur l'herbe" (1863)	23
5	Marcel Duchamp (1887–1968), "Étant donnés," 1° la chute d'eau, 2° le gaz d'éclairage . . . (Given: 1. The Waterfall, 2. The Illuminating Gas . . .); exterior view of Spanish wooden door (1946–66)	35
6	Marcel Duchamp (1887–1968), "Étant donnés," 1° la chute d'eau, 2° le gaz d'éclairage . . . (Given: 1. The Waterfall, 2. The Illuminating Gas . . .), (1946–66)	36
7	Marcel Duchamp (1887–1968), "Roue de bicyslette" (Bicycle Wheel) (1913)	37
8	Marcel Duchamp (1887–1968), "En prévision du bras cassé" (In Advance of a Broken Arm) (August 1964, fourth version, after lost original of November 1915)	38
9	Marcel Duchamp (1887–1968), "Fountain" (1917). Photograph by Alfred Stieglitz (1864–1946)	39
10	Marcel Duchamp (1887–1968), "Nu descendant un escalier n° 2" (Nude Descending a Staircase, No. 2), (1912)	40

Preface

This book was being written long before it was conceived. It is the end point of a lifelong concern with social values as manifested in the arts, in religion, in philosophy, in human experience itself. The chapters that follow were written independently over several decades to the very present. Not only do they represent my most recent work; more importantly, they also document a long-standing and growing concern with the formative presence of the social in aesthetics, as well as in ethics and philosophy, itself. More particularly, this book reflects my thinking on what can be called social aesthetics.

Social aesthetics is a field of inquiry that has been waiting to be discovered, and a literature is gradually emerging. This book reveals the value of its critical presence. The book is also a foray into the domain of what I call "negative aesthetics," aesthetic perception that is not intrinsically rewarding but disconcerting, exploitative, injurious—perceptual experience that uses the aesthetic in negative ways. Lest this seem perverse, we need to be reminded that such occasions constitute a great part of our environmental experience in so-called "advanced" commercial-industrial societies.

The human environment is not only the constructed surroundings in which people carry on their lives; it is also a thoroughly social construct, the product of more or less considered decisions in meeting needs and wants, the outcome of impulse, taste, custom, or immediate considerations. As such, it is inseparable from its inhabitants and its inhabitants from it. That is one reason why I do not speak of "the environment" but always of "environment" *ipso facto*, for every environment as lived is a human environment.

How does this affect our understanding of environment? As the product of human making, environment is never separate from its makers. It does not lie beyond us; it is, so to speak, our home, and like every home, it reflects the spirit and quality of those who fashioned it. As such, environment is intimately social.

It is evident that a social tonality pervades much of my work even when it is not explicit. By identifying critical themes, this book begins to recognize some of the parameters of social aesthetics and to suggest their implications. These chapters all pursue social issues or implicate social themes. They are evidence of the claim that aesthetic values may have social implications and, conversely, that social values may implicate aesthetic ones. There is obviously more to be done here, and it is my hope that others will find the aesthetic a powerful instrument of social critique and carry the inquiry still further.

Also included in this book is an annotated bibliography of my writings on social aesthetics dating back nearly sixty years. It shows the evolution of this concern from an origin in ethical and aesthetic theory to environmental aesthetics, proliferating into a wide-ranging exploration of the aesthetic manifestations of social values. My hope is that this demonstration of the breadth of the social will suggest still other directions and ways to pursue this theme.

Acknowledgments

A concern with social aesthetics is the culmination of my long involvement with the world of the arts. It is a fascination that began in childhood with the devoted study of musical composition and piano performance. A succession of inspiring teachers encouraged my pursuit of instrumental skill and musicianship. As my horizons widened from music making to a fascination with understanding its mysterious hold, the scope of my involvement widened to embrace the other arts and pursue philosophical aesthetics. At the same time, music has remained my paradigmatic experience.

How does social philosophy enter into inquiry in aesthetics? For this I must credit my principal advisor, Marvin Farber, who never lost sight of the social premise of philosophy. I endeavored to show this in my doctoral dissertation on John Dewey's logical theory, and it reappeared in my early papers in ethical theory, which identified the social as an implicit factor. A social aesthetic gradually emerged as an explicit theme as my work on environmental aesthetics enlarged its scope from the natural environment to the urban environment and the human presence in the landscape. This present book makes the social premise explicit largely (but not entirely) in its negative manifestations.

Working under the penumbra of pragmatism in a hostile philosophical landscape, an aesthetics of engagement gradually unfolded, revealing its insights and applicability. One of the earliest to understand and encourage what I was attempting was Mădălina Diaconu, who immediately recognized the importance of the phenomenological concern with the directness of sensory perception and with whom I quickly developed an ease of cognitive understanding and communication. I was encouraged in these explorations by my Finnish colleagues, especially Yrjö Sepänmaa, whose commitment to the broader, social scope of environment in his concern with civility confirmed my explorations in that direction. There are others whose confidence in the value of my work buoyed my spirits: Krystyna Wilkowszewska, Cheryl Foster, Katya Mandoki, Cheng Xiangzhan, Max Ryynänen, Aleksandra Łukaszewicz, and Giovanni Mateucci notable among them. The encouragement and support of these remarkable scholars did much to confirm my confidence in the soundness of my elaboration of an aesthetics of engagement. Others, both students and colleagues, recognized the importance of my leading insights, and to them I owe the encouragement that only genuine support can provide.

I am particularly grateful for the sympathetic response of my editor, Colleen Coalter, and the support of her able assistant Suzie Nash. I am indebted to the reader of my completed manuscript for the careful attention and suggestions that were offered. Finally, these acknowledgments would not be complete without recognizing the careful and devoted contributions to the preparation of this book by Lynnie Dall Lyman. She has for many years assisted my research with patience and ingenuity, helping me overcome technical difficulties and practical obstacles with equanimity and good humor.

I must express special gratitude to my long-time colleague and friend Yuriko Saito. Her encouragement, support, and counsel have been the mainstay of my professional efforts over many years, and her wise judgment has been my standard.

Like all of my writing, this book reflects the influence of the literate sensibility and cognitive acumen of my wife, Riva Berleant. She has always served as my touchstone in evaluating and elaborating my ideas. Her scope of knowledge and penetrating judgment helped keep my searches and speculations on track. I have long benefited from her extraordinary knowledge and steadfast support, and this book is gratefully dedicated to her.

To all my warm gratitude.

Arnold Berleant
Castine, Maine, 2022

Permissions

The author gratefully acknowledges permissions granted by the journals and original publishers of the chapters that appear in this book.

"Transformations in Art and Aesthetics." In *Aesthetics of Everyday Life, East and West*, edited by Liu Yuedi and Curtis L. Carter, 2–13. Newcastle upon Tyne: Cambridge Scholars Publ., 2014.

"Objects into Persons: The Way to Social Aesthetics." *Aesthetics Between Art and Society: Perspectives of Arnold Berleant's Postkantian Aesthetics of Engagement. Espes* 6, no. 2 (2017): 9–18.

"Duchampian Reflections on Descartes." *Festschrift Liber Amicorum for Arnold Berleant. Popular Inquiry* 10 (2022): 6–10.

"The Cultural Aesthetics of Environment." *Annals for Aesthetics*, Fiftieth Anniversary Issue 46B (2010): 39–50.

"Some Questions for Ecological Aesthetics." *Environmental Philosophy* 13, no. 1 (Spring 2016): 123–35.

"The Critical Aesthetics of Disney World." *Journal of Applied Philosophy* 11, no. 2 (1994): 171–80.

"The Co-optation of Sensibility and the Subversion of Beauty." Filozofski vestnik XXXVI, no. 1 (2015).

"Art, Terrorism and the Negative Sublime." In *Sensibility and Sense: The Aesthetic Transformation of the Human World*. Exeter: Imprint Academic, 2010.

"Reflections on the Aesthetics of Violence." *Contemporary Aesthetics*, guest editor Emmanouil Aretoulakis, Special Volume 7 (2019).

"The Sublime Troubles of Postmodernism." *Arts &* Cultural Studies Review (Przegląd Kulturoznawczy) 4 (2021).

"Getting Along Beautifully: Ideas for a Social Aesthetics." In *Aesthetics and Environment, Variations on a Theme*. Farnham and Burlington, VT: Ashgate, 2005.

"Aesthetics and Community." *Journal of Value Inquiry* 28 (1994): 257–72.

Part I

Wherefore Aesthetics?

1

Questioning Aesthetics[*]

Inquiry in Aesthetics

Aesthetic inquiry originated in the effort to recognize and understand the distinctive experiences of value in nature and in the arts. While long a matter of interest, aesthetics was identified as a discipline in Western philosophy only in the latter half of the eighteenth century. In the following century and with increasing frequency, new directions in the arts, in combination with dramatic social changes, led to the proliferation of innovations in media, style, and content. These changes raised doubts about the legitimacy of those developments and stimulated speculation about their significance. This process has continued to the present day with growing intensity, raising questions about the identity of art, its experience, and its value, and about the very enterprise of aesthetics.

The title of this chapter could then be read as an invitation to critique the value and appreciation of art and nature and to question the practice of aesthetics as a scholarly discipline. Is there a distinctive contribution that aesthetic inquiry can make? Does art have a unique identity? Can it be defined? What is its relation to artistic practice? Can aesthetics contribute to our understanding of radical changes in artistic style and practice? How subservient has aesthetics been to religious and moral strictures, to social conventions, and to fashionable academic ideologies? How does it bear on innovations in style, content, materials, and uses of and in the arts? What is its relation to the practices of artists in different media and traditions, past as well as present? Such a critique could serve a useful purpose, to be sure, in aiding our understanding and appreciation, but it could easily lead to quibbling rather than to illumination and devolve into academic platitudes.

---

[*] This chapter is based on a presentation at the conference, "Questioning Aesthetics," held at the Rhode Island School of Design on March 11, 2016.

But questioning aesthetics can go further by pursuing a critique of the academic practice of aesthetics as a scholarly discipline. This would query its scope and its limitations, condemn its subservience to social convention and academic fashion, and lament over its estrangement from the practices of artists. In the effort to identify the place of aesthetic inquiry, it is often observed that the word itself was taken directly from the Greek *aisthēsis*, perception by the senses. From this we might claim that aesthetic inquiry has the obligation to engage with the very ground of sensory experience and to consider the forms, structures, and meanings that have been formed on that ground. And because aesthetics rests on sense experience, it is foundational as well as primary.[1] This places an aesthetics that questions on the most fundamental level of inquiry. Such inquiry, foundational and formative, thus suggests a questioning of aesthetics that comes from the fact that aesthetics is grounded in sense perception. This could go still deeper and farther through its concern with the primacy of sense experience. Sensory experience is fundamental in both aesthetics and the arts, and it has the capacity to be deeply critical. Perceptual experience is never pure sensation but is thick with associations, history, and meaning, as well as somatic memory.

There is, then, an adjectival meaning in a questioning aesthetics. It considers aesthetics as an inquiry that questions by its very nature, aesthetic questioning, aesthetics as a distinctive kind of critical query. Here its scope is boundless, and aesthetics quickly becomes a critique of our sensible perception of the human world—of its institutions, its practices, its justices and injustices, its sense of things, all on the basis of the perceptual conditions they inhabit, entail, and promote. What might such a critique reveal? Where might it lead if aesthetics became the questioner? What is an aesthetics that questions?

It is clear that questioning aesthetics can mean several distinct things. One consists in raising questions about aesthetics as a field of inquiry. Where does aesthetics belong in the domain of scholarship? What issues should aesthetics be concerned with? What values does aesthetics center around and certify? How does their relevance vary? What kind of theoretical account best captures the workings of the aesthetic? Questioning aesthetics here means questioning the discipline, a purgative process that is useful for any field of inquiry.

But what, in contrast, is the peculiar character of the aesthetic that places things in question? How does aesthetics question? What kind of questioning is aesthetics especially capable of undertaking? It is, I think, a questioning that judges by an aesthetic standard. That is, it starts from sensible experience and evaluates things by perceptual criteria. Of what, specifically, is aesthetics an appropriate critique?

This adjectival meaning assigns a critical function to aesthetic inquiry. It suggests that aesthetic inquiry can provide the grounding for a critique of practices by their consequences for the sensible world of human life. Here is the basis of an inquiry into social and political policies and practices. An implicit humanism colors such a critique, for the qualitative, perceptual richness of experience becomes the standard of judgment. In a sense, these two meanings of "questioning aesthetics" may be inseparable because a questioning aesthetics suggests a direction in responding to the question of what aesthetics is. The chapters in this book exemplify the capacity of aesthetics to provide the basis for a critical evaluation of social practices.

A Questioning Aesthetics

That this not seem too convoluted, let me suggest how questioning of and by aesthetics relates to the human environment, to forms of engagement, and to promoting sustainability. Both engagement and sustainability embody ethical concerns, the first for the contribution of aesthetic experience to the quality of living and the second for ways of life that maintain a balance of production and consumption, of use and replenishment, a balance that is increasingly disrupted and threatened to the point of rendering the human future precarious. Our faith in a technological fix for the ills of excess has reached the blank wall of impossibility when exhausted resources cannot be replenished and environmental damage cannot be reversed. We are facing the fact that we cannot insulate ourselves from the consequences of unrestrained environmental consumption and thoughtless environmental depredation. The fact is that we have become consumers of environment and are eviscerating the very ground of our sustenance. Hence we must confront the inescapable criterion of sustainability, which includes a concern for attending to the aesthetic values inherent in the survival of civilizations that are more than simply biological persistence and embody values that are necessarily human but also humane. Indeed, the very subject of survival requires a concern for environment, just as the survival of human civilization requires safeguarding aesthetic, qualitatively perceptual values to achieve a global civilization that is both ecologically sound and morally humane.

A social dimension implicit in aesthetic values appears in many forms. I identify these as "themes" in the chapters that follow. The ones I have chosen to exemplify are critical in the sense that they call attention to or take issue with current practices that diminish human well-being by negating aesthetic values.

Positive themes that have both social and aesthetic import are possible, as in practices that exemplify social harmony, cultural creativity, cooperation, and generosity. These may be implicit here or notable by their absence. Moreover, the social fuses with the ethical in multiple forms so that these themes might be conceived as a mode of social ethics. While more and different values are surely implicated, it is necessary to assert the critical place of the aesthetic. Concern for aesthetic values offers the basis for insight that allows a vigorous critique of harmful practices that are revealed in studies of the aesthetics of community, of mental health practices, and of education, to cite just a few. Here the quality of sensory perception becomes the criterion for evaluative judgment.

This suggests answers to the challenges of questioning aesthetics and for several reasons. One lies in challenging the tradition that limits aesthetic value to natural beauty and the arts. While these may be paradigmatic modes of aesthetic gratification, a fulfilling environment embraces more than dramatic scenery and accommodating landscape design. It denotes a contextual condition that implicates and includes the human percipient. Environment is a collective term for the multiple settings of human life activity in their dystopic forms as well as in their benign ones.

It is essential, then, to recognize that environment is not an external, separate place or phenomenon. And the arts are more than objects and occasions for delectation; they can enter into the very substance of human life experience. Both the arts and environment may offer conditions for aesthetic engagement. So the second form of aesthetic questioning, a questioning aesthetics, introduces the need for normative criteria. It invites us to identify, in the range of aesthetic perception, values that are negative and harmful in environmental experience. Aesthetic questioning can also assist us in identifying those aesthetic values that enlarge and enrich our life experiences and lead us into harmony with the world we have created and inhabit.[2]

Sensible Experience

In sum, we must recognize that a questioning aesthetics concerns the central place of sensible experience. Sensory perception is foundational and carries the capacity to be deeply critical. For sense experience is never pure sensation but is filled with associations, history, somatic memory, and meaning. Because aesthetics rests on sense experience, it is foundational as well as primary. The chapters in this book exemplify the capacity of aesthetic inquiry to provide the grounding for a critical evaluation of social practices.

A social dimension implicit in aesthetic values appears in many forms. The themes I have chosen to exemplify these values are critical in calling attention to or taking issue with current practices that employ aesthetic values as vehicles to diminish human well-being. Positive uses are also possible, as themes that incorporate practices exemplifying social harmony, cooperation, and open generosity. In multiple forms the social fuses with the ethical so that these practices might be conceived equally as modes of social ethics. Often other values may be more apparent and the aesthetic likely to be obscured. Aesthetic inquiry, however, offers a revelatory perspective that can encourage a vigorous critique of harmful social practices. Studies in the aesthetics of community, the aesthetics of mental health practices,[3] the aesthetics of education, and other forms of social practice would reveal systematic ignorance and abuse of aesthetic possibilities in perceptual experience. While the values inherent in the beautiful in nature and art are exemplary, they represent the magical possibilities of aesthetic fulfillment, for sensory perception is embedded in all experience and so, too, then, is aesthetic value.

So it is that a questioning aesthetics gives aesthetic values and interests central importance, for the ubiquity of aesthetic perception implicates the full range of sensible experience. And the normative question encourages issues concerning the negative domains of perceptual experience and the necessity for the aesthetic critique of environment. A questioning aesthetics is therefore fundamental, for it promotes inquiry grounded in and on our perceptual world. When aesthetics questions, everything must be prepared to answer.

2

The Transformations of Aesthetics

Recent decades have witnessed a dramatic broadening in the scope of aesthetic inquiry. No longer focused exclusively on the arts and natural beauty, the mainstream of aesthetics has entered a delta from which its flow has spread out into many channels before reaching the ocean of civilization. Several decades ago, environmental aesthetics began to attract interest and has grown to be an important focus of present-day inquiry in aesthetics. Along with environmental ethics, it has become part of the broader scope of environmental studies and the environmental movement in general. This expansion has continued, interpreting environment not only as natural but also as social.

Similarly, the arts, themselves, have displayed a succession of changes over the past century and a half, increasingly rejecting traditional paradigms of representation and incorporating the everyday world into their subject matter and practices, along with active participation by their audiences. The aesthetic has further extended into social relations and practices, into political critique, into everyday aesthetics, and into urban aesthetics. It would seem that art has overstepped all boundaries, boundaries between art and nonart, between artist and perceiver, between art and life.

Scholars committed to the study of the fine arts and traditional forms of natural beauty may consider this enlargement of the arts and extension of aesthetics a corruption of standards. This, of course, ignores the fact that, as an area of scholarship, aesthetics is of comparatively recent origin, only beginning formally with Baumgarten's *Aesthetica* in 1750. Less dogmatic scholars may take these changes worth inquiry in their own right and perhaps signifying a change in the condition of aesthetics. I should like to the follow this second course here, for I think that these developments signify not only greater inclusiveness but also a fundamental alteration in the nature of aesthetic inquiry, itself. Put more directly and succinctly, the scope of aesthetics has changed from an aesthetics of objects to an aesthetics of experience, an aesthetics of sensibility. This essay proposes an account of how this has come about and what it signifies.[1]

The Transformations of Art

Developments in the visual arts since the late nineteenth century display a fascinating succession of movements and styles. Among the most notable movements are Impressionism, Post-Impressionism, Fauvism, Expressionism, Cubism, Futurism, Surrealism, Dada, Abstract Art, Pop Art, Op Art, and Conceptual Art. These changes provide a surprising array of encounters for the museumgoer and rich material for the art historian. They are, however, more than changes in style, and they display more than degrees and variations in representation and abstraction. These changes seem to puzzle the mind as they dazzle the eye, posing seemingly bizarre innovations that present insoluble obstacles to efforts at understanding the meaning of modern art and frustrating attempts at determining its boundaries. Let us cast an eye over this succession of movements to see if there is some underlying logic to their sequence.

Impressionism, to begin, is usually explained as an attempt at capturing the fleeting effects of light, especially sunlight, on objects and landscapes. Things seem to lose their solidity and appear to vibrate with solar energy, dissolving into vaguely defined, multicolored hues as the atmosphere is charged by sunlight. With Post-Impressionism, objects regained solidity and radiated a strong presence, while Fauvism flourished with untamed brushwork and intense hues. In Expressionism objects were colored in the rich tones of powerful emotion, but this was then replaced by the dissolution of solidity into the geometrical structures of Cubism, sometimes broken up into their parts, rendered multiperspectivally, or made transparent by displaying their inner structure. Futurism, in contrast, transmuted the solidity of objects into the disconcerting dynamism of frenetic motion. With the iconoclasm of Dada, ridicule was cast at the once noble objects of artistic idealization and bourgeois contentment by introducing the prosaic and irreverent into the sanctorum of art, while Surrealism transformed the world of ordinary objects into the bizarre distortions and irrational juxtapositions of dreams.

As the visual arts became emancipated from the constraints of representation, the figurative center of art was increasingly abandoned. Representational subject matter became unimportant and the purely pictorial elements of hue, texture, form, and composition became the source of rich originality. Artists forsook any attempt at capturing the world of objects and used color and form for their visual effect, alone. One could consider Pop Art the antithesis of abstraction, where common objects and commercialized forms take center stage larger than life, or it could be the apotheosis of abstraction, presenting stylized illustrations as purely illustration. Abstraction reappeared in the subtle variation of repeated simple forms for their pulsating effect on the eye, ingeniously exploited by Op Art, while in Conceptual Art the object disappeared from space and became only an imaginative construction.

This kaleidoscopic survey of the modern course of the visual arts may verge on parody, but at the same time it reveals a fascinating process of transfiguration. In this succession of movements one may see imaginative transmutations of the art object under the influence of light, of the eye, of emotion, and of dreams, along with varying degrees of manipulation of the object's structure, its solidity, and its variability under the influence of thought, theory, and imagination. This might be seen as a history of the iconoclasm of the modern artist, constantly defying conventional expectations and traditional modes. That would turn it into an account of art movements that increasingly reject traditional paradigms and incorporate the everyday world and viewer participation into the visual array. This history could then be read as an account of the vagaries of artistic imagination coupled with unbridled irreverence. To be sure, one can often find such expressions in manifestations of the artistic temperament and its inclination to notoriety.

However, I should like to suggest another, very different reading. This is to consider the course of modern art as a narrative of transformation, not of objects but of experiences. Indeed, these developments may signify a shift from object-based art to experience-based art. Such an account displays not so much a sequence of distorted or abandoned objects as a sequence of ways of seeing. The object becomes less important as the visual effect increases in significance until, in abstract and conceptual art, the object, as such, disappears entirely. From its dissolution into light and color in Impressionism, into the tactile sense of its pure physicality and weight in Post-Impressionism, its transformation into a stimulus for evoking an emotional response in Expressionism, its structural dissolution in Cubism, its physical reduction to movement in Futurism, its replacement by parody in Dada, its oneiric transmutation in Surrealism and into an ocular stimulus in Op Art, its disappearance in abstract art in favor of the sensibility of pictorial qualities, the lampooning effect of its parody in Pop Art—all these made the object less important if not unimportant. In its place is art's relation to the spectator.

But to put it this way is actually misleading because it masks a crucial difference: the audience in art is no longer a spectator but has become rather a participant and co-creator, absorbing the visual or textual materials, responding at times physically to its stimulation, and intellectually as well as emotionally to its social critique (i.e., Futurism's glorification of war, Dada's critique of bourgeois society), and, by its participation, activating the art object. It is essential here to understand that this transformation in the arts did not turn appreciation into pure subjectivity, into psychological effects disconnected from the body, the art work, and the situation. Rather these arts demanded sharpened awareness and acute perceptual attention to their sensible qualities. They required recognizing the effects of art as conscious bodily experience, physical as well as mental. Often this was required by the perceptual demands of the art work for active participation in an appreciative process that collaborates with the artistic one. Indeed, these traditionally separate functions were fused in experiencing art. We have, in short, the transformation of an art of objects into an art of experiences.

What does all this signify? To respond to this question, let me turn to the scholarly analogue of the artistic process.

The Transformations of Aesthetic Theory

While art has undergone a series of transformative changes, aesthetic theory has largely remained mired in the framework and concepts of the eighteenth century, grounded mainly in Kant's aesthetics. I have written at length elsewhere about the persistence of obsolescent concepts such as aesthetic disinterestedness, contemplation, purposiveness without purpose, the quest for universality, and the subjectivity of aesthetic judgments, as well as questioning distinctions such as between pure and dependent beauty, the sensible and the supersensible, and the separation of aesthetics and morality.[2] Important as these ideas may have been two centuries ago in establishing aesthetics within the framework of a systematic philosophy and giving legitimacy and independence to the arts, these concepts have become increasingly irrelevant to the actual practices of artists and the appropriate appreciative experiences of the art public.

Despite being constrained by obsolescent and increasingly irrelevant aesthetic concepts, aesthetic inquiry has, in recent decades, pursued a number of directions that reflect the expanded scope of the arts and aesthetic appreciation. The art public has become more willing to accept the use of innovative art materials and concepts and the widening range of art experiences that extend beyond the museum and into the home, the workplace, the street, and the field. More significant still is the complete alteration of aesthetic appreciation from the receptive contemplation of objects to an active aesthetic engagement with the materials and conditions of art works. Nor is it any longer clear or even possible to separate aesthetic value from moral value as the social significance and uses of art and the aesthetic have come into greater prominence. Further, the increasingly political utilization of the arts belies their traditional exclusivity.

Along with innovations in the arts has come an enlargement of the scope of aesthetic experiences. This has encouraged new interests and directions in both artistic activity and aesthetic experience over the last several decades, and these changes have stimulated aesthetic theorizing. Among the new domains of theoretical investigation are environmental aesthetics, the intersection of aesthetics and politics, social aesthetics including relational aesthetics, and everyday aesthetics. The progressive broadening of the scope of aesthetic inquiry away from the conventional venues of traditional art began by focusing attention on environmental aesthetics.[3] It started with a return of attention to nature and an exploration of modes and conditions of appreciation that differ greatly from the contemplation of discrete objects and distant scenes. Walking in the woods, paddling a stream, hiking in a wilderness area, driving down a highway or along a rural road in an agricultural landscape, and sailing a boat were recognized as occasions for aesthetic pleasure, occasions where an intrinsic part of the enjoyment lies in entering into some activity in the landscape. At the same time, recognition grew that aesthetic engagement in environment embraces more than the appreciation of nature: a large part of environmental experience in the developed world takes place in cities. Urban aesthetics began to enter into environmental discourse and, including the built environment, expanded the conditions and possibilities of appreciation. Even outer space became a subject for aesthetic awareness.[4]

Recognizing an aesthetic interest in environment has had powerful implications for aesthetic inquiry more generally. It means that aesthetic inquiry had to concern itself not only with art objects but also with aesthetic situations. And this shift was not a conceptual one but a substantive one. The focus of appreciation was no longer on a discrete object, that is, binary, but within a situation, that is, contextual. And the traditional dualistic assumption of Western philosophy that considered appreciation a subjective response to an external object became increasingly challenged and irrelevant. I have proposed replacing that obsolete model with the concept of *aesthetic engagement* in order to reflect the embeddedness of the appreciator in every environmental context. A related development is the formulation primarily by Chinese environmental aestheticians of ecological aesthetics or eco-aesthetics.[5]

Once environment gained aesthetic legitimacy, it led to other enlargements of the venues of aesthetic appreciation. One of these lies in discerning aesthetic values in social situations, where the aesthetic is encountered in settings involving different forms of human relationships, such as friendship, family, and love. Aesthetic values are also present in other associations, as well, but often in a negative form. Indeed, negative aesthetic values are common in urban life, commercial situations, voluntary associations, and, indeed, all forms of social relations. Such contexts have led to recognizing perceptual experiences common in social situations that are negative in character and to identifying such forms of aesthetic negativity as an aesthetic affront, as aesthetic pain, and aesthetic depravity. Acknowledging negativity in aesthetic experience has led to broadening the scope of aesthetics to include the full range of negative values in perceptual experience. And because these values identify harmful practices, aesthetic theory merges with ethics to form a powerful instrument for social criticism.[6]

A similar development in aesthetic theory is the idea of relational aesthetics that was advanced by the French critic Nicolas Bourriaud.[7] Applied to the work of a number of contemporary artists, relational aesthetics recognizes that their art creates a social space, a context for human relationships. The art work then becomes an occasion for human interactions and the audience joins in to become a community.[8] This is a genuine enlargement in our understanding of aesthetic experience, but under the influence of traditional aesthetic theory, the art world has co-opted and undermined the insight of relational aesthetics by the practice of replacing the term "relational aesthetics" with "relational art," thus turning a situation into an object and entirely evading the point of relational aesthetics. Its insight remains valid, nevertheless.

Political aesthetics is yet another broadening of inquiry closely allied with social aesthetics. Jacques Rancière has called attention to the political implications of sensibility: its distribution, its control, and its uses, and he develops this in the service of an argument for radical democracy.[9] Going about this from another direction, Crispin Sartwell has interpreted the force of political ideology from the fact that it is actually an aesthetic system, and he sees politics operating by creating an aesthetic environment.[10] Employing similar materials, Davide Panagia has related the force of an idea to the bodily sensations that accompany it. He finds sensation at the source of political thought and the aesthetic as the source of political action.[11] My recent work has joined closely both the social and the political implications of the aesthetic. Recognizing that the heart of the aesthetic lies in sensibility, I have claimed that developing the awareness and capacity of aesthetic sensibility leads to immensely broader and richer social experience. At the same time, through an awareness of negative aesthetics and the negative sublime, aesthetic sensibility provides a powerful tool for criticism by recognizing the human consequences of exploitative commercial and political practices.[12]

Perhaps the best-known development to emerge from the liberation and expansion of aesthetic experience is the aesthetics of everyday life. Although there is presently a flowering of work on everyday aesthetics, the possibility of aesthetic gratification in ordinary objects and events has long been recognized, even if degraded and dismissed by prevalent philosophical theory. Widely valued by poets, especially Romantic poets and those in Asian traditions, the aesthetic in everyday situations has also been recognized by novelists.[13] It may be most convenient, though, to locate its contemporary intellectual origins in John Dewey's *Art as Experience*.[14] In that book Dewey argued against the separation of art from life by basing aesthetic experience on the biological and cultural conditions of human life. He located the aesthetic, not in an internalized awareness of sensation and feeling but in "a complete interpenetration of self and the world of objects and events."[15] Further, Dewey maintained that "the esthetic . . . is the clarified and intensified development of traits that belong to every normally complete experience."[16]

I shall not attempt a chronology of the development of the present interest in the aesthetics of everyday life. Instead, let me mention some significant stages in its emergence. An important source came from the innovations that were occurring in the arts in the mid-twentieth century. A prime influence was the work of the American composer and theorist, John Cage. Experimental and innovative, Cage's interest in aleatoric (chance) music became widely known through his piano work of 1952, $4'33''$, which consisted in attending to the chance sounds that occurred during that interval of time. Happenings, a predecessor of present-day performance art that originated in the 1950s, eliminated the separation between the art work and the viewer, who became instead a participant in the work, which often comprised the unscripted, chance events of an ordinary situation.

Such innovative developments in the arts had a profound effect on concurrent work in aesthetics. Beginning in the 1990s, a series of steps in the expansion of aesthetic appreciation were taken that resolutely rejected the traditional separation of art from life activities in the conviction that the scope of the arts has no limits. Two books published in 1992 made an extended case for a broader and more inclusive understanding of the aesthetic that incorporated all activities within the purview of art. David Novitz's *The Boundaries of Art*[17] abjured all limits to art and extended the aesthetic to personal and social relationships and from these to politics. Arnold Berleant's *Art and Engagement*[18] extended an argument he had first made in 1970 for reconstructing aesthetics under the influence of innovative developments in the contemporary arts.[19] That argument explored the philosophical implications of considering aesthetic appreciation in both traditional and contemporary arts as active perceptual engagement. Two decades later, his book elaborated a theoretical position for the enlargement of aesthetic experience that would include the objects and events of daily life based on the practices and experience of the arts, themselves.

Since these publications, there has been a proliferation of work developing and detailing the unconstrained extension of the aesthetic. The aesthetics of everyday life is the most recent stage of this progressive broadening in the scope of aesthetic appreciation and inquiry that had begun with environmental aesthetics, and important work has already appeared. *The Aesthetics of Everyday Life* is a collection published in 1995 that included essays on such topics as social aesthetics, the aesthetics of place, unplanned building, landscape, sport, weather, smells and tastes, and food.[20] Katya Mandoki's *Everyday Aesthetics* (2007), an English-language version of a book that had originally been published in Spanish in 1994, was the first extended treatment of the subject.[21] *Everyday Aesthetics* is a far-reaching study of aesthetic theory with extraordinary scope and originality that centers around the crucial role of aesthetics in the contemporary highly technological and complex societies in which we now live. This was soon followed by another volume with the same title and an equally distinctive and original focus, Yuriko Saito's *Everyday Aesthetics*.[22] Richly informed by the author's native Japanese culture and her long experience teaching at a school of art and design, this book details the pervasive presence and influence of the aesthetic over the many facets of daily life, remarkable and unremarkable alike. The most recent addition to these extended treatments is Thomas Leddy's *The Extraordinary in the Ordinary: The Aesthetics of Everyday Life*.[23] Leddy develops an extensive critical review of much of the literature, as well as the current scholarly debates, leading to his own contribution in the form of a phenomenological approach to aesthetics. He proposes the concept of "aura" to identify the quality an object can have when experienced as aesthetic. It is a quality that is not confined to art objects but to the culturally conditioned experiences of daily life.

Aesthetic Engagement

I have depicted a broad landscape on these pages, rather like one of Constable's wall-sized canvases, and I hope it shares its realism in offering a historical and theoretical perspective on developments in art and aesthetics. For besides the greater range of interests and applications in aesthetics, these developments have demonstrated the obsolescence of traditional concepts. To close, let me suggest some implications that emerge from the trends in aesthetic experience and theory I have been detailing here.

To begin, it is clear that there is a sharp dislocation between the practices of many contemporary artists, their creations, and the experience and behavior of the art public and the strictures of aesthetic theory, especially as it had been formulated by Kant. That theory is grounded in a separation between the subjectivity of aesthetic experience and the objectivity of the art object, in a separation between beauty and utility, and in the sequestering of the arts and natural beauty in museums and privileged views and away from the ordinary course of human life activities. While such a theory may be thought to honor the special aesthetic forcefulness of the noblest artistic creations, it does so at the cost of severely constricting the scope of aesthetic appreciation, and this belies the prevalence of aesthetic value in human cultures. Is it possible to have a theoretical frame that retains the validity of the powerful experience of great art and awesome natural scenes while, at the same time, recognizing and accounting for the fact that aesthetic interests pervade every domain of human experience?

I believe that this is indeed possible, and that we need concepts that can accommodate both in proper proportion. These can be developed by enlarging the scope and understanding of aesthetics. First, we need to overcome the fragmentation that results from the many divisions drawn by traditional theory, as between the appreciator of art and the art object, between beauty and utility, and between cognitive and noncognitive experience. We need, in fact, a unifying concept that can admit connections, mutual influences, and reciprocity without sacrificing the aesthetic. Such a concept may be found in the idea of an *aesthetic field*, an idea that embodies the insight that the presence and functioning of aesthetic values occur in a context that encompasses the principal factors that contribute to such experience. The aesthetic field can accommodate artistic innovation and expanded occasions for appreciation at the same time that it enfolds the appreciative experience of the traditional arts. For it embraces the four functional constituents present in all: the objective, the appreciative, the creative, and the performative, none of which is independent of the others.[24]

The central idea in appreciation now becomes *aesthetic engagement*, which recognizes the unqualified participation that active appreciation requires and that the contemporary arts increasingly demand. We also need to recognize that the art object is no longer the sole repository of aesthetic value and to accept that it need not occupy an elevated status. For now the art work can be something of ordinary use or no object at all but a perceptual experience or even only an idea. Nor need it be complete and polished but simply a processive event like much of daily life. The context of appreciation has also changed along with the unity of the art object, both of which now share the incompleteness of ordinary experience. That is why the human environment has become the wider locus of the aesthetic and the context in which specific questions need to be considered. The new landscape of aesthetics invites us to enter.

Part II

The Complicit Participant

3

Objects into Persons

The Way to Social Aesthetics

Figure 1 Johannes Vermeer (1632–75), "Girl with Pearl Earring" (1665). Medium: Oil on canvas. Dimensions: 44.5 cm × 39 cm (17.5 in. × 15 in.). Public Domain. *Source*: Wikimedia Commons

Figure 2 Rembrandt (1606–69), "Self-Portrait" (1655). Medium: Oil on walnut, cut down in size. Dimensions: height 48 cm (18.8 in.); width: 40.6 cm (15.9 in.). Public Domain. *Source*: Wikimedia Commons

Figure 3 Amedeo Modigliani (1884–1920), "Nu couché" (1917). Medium: Oil on canvas. Dimensions: height: 89 cm (35 in.); width: 146 cm (57.4 in.). Public Domain. *Source*: Wikimedia Commons

Figure 4 Édouard Manet (1832–83), "Dejeuner sur l'herbe" (1863). Medium: Oil on canvas. Dimensions: 208 cm × 264.5 cm (81.9 in. × 104.1 in.). Public Domain. *Source*: Wikimedia Commons

Aesthetic Sensibility

Social aesthetics may seem to be a strange combination of terms. People usually associate aesthetics with the arts—their experience, their appreciation, their value. What can this have to do with society except in the most general sense? Actually, this customary way of thinking about aesthetics is needlessly narrow as well as vague. The purview of aesthetics can be broadened to embrace the natural and built environments, and the social environment, as well. Not only do activities concerned with the arts and natural beauty have a place in social life, but the values we recognize in such experiences are found more widely in social experience.

It will be useful to begin explaining this by returning to the meaning of "aesthetics." Definitions do not solve philosophical problems, nor do etymologies. They can, however, help us recover the scope and issues with which we are concerned. As already noted, the word "aesthetics" comes from the Greek word *aisthēsis*, which literally means "perception by the senses." It began to be used in the mid-eighteenth century to refer to philosophical problems concerning the meaning and judgment of beauty in art and nature, although those issues had been discussed by philosophers since classical Greece. It is important to keep the etymology of "aesthetics" in mind in dealing with such questions because it reminds us that sensory experience has a central place in the meaning and value of art and natural beauty.

Another important concept here is "sensibility." Sensibility is at the center of the aesthetic values we ascribe to art and nature. That is because sensibility connotes more than simply sensation; it includes a developed awareness of perceptual experience, something more like perceptual acuity. That is why we can understand aesthetics to involve the philosophical study of both sense experience and its refinement, in brief, as the theory of sensibility. Aesthetic sensibility is a valuable dimension of human experience. Most people have a strong response to the beauty of a colorful sunset and a panoramic landscape. It is also clear that such appreciation need not be limited to nature or to the arts. Acute perceptual awareness can be part of all experience, including social experience. Some of the arts exhibit the aesthetic force of social relations in powerful ways, arts such as theater and film and, perhaps less directly, poetry and the novel. Moreover, a sensitivity to the perceptual nuances in human relationships adds greatly to the richness of social experience, and this sensibility can be called aesthetic.[1]

These experiences are generally called "aesthetic experience." They are regarded as valuable and so may be considered a form of normative experience.

It is important to recognize that acknowledging aesthetic experience as valuable does not commit us to considering such experience as necessarily positive. It is possible, and even common, for aesthetic experiences to be negative to varying degrees, although this is not often recognized or discussed.

Aesthetic appreciation is the valuing of such experience, from basking in the warming brightness of spring sunshine to discerning the weariness in the sitter's eyes in Rembrandt's late self-portraits. Although such experiences are widely had, there is considerable debate about how they are to be understood and explained.

Since the eighteenth century, aesthetic appreciation has commonly been explained by following a cognitive model. On the one side stands the appreciator and on the other the object of appreciation. It is claimed that appreciating an object aesthetically requires that one regard it for its own intrinsic qualities and on its own terms independent of its utility or other extrinsic values. The word usually used to describe this attitude is "disinterested." Kant proposed the concept of disinterestedness to identify the specifically aesthetic character in the appreciation of beauty: appreciating an object for its own sake and not for external reasons or uses. Disinterestedness does not mean lack of interest but rather not having appreciation distracted by outside interests. One should appreciate the object for its own sake, not for its extrinsic value. Disinterestedness thus is a kind of aesthetic objectification. While aesthetic value may be found in practical objects and situations, it is considered to have a lower value than "pure beauty."[2]

Although still widely accepted, disinterestedness has been strongly criticized in recent times for widely disparate reasons. Bourdieu developed a sociological critique of disinterestedness, regarding it as a social construct that is class-oriented, an insidious intellectual basis for bourgeois self-esteem. Disinterestedness, he held, is a means of supporting the social *status quo* by using an aesthetic criterion to mask and justify class taste and its superiority.[3]

I have long been developing an alternative approach to understanding aesthetic value that I call "aesthetic engagement." Rather than using a cognitive model or a sociological analysis to explain aesthetic appreciation, this approach uses an experiential model. It is based on a phenomenological analysis of the direct experience of aesthetic appreciation, an experience commonly had of full participatory involvement in a situation that may include a work of art, a performance, an architectural or environmental location, or a social situation. In aesthetic engagement there is no separation between the components but a continuous exchange in which they act on each other. I call this situation "the aesthetic field."[4]

The aesthetic field recognizes four principal components. There is an appreciator, the person experiencing aesthetic value. Then there is the focus of that appreciation, usually an object such as a work of art, a building, or a landscape. The object, however, need not be physically separate, as in appreciating a poem, a novel, or music, and, indeed, it may even be a mental thought or image, as in conceptual art. Nor need it literally be an object. It is, rather, the point of focused attention. A third component is the activity or event that brings the object of focus into experience: the artist, the processes of nature, or the perceptual act of identifying an object of appreciation, as in found art. Finally, the fourth feature is the factor that activates the field or situation, such as the performer or the engaged perceiver. It is important to note that a performative element is present in all art and aesthetic appreciation, for the appreciator who is actively engaged is, by that fact, "performing" the work by attentively viewing a painting or reading a novel.

This brief account is only a bare outline but it is enough to show the integrative nature of the aesthetic situation and the interconnection and interdependence of all its components. For the aesthetic field is not a combination of separate elements but a single whole.[5] That is what is implied in describing the appreciative experience by the term "engagement." Aesthetic engagement, then, conveys the integrative involvement in the normative experience we call "aesthetic."

While aesthetic appreciation as engagement is, perhaps, more readily associated with our experience of the arts, it is not confined to them, for we can have such appreciation with nature. People are often powerfully affected when encountering natural beauty in a sunrise or sunset, a flower, or a dramatic landscape, but aesthetic appreciation also occurs in other contexts. There is aesthetic value in a fine meal, in the pleasure of driving an automobile that functions perfectly, and in the somatic satisfaction of participating in a group activity, such as a sports team or a social organization. The fact that aesthetic value in these cases is not the only value involved does not diminish its significance but rather recognizes its pervasive presence.

In recent decades, environment has emerged as a major interest in aesthetics. Questions have been raised about what is included in the meaning of environment and how environments can be appreciated aesthetically. Consider first the idea of environment. You will notice that "the" environment is not referred to but simply the term "environment" is used. This is done deliberately because to speak of "the" environment turns environment into an object separate from the perceiver. This practice of objectifying things in order to study them, a cognitive model, is a long-established feature of scientific inquiry. It has obviously had considerable success in the physical sciences and in some practical situations. Whether that approach should be used in the human sciences, however, is open to question.

In my view, the world in which humans participate cannot be entirely separated from the human presence. There is rather a reciprocal relation between people and the things and conditions with which we live. And when environment involves human interests, it must necessarily be understood in relation to humans and not as an array of independent objects. We can find support for this in the work of social psychologists such as Kurt Lewin and J. J. Gibson. Lewin envisioned a social world comprised of vectors of force between participants and the things and conditions with which they interact. These vectors invite particular behaviors, and this led Lewin to call them by the German term *Affördungsqualitäten*, translated into English as "invitational qualities." More recently, the perceptual psychologist J. J. Gibson studied the ways in which the design and appearance of environmental configurations and objects encourage particular responses in human behavior. He called these connections "affordances" for behavior, clearly influenced by Lewin's terminology and resembling his observations. The work of Lewin and Gibson is important and instructive for it suggests that environment is not just open space filled with arrangements of independent objects but rather is a field of forces in compelling relationships of attraction, repulsion, and neutrality or indifference. Environment is, then, a field that includes the human participant.

When environment is experienced aesthetically, sensory features assume primary importance. This is the environmental meaning of aesthetic engagement. The human environment not only includes things in the natural world; it also comprises most significantly humans as individuals and groups in their social and environmental relationships. For the human world is a social world. Moreover, there is an aesthetic dimension in human relations that often goes unrecognized. To point this out does not mean that human relations are always necessarily or primarily aesthetic but that an aesthetic factor may be present and at times may predominate.[6]

The aesthetic occurs as a condition that has different aspects that are depicted in the aesthetic field. The aspect of *focus* is critical here. The human is the center of attention, both perceptually and psychologically, as a physical, biological being and a cultural construction, and as a behavioral entity in our actions and responses.

As the aesthetic of humans becomes more pronounced in experience, it may merge with the moral, since the human presence is the focus of both aesthetic and moral value. For the irreducible value of human being is inseparably moral and aesthetic. There is a moral obligation, indeed a moral compulsion, to preserve and to honor a human life as there is to preserve and honor an outstanding artistic achievement. Their very existence is their aesthetic and moral claim.

Social Aesthetics

It is now easier to see how aesthetic engagement relates to human relations and may, at times, suffuse a social situation. This may occur in group activities when a shared enthusiasm develops that leads to a sense of expansiveness in a common situation and delight in its pursuit. This can be seen in team sports, in choral singing, between individuals in amorous relations, and perhaps in a most negative manifestation, in the total self-abnegation of a terrorist group.[7]

What becomes clear is the pervasiveness of aesthetic engagement and its value in describing aesthetic appreciation both in art and nature and in human relations, as well. In the most general sense, aesthetic engagement occurs in social situations that lie outside the arts when aesthetic perception predominates in social relations. Some psychological theorists have recently identified similar occasions as "direct social perception" (DSP) and "basic empathy" (BE).[8]

The idea of the aesthetic field can be useful here. As we have seen, the aesthetic field describes the context of interacting perceptual forces, and aesthetic engagement may at times characterize the perceptual experience of a social process. When it is an integral part of social relations, aesthetic engagement transforms that process, turning relationships governed by a utilitarian standard that objectifies people into a perceptual context of interdependencies. By recognizing the presence of the aesthetic, its influence can be enhanced by creating conditions that encourage aesthetic engagement. This may be through educational practices and environmental designs that facilitate an awareness of the aesthetic dimension of experience in situations that may be personal, social, natural, or cultural and that transform people as objects into people as persons.

To turn to the paintings presented at the beginning of this chapter, we may ask if these images look any different after having considered the ideas just offered. Do they have anything significant in common? There are, of course, many common features. All the paintings are figurative; all depict people in various places and situations. As art works they were made using similar materials and techniques, and much more that is of varying and perhaps lesser relevance. But there is one feature of each image that has special significance.

Japanese printmakers have noted that there is a location in a print called the "crying point." This is the specific place that brings the entire print together and makes it work, *activates* it, so to speak. What makes the crying point important here is that it is not just a visual feature but the place in a print that evokes a visceral awareness that connects the print to the viewer, the work to its act of appreciation.

Now each of these paintings has a feature that acts in a similar way: the eyes. Each painting is not merely an object that depicts the likeness of the sitter. It invites the viewer to make contact, to engage with that *person*. The eyes in each painting are not just a feature of the face: they *look* at us. They look at and connect with us, and we are led to gaze back at a *person*. The eyes are the crying point, so to say, not just the crying point of the painting but the crying point that activates the aesthetic field in which the painting and the viewer participate. For the eyes create a human relationship in which the image ceases to be simply a likeness, an object, and becomes a person with whom we enter into a relationship. This is a vivid instance of aesthetic engagement.

The aesthetic is not a substance, an object, a quality, or a feeling but the distinctive experiential character of a situation. The aesthetic does not displace the occasion on which it occurs but, so to say, colors it, gives it a special, distinctive tone that we call aesthetic. An environmental situation is no less an environment when it is experienced aesthetically; it acquires a different, distinctive character. What is it that makes a social occasion aesthetic? To answer this question we must return to the field experience that describes the aesthetic.

As noted earlier, aesthetic engagement is an experience that displays four principal aspects: creative, performative, appreciative, and focused. While we can distinguish these aspects, they are not separate but thoroughly interpenetrate each other in aesthetic experience. Such experiences are most widely recognized in our engagement with the arts, but they also occur in different environmental settings, both natural and built, and in everyday life situations. Moreover, as this chapter endeavors to show, the aesthetic may have an often unrecognized presence in a social environment. We can find it coloring the complex features of many social occasions. And when they are strongly present as a perceptual ensemble, we can consider that situation aesthetic.

Consider common social situations that typically evoke conventional, impersonal roles that position people as objects. Education easily devolves into teacher and student, commerce into salesperson and customer, business into representative and client, entertainment into performer and audience, a work environment into supervisor and worker, a medical visit into doctor and patient. These are binary types of relation between people objectified in impersonal roles whose places are occupied by human objects, relationships in which mechanical patterns replace the human exchanges and in which one of the pair is dominant and the other subordinate. How could this be otherwise? How can there be an aesthetic in such relationships? Don't we need these templates to conduct typical human affairs easily and efficiently?

Efficiency, however, is a mechanical value, a value in which the smooth operation of component parts is the mark of success. Yet efficiency is not a human value but a mechanical one. People require time and attention, time to acclimate themselves to the conditions of a situation and adapt to its requirements in order to function easily and well. And the unique value in and of individual people needs to be recognized and honored. How can the aesthetic transform such situations?

The educational process provides another case.[9] What would transforming the student from a receptive object of education into an interested, attentive learner? An aesthetic model would display curiosity about the investigative process underlying the material being studied with interest in how it develops into justifiable knowledge, joining teacher and student in a collaborative quest. Such a situation would exemplify the four functional features of an aesthetic field: the scholar or scientist being the creative factor, the material being studied the focus, the teacher the performative factor, and the student the appreciative one. All join together, sharing their functions in the pursuit of understanding as a perceptual experience. It is important to acknowledge the powerful influence of environmental factors in conducing to aesthetic engagement: space, quiet, visual and physical comfort, and stimulation all contribute. This analysis is, of course, abstract and minimal, but perhaps it shows the interdependent character and condition of aesthetic education.

Efforts are being made to recognize a social aesthetic in medical situations, particularly in patient care.[10] What would change the stereotypical roles of medical professional and patient into an occasion of aesthetic engagement? As in the aesthetic appreciation of art, there is a focus of attention, in this case on the medical situation: the disease, infection, abnormality, disability, or other condition. A professional who is aesthetically aware performs a function by actively pursuing a plan of treatment designed to take into account not only the standard protocols but the particular characteristics, needs, and perceptions of the individual being treated. The term "patient" tends to institutionalize and prescribe a passive role. When aesthetically engaged, the individual undergoing treatment becomes an active participant, a collaborator in the process, understanding and appreciating everything that is done and making every effort to promote the optimum conditions for successful treatment. In this situation, as in all instances of aesthetic engagement, a human exchange takes place on a perceptual level, with eye contact, shared feeling, and interest that is palpable. Environing conditions also play a critical supporting role, where the space and decorative features of the treatment facility are carefully chosen, and distracting ambient sounds and other common disruptive conditions are monitored and modified so as to be conducive to healing.

The aesthetic field can illuminate and transform other social situations: in business, in commerce, in entertainment, and in routine activity involving manual labor or regular, simple patterns of activity. It is important to see the aesthetic not as a mechanical operation but as an experiential, perceptual process in which all four factors reciprocally influence each other. Such active perceptual engagement can transform the experience and influence the outcome. Perceptual awareness in human exchange can transfigure mindless, mechanical action, turning it into an activity of creative engagement. Such a social aesthetic expresses Aristotle's description of true friendship as between "friends [who] wish alike for one another's good."[11]

Social Aesthetics as Engagement

Aesthetic engagement is an experience of aesthetic appreciation that transforms a physical juxtaposition into a social relationship in which a personal encounter takes place. It projects the aesthetic connection we can experience in the arts into our engagement with other people and with things, as well, turning our encounter with separate, impersonal objects into personal relationships.[12] Moreover, the paintings with which we began are not anomalous cases peculiar to portrait and figure painting; in a manner of speaking every painting looks back. So does every art work. So, too, can every "thing" in the human world. This is implicit in the idea of aesthetic engagement and why it is central to a social aesthetic. Indeed, a social aesthetic shows us how to create and live in a human world: how to humanize the world. By centering on the aesthetic, we see how human relations may resemble the experience of the holy in religion, the recognition of the sanctity of human life in ethics, and the ultimate value of the individual in the philosophy of democracy. The aesthetic embodies the defining value in each.

We have now traversed the conceptual stages that lead to an understanding of social aesthetics. Beginning by recognizing sense perception as central in aesthetic experience, we came to see how a developed sensibility underlies aesthetic appreciation. Acknowledging the participatory nature of such appreciation led to rejecting disinterestedness as its defining feature in favor of aesthetic engagement. The idea of an aesthetic field provided the basis for describing the complexity and the integral, contextual character of aesthetic experience.

This understanding of the aesthetic leads to the recognition that such experience is not confined to the arts but extends to environments and to the human world, more generally. The pervasiveness of the aesthetic thus provides a different model for grasping human values. For aesthetic perception pervades the human world and, because experience is broadly social, we are led to recognize the omnipresence of a social aesthetic.

This is not simply a conceptual relationship. It has endless practical ramifications for all human activities, both necessary and freely chosen, and for the quality of human life most generally. A social aesthetic may characterize personal relationships, vocational situations, educational, therapeutic, and creative activities, and, ideally, political processes. Because human life is thoroughly and pervasively social, social aesthetics offers a basis for a humane worldview, one that both redeems our humanity and guides us in fulfilling it.[13]

4

Duchampian Reflections on Descartes[*]

Preamble

The claim has been made that Descartes's famous argument in the *Meditations* is flawed because it is essentially circular.[1] This is because Descartes claimed to prove his existence, not by using the method of doubt but rather by adopting that method. That is, by doubting, Descartes had to postulate a doubter, that is, a thinking being: it does not prove the existence of one: the simple act of doubting requires a doubter. Interestingly, the essential insight at the heart of this argument has reappeared in a newly illuminating form in the work of Descartes's twentieth century compatriot, Marcel Duchamp. Here, however, it does not have a vitiating implication but rather an illuminating one, for the presence of a participating perceiver is central to the aesthetic impact of much of Duchamp's enigmatic art. Rather than standing as an odd deviance from tradition, his art draws us to recognize an essential factor usually unnoticed: the essential presence of a perceiver in the aesthetic field or situation. So inadvertently, Duchamp has become the Descartes of art by demonstrating the essential presence of a perceiver in art with greater success than Descartes did for philosophy.

The effect of this on appreciation is not to diminish the stature of Duchamp's art but rather to strengthen it, for the presence of a participating perceiver is essential for its impact. This is central in grasping the import of Duchamp's art. Moreover, rather than standing as an odd deviation from tradition, Duchamp's participatory art rather leads us to recognize an essential factor in aesthetic appreciation *en tout* that usually goes unnoticed and unrecognized: the essential presence of a perceiver participating in the aesthetic field. Thus, Duchamp's art is not an art of objects but an art of situations, in a manner of speaking an art

---

[*] This is a slightly revised version of an essay that originally appeared in *Festschrift Liber Amicorum for Arnold Berleant, Popular Inquiry,* Vol. 10, 2022.

of environments. So inadvertently, Duchamp has become the Descartes of art to better effect than Descartes was the Duchamp of philosophy.

Duchamp's Provocative Art

The reputation of Marcel Duchamp (1887–1968) as a controversial artist has persisted for more than a century following the New York Armory Show of 1913 in which his "Nude Descending a Staircase" was first displayed, and his notorious "Fountain," one of a succession of "Readymades," that was first exhibited in 1917. Duchamp's art was shocking both in conception and execution and continues to be enigmatic. Standing outside the conventional expectation of how painting and sculpture should look, these works remain difficult to assimilate into the history of visual art. Little has happened in the art world since then that can be considered more anomalous. Rather than ascribing these works to the scandalous intent of Dada, they have greater significance for the history of art. This is not so much as exceptions to the gradual unfolding of the technical and perceptual possibilities of painting and sculpture, but because they prefigure a dramatic change in our understanding of the experience of appreciation.

Duchamp's art is striking on many counts: it is enigmatic, disconcerting, even disruptive, yet strangely fascinating. Appearing near the close of Cubism and moving in the bizarre and even satirical direction of Dada, his work is both the culmination of that of his predecessors and an anticipation of what would follow. Duchamp's artistic innovations require more than minor adjustments to new forms of representation and execution. His art is deeply disturbing; it attacks us viscerally. His innovations prefigured many of the late twentieth century conceptually and perceptually disconcerting effects that art would come to have on the benign convention of aesthetic appreciation and the world that art evokes. Even given his originality, it may still seem strange to think of Marcel Duchamp as an environmental artist, much less one whose work has philosophical implications. Is there a master key that opens the many doors to Duchamp's art works?

I would like to suggest that a hidden factor vitalizes Duchamp's art, a factor that it is important to recognize, not only in order to understand the art but, in point of fact, to complete it. While it figures in his early work, this factor is most dramatically present at the culmination of his creative trajectory. His late work, *Étant donné*, is the door, both literally and metaphorically, that provides the entry to his artistic project. A clue may be found in Duchamp's reflective comment on having largely given up painting after the *Nude Descending a Staircase*: "I was interested in ideas—not merely in visual products."[2] From his late work *Étant donné* we can read back to a guiding artistic insight in the succession of Readymades and even to the early *Nude*. Moreover, this factor has philosophical significance of overriding importance. But more of that later. Let us begin at the end with some observations on *Étant donné*.

Étant donné (literally, *Being Given*) preoccupied the artist from 1946 to 1966. It followed and was contemporaneous with the succession of Readymades, Duchamp's distinctive artistic innovation. *Étant donné* can indeed be thought of as the fulfillment of that artistic project: a more complex and complete Readymade. Consider how we encounter it. Approaching this work,[3] one is confronted by a heavy Spanish wooden door with a pair of holes located at eye level in the center. Nothing else is visible until one approaches the door and looks through the holes.

Figure 5 Duchamp (1887–1968), "Étant donnés," 1° la chute d'eau, 2° le gaz d'éclairage . . . (Given: 1. The Waterfall, 2. The Illuminating Gas . . .); exterior view of Spanish wooden door (1946–66). Philadelphia Museum of Art: Gift of the Cassandra Foundation, 1969, 1969-41-1 © Association Marcel Duchamp / ADAGP, Paris / Artists Rights Society (ARS), New York 2023

There the viewer encounters a physical scene consisting of a female nude lying supine directly before one's eyes, sprawling disheveled on a bed of twigs and vegetation. She is holding a gas lamp in her extended left hand while, just beyond in a distant landscape, a flowing waterfall produces a misty vapor. It is left to **the** viewer to interpret the scene, but more than interpret it, for by peeping through the holes, **the** viewer inadvertently participates in the environment as a *voyeur*. Sometimes conveniently called an assemblage, *Étant donné* is better considered an inclusive environment comprising the observer, the door, and the scene beyond it. This is a disconcertingly clever construction.

Figure 6 Duchamp (1887–1968), "Étant donnés," 1° la chute d'eau, 2° le gaz d'éclairage . . . (Given: 1. The Waterfall, 2. The Illuminating Gas . . .), (1946–66). Philadelphia Museum of Art: Gift of the Cassandra Foundation, 1969, 1969-41-1 © Association Marcel Duchamp / ADAGP, Paris / Artists Rights Society (ARS), New York 2023

Étant donné is further significant because it can be understood not only as a participatory environmental construction but as the elaborate explicit and culmination of the series of Readymades that preceded it. For in recognizing the Bicycle Wheel, the viewer supplies the context of a bicycle in the manner of conceptual art, just as viewing the snow shovel of *In Advance of a Broken Arm* requires the implicit presence of a shoveler to complete the work.[4] In a similar way though perhaps with a disconcerting twist, *Fountain* implies a potential user to complete the context. This piece in particular can be seen as a vivid instance of what the perceptual psychologist J. J. Gibson called an "affordance," a design or environmental feature that invites a certain behavioral response in the perceiver.[5]

Figure 7 Duchamp (1887–1968), "Roue de bicyslette" (Bicycle Wheel) (1913). © Association Marcel Duchamp / ADAGP, Paris / Artists Rights Society (ARS), New York 2023

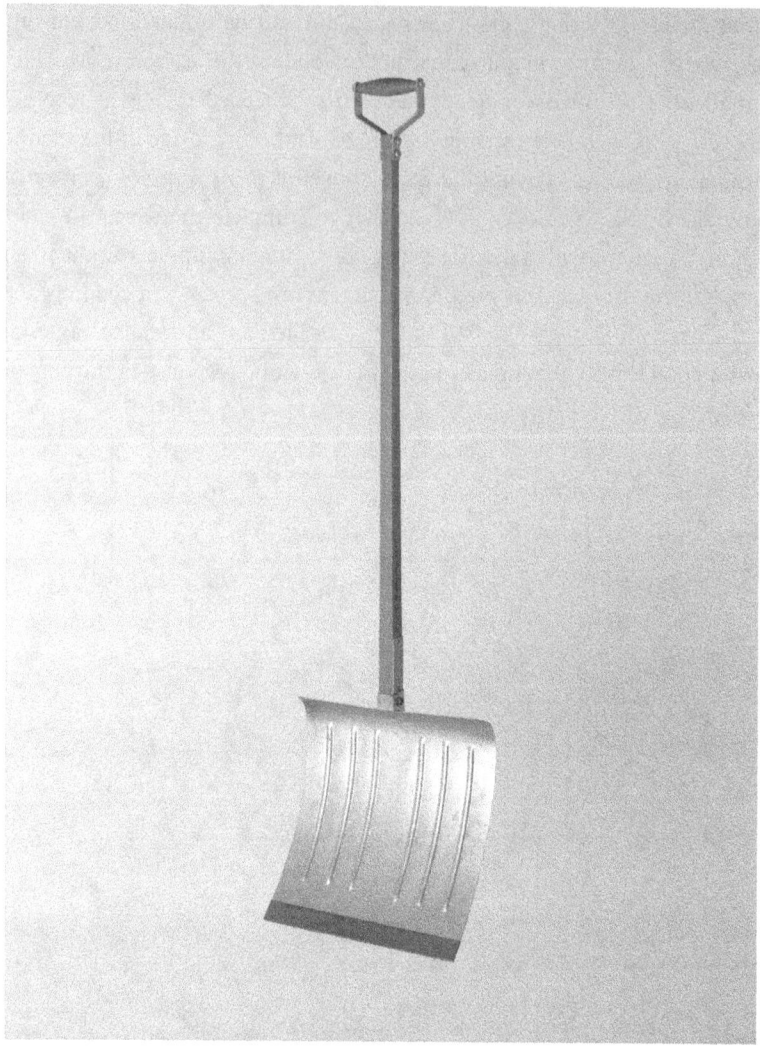

Figure 8 Marcel Duchamp (1887–1968), "En prévision du bras cassé" (In Advance of a Broken Arm) (August 1964, fourth version, after lost original of November 1915). Medium: Readymade. Dimensions: 132 cm high. Metropolitan Museum of Art: Gift of The Jerry and Emily Spiegel Family Foundation. Digital Image © The Museum of Modern Art/Licensed by SCALA / Art Resource, NY © Association Marcel Duchamp / ADAGP, Paris / Artists Rights Society (ARS), New York 2023

It is clear that these works anticipate conceptual art, for they require to be experienced as tangible parts of larger, more extensive virtual works contributed to by the awareness of the appreciator. Viewing Readymades in the conventional way as contemplative objects not only obstructs the appreciative experience but

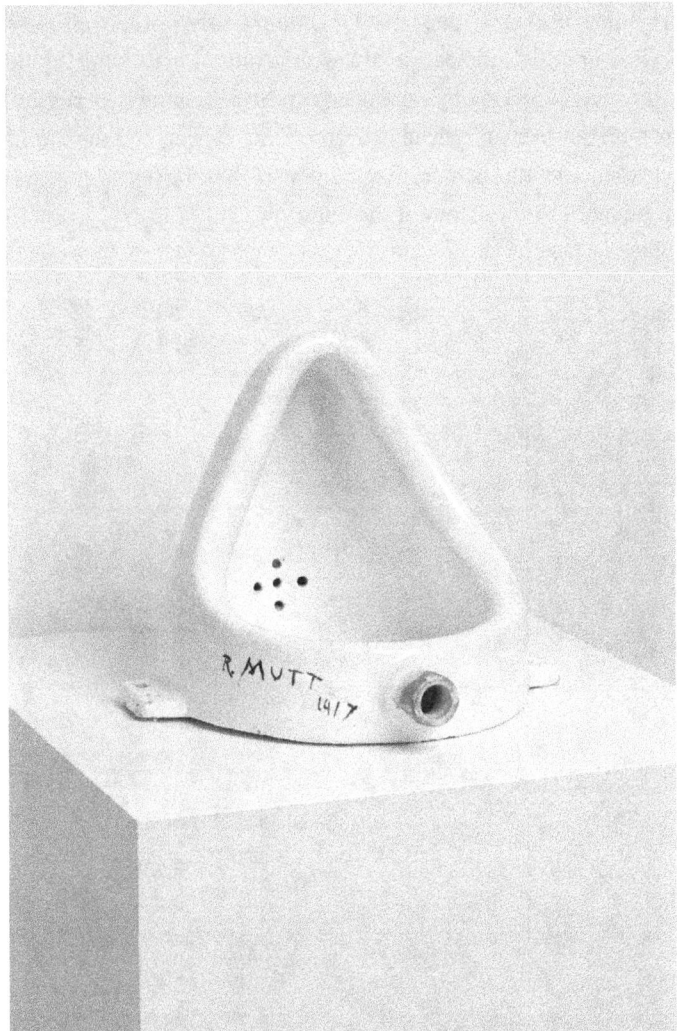

Figure 9 Duchamp (1887–1968), "Fountain" (1917). Photograph by Alfred Stieglitz. © Association Marcel Duchamp / ADAGP, Paris / Artists Rights Society (ARS), New York 2023; photograph © 2023 Artists Rights Society (ARS), New York

misses the point. Moreover, there are also overtones here of found art and of performance art, later twentieth century innovations that Duchamp remarkably prefigured. Taken collectively, moreover, these works may be understood most comprehensively as environments that incorporate the appreciator as a participant. *Étant donné*, then, makes explicit by overt behavior what is implicit in the extended series of Readymades that were fabricated during the twenty years over which it was constructed.

Perhaps one may even suggest that Duchamp's early work, *Nude Descending a Staircase*, was a graphic anticipation of the same intention to bring the viewer into the work. For encountering this painting can be a somatic experience. Because of its large size, the scene physically confronts the viewer, and the motility of the nude is represented with such dramatic intensity that the figure appears not only in motion but about to walk out of the painting.

Figure 10 Duchamp (1887–1968), "Nu descendant un escalier n° 2" (Nude Descending a Staircase, No. 2), (1912). © Association Marcel Duchamp / ADAGP, Paris / Artists Rights Society (ARS), New York 2023

Philosophical Significance

These observations may be taken as a commentary on Duchamp's art. But we can go further by suggesting that it also has important philosophical significance. Let us turn to a different case, one that provides an improbable comparison with Duchamp. There is a curious parallel between Duchamp's innovative *oeuvre* and the strikingly original argument of an earlier transformer of Western culture, the French philosopher and mathematician René Descartes. Although Descartes lived three centuries before Duchamp, the influence of his innovative ideas grew over the intervening period to become, in the twentieth century, one of the dominant cognitive features of Western culture. In comparing their distinctive contributions, both men seem to offer parallel situations apparently in inverse form: While Duchamp revealed a hidden participant in the aesthetic encounter, Descartes made a case for the subjective self-substantiation of cognitive consciousness.

This is not the place to review the long tradition of subjectivism in Western philosophy, a history that had its beginnings in Plato's *eidos* and underwent various transformations over the centuries that followed. During that period, subjectivism became an entrenched and powerful influence in Western thought, achieving its consummation in the *cogito* of Descartes. From the seventeenth century on, subjectivism pervaded philosophical thought, culminating in the transcendental metaphysics of Kant and the pure phenomenology of Husserl.

Descartes's argument, reiterated by Husserl in his *Cartesian Meditations* (1931), stands as an exemplary statement of the basic claim for the subjective foundation of knowledge.[6] As he recounted it in the *Discourse on Method* and the *Meditations on First Philosophy*, Descartes resolved to review, under the most stringent conditions, the foundations of his belief. He did this by applying the test of doubt to every opinion he held. Only that which he could conceive clearly and distinctly and without a trace of doubt would he be justified in accepting as true. And conversely, whatever he found that he was able to doubt, he must reject as insufficiently dependable to be accepted as true belief. And so, on the basis of the *dubito*, Descartes began his inquiry by rejecting the veracity of nearly everything he had come to believe as true. At this impasse he found that there is only one thing he can conceive clearly and distinctly, one thing he cannot doubt. That is the fact that he is doubting and, consequently, that he exists as a thinking being. From this he proceeded to reconstruct the world with the reassurance of a God who could not deceive him.

Descartes thus proceeded by employing doubt methodologically: the *dubito* became the standard to judge the truth of an idea. From the uncompromising application of the standard of doubt to all beliefs and, with the reassurance of a God who would not deceive him, Descartes's inability to find a single belief which he cannot doubt itself provides him with one: the fact of his doubting is the only thing he cannot doubt.[7] His rigorous method thus appears to have been successful, and Descartes was then free to reconstruct his familiar world. Most crucially, he ultimately arrived at a clear and distinct idea of his personal existence.

An Implicit Presence

Yet on reflection, Descartes's argument is fundamentally circular. This is because his proof of his personal existence as a doubting, that is, a thinking being follows, not from using the method of doubt but from his decision to adopt that method. That is, doubt cannot be exercised before being recognized and accepted as a mode of thought. And doubt as a mode of thought must be assumed, before it can be used. Doubt cannot prove its own existence; it must first be stipulated. The readymade *In Advance of a Broken Arm*, the snow shovel, cannot stand alone but presumes a situation of use by a prospective user. Similarly, doubt does not just appear in consciousness. It is a response to a previous perception, belief, or other thought. Just as Duchamp's art implies an omnipresent participant in relation to the readymade, so Descartes's doubt implies a doubter in order to be exercised. Each has a correlative participant. As the snow shovel presupposes a shoveler, so doubt presupposes a doubter. Thus in Descartes's *cogito* there lives a thinker present "in advance of doubting," so to speak.

The purity of Descartes's rationalism is impressive. Because his procedure rests on assumptions and leads to conclusions congenial to the tradition of subjectivism, it has been remarkably convincing. Yet the logic of Descartes's train of inferences is defective. While apparently plausible, it is inherently circular because it rests on assuming (a doubting being) in support of what he intends to prove (the existence of a doubting being).

Thus doubt cannot be a starting point because it presupposes a thinking being, just as Duchamp's art projects a participant, and the parallel of Descartes with Duchamp is not inverse but exact. A human presence is implicit in philosophy as it is in art. Nor can a mind begin the reconstructive process since, despite persistent mythologies, "mind" is not a free-floating entity but a concept that hypostatizes self-conscious awareness and inheres in biological, historical, cultural beings. The situation thus precedes the event. Similarly, Duchamp's art requires a user for its completion. It exhibits a mastery of aesthetic reciprocity, of what, in logic, would be called circularity. Like the cogito, it is self-justifying.

Can art be a guide to philosophy? Perhaps it may be concluded that circular thinking leads to more effective art than to sound philosophy. We had to wait three centuries for one French cultural revolutionary to comment so eloquently on another. Who, then, is the voyeur in the *Meditations*?

Part III

Environment as Cultural

5

The Cultural Aesthetics of Environment

Considering environment aesthetically is a comparatively recent development. The focus on the aesthetic dimension of environment began in the 1970s and gained increasing prominence. Appearing sporadically at first, interest in environmental aesthetics developed during subsequent decades in the United Kingdom, Canada, and the United States and more insistently and intensively in Finland. Beginning in the 1990s, the aesthetics of environment gained considerable attention in China. Environmental aesthetics can now be considered an established domain of inquiry that is international in scope and that draws on and influences several disciplines. It appears most prominently in philosophical aesthetics, environmental psychology, and landscape design, and it is a recognized focus in the visual arts, literature, and the environmental sciences.

Interest in environmental aesthetics has indeed become a global phenomenon, cutting across philosophical styles as well as cultural traditions. Much remains to be gained by continuing this momentum. Yet while we all face similar environmental problems, ways of thinking about environment vary. Different cultural traditions, different philosophical cultures, and different conditions of life influence the way we understand experience, environment, aesthetics, ecology, and their place in life experience. There are obvious reasons for this variety. At the same time, environmental issues are no longer only regional but involve changes whose effects spread without limit atmospherically as well as geographically. There are compelling reasons, therefore, to consider whether there is any commonality on which these differences can converge.

Common problems invite coordinated solutions. It would greatly assist cooperative action on environmental issues if we shared a similar understanding of the ideas that are central to this situation. Encouraging as the global interest in environment may be, it is nonetheless the case that research on the aesthetics of environment displays significant differences in the meaning of its central ideas.

It may therefore help reduce the inconsistencies and confusion in what is meant by the key concepts by clarifying their meanings. In such a spirit, I should like to offer some reflections on how we might bring together the sometimes disjointed thinking on the underlying issues.

It seems obvious that any inquiry should begin with a clear understanding of the basic concepts involved. This may seem obvious but it is not easy to do for, as is well known, our concepts are so embedded in historical uses and cultural matrices that ideas that seem intuitively simple and unambiguous may well embody confusion and even contradiction. As an interest in environmental aesthetics has grown beyond the attention of a few widely scattered scholars to enter into national and international discussion, problems with clarity and difficulties in communication have become increasingly troublesome. A comprehensive analysis of terminology would be a worthwhile undertaking, but it is not possible in a brief chapter to offer more than one perspective on this. For the purposes of the present discussion, let me present approximations of our foundational concepts that may provide a common place of reference if not a common ground.

Words About Environment

Let me begin with the observation that no concept in philosophy is self-evident, simple, or self-contained. Every basic idea is unavoidably caught in a network of theoretical assumptions and implications. Any apparent obviousness belies these hidden debts and allegiances. Culture and theory thus combine to oblige us to begin with complexity. There are no simples in philosophy. This is clearly the case with the three basic ideas that inform our discussion: environment, aesthetics, and ecology.

It might seem obvious to consider *environment* the foundational idea of this inquiry. Surely it is the overall focus of our concern. It is commonplace to speak these days of an environmental crisis, and this is not only a manner of speaking. People across the globe are increasingly distressed by erratic and unseemly weather events: disrupted seasonal changes, freak windstorms, record floods, and tidal waves, not to mention more anticipated if not welcomed environmental disturbances like hurricanes, volcanic eruptions, and earthquakes. Added to these so-called natural disasters are those caused by human action and error. I am inclined to think, however, that rather than beginning with an understanding of environment, the discussion might better terminate in an enlarged sense of environment. That is, our confrontation with environmental issues such as weather and climate change is a result of the consequences of people's attitudes and practices and not because of any conceptual order. As one of the leading ideas, environment invites a larger, more inclusive understanding than climatological changes and crises.

Yet the very breadth of environmental concerns makes a clear focus difficult. Environment embraces many regions and perspectives: preservation, conservation, resource protection and use, land use and planning, public policy, recreation, and enjoyment, to name some of the most obvious. All are relevant and all are important, but the concern here is with a clearer understanding of environment and its issues. Perhaps it would serve to focus on an *aesthetic* interest in environment as fundamental. In some sense, it *is* fundamental because our *sensory* engagement with environment precedes and underlies every other interest. I say this because sensory perception lies at the heart of the meaning of aesthetics and is central in aesthetic experience, and the sensible experience of environment stands at the center of every other environmental interest and use.

It might seem, then, that since our concern here is with aesthetics, that is, environmental aesthetics, *aesthetics* should be our point of departure. Whether we take aesthetics here in a fairly narrow sense to mean the beauty of environment or consider it broadly as sensible experience in general, that is, as the range of sensory perception, aesthetics is necessarily a central point at which environmental concerns intersect human experience and activity. We might even claim that the aesthetic should not only be our starting point but is also our ultimate end as the fundamental understanding of direct perceptual experience.

These two ideas, environment and aesthetics, are clearly at the heart of this inquiry. But there is a third: *ecology*. This may seem like a late addition to the discussion; and, as I noted earlier, ecology has only more recently assumed an important place in our understanding of environment. Indeed, as a region of scientific theory and investigation, ecology emerged only in the late nineteenth century. And while it began as a biological theory about the interdependence of organisms in particular environments considered as ecosystems, its basic concept has spread throughout the social as well as natural sciences.

Ecology may seem to be derivative, a way of thinking about environment that has only secondary interest here, and until recently ecological concerns have not had a prominent place in environmental aesthetics. Indeed, ecology figures most prominently in discussions of environmental aesthetics by Chinese researchers. Is this a cultural difference or does it entail a theoretical divergence?

Reviewing the theoretical underpinning of an aesthetics of environment, one may conclude that ecology can make a significant, indeed a determinative contribution. By starting with an ecological orientation, we gain an illuminating perspective on this inquiry, for an ecological outlook transfigures our understanding of both environment and aesthetics. In fact, ecological aesthetics can serve as the leading idea here, an idea whose meaning decides all that follows. Let us see how that is.

An ecological perspective considers environment as a system of interacting, interdependent participating factors. Environment then becomes a complex whole. Because of this interdependence, an ecosystem is not the sum of independent parts or organisms. Rather it is an unstable complex in precarious balance striving to sustain its coherence. I use the word "complex" rather than "whole" because the coherence of an ecosystem is the outcome of a dynamic process involving a multitude of organisms, objects, factors, and conditions. It may achieve balance but that is as a complex, never a unity. We can think of an ecosystem, then, as a context rather than a thing or an object.[1]

Considering environment from an ecological perspective transforms our understanding. It leads to discarding the common meaning of environment as surroundings in favor of reenvisioning it as an all-inclusive whole, embracing humans, when present, together with other living organisms and the physical conditions with which they live, including geographical features and climate. Because ecology envisions these as interconnected, it is necessary to think of the constituents of environment as all-inclusive and continuous. In this sense, environment is holistic: nothing outside, nothing apart. It is clear from the conception of ecology that there are ethical as well as aesthetic implications: An ecological aesthetics is inseparable from an ecological ethics.[2]

Humans, then, should be understood as participating parts of their context, understood and experienced from within. From the human standpoint, in relation to people's lives, environment becomes experience. Thinking ecologically, environment must be understood as *contextual* experience. Aesthetics fastens on the sensible aspects of that experience, and so environment, considered aesthetically, is perceptual. Thus the language of environmental aesthetics brings us to the idea of *experience*, for our understanding of experience is fundamental to everything we say about environment.

The Matrix of Experience

Experience has been an important idea in the history of philosophic thought, beginning with the pre-Socratics and extending to the very present.

Generally considered synecdochically as sense experience, its transitoriness and ephemerality have troubled philosophers in their search for coherence, regularity, and stability. Thus a dialectic developed around change in favor of permanence, denigrating change as unworthy and destructive of human good in comparison with the ideal of absolute permanence, of things *sub specie aeternitatis*. Experience has a history that runs the length of philosophic time, yet oddly enough, the history of experience remains to be written. In our present discussion, understanding experience is basic to understanding environment.

Starting with experience may seem a strange way to pursue a discussion of environment. Environment, of course, is usually thought of in a scientific or quasi-scientific, objective sense as *the* environment, a definable subject matter, something to be studied by various branches of physical science, such as physical geography, climatology, and ecology. These identify environment objectively, as an object, but it is an object that becomes more personal when we ponder the effects of global warming, since all living creatures, humans included, are affected by climate change and its consequences. These affect the habitability of various regions of the earth's surface, they influence agriculture and food production, and they force us to cope with the effects of changing temperature gradients and new and more extreme weather patterns. It is convenient when considering global climate change to externalize environment, to speak of *the* environment as if environment were something apart from ourselves about which we are concerned.

But this, I think, offers only a partial and misleading understanding. It is partial because it fragments environment by circumscribing and objectifying environmental experience, abstracting it into separate parts, and treating problems as isolated events requiring specific, local solutions. It is misleading because, by regarding these abstractions as if they were real and objective, it takes a derivative understanding as if it were the basic one. The lesson of ecology is that, in relation to human needs and human uses, there is no environment out there apart from and distinct from us.[3] This leads us to recognize that the fundamental meaning of environment is its human meaning, more pointedly, its meaning in experience. And environment is not experienced objectively but always here with us, where we are. By beginning with experience, then, we begin with ourselves, with the human world of which we are an integral part. And when we come to speak of environment, then, it only falsifies things to think that we can objectify environment and consider it independently of human place, participation, and use.

The intent here has been to offer an orderly progression of the leading ideas of environmental aesthetics. Oddly enough, what has emerged is actually two orders. We began with environment, turned next to discuss aesthetics, and followed with ecology. And we concluded by interpreting all within the matrix of experience. This is a logical order: with environment as the broadest concept, which we then combine with aesthetics and arrive at a special sense of environmental aesthetics as ecological.

There is another order, however, one that is truer to experience. Indeed, when we cast our ideas in the language of experience, the order becomes inverted. For starting with experience, all experience is actually contextual and so can be understood ecologically. And as experience is primarily perceptual, it is always aesthetic. Finally, taken most broadly, we come to understand the idea of environment as ecological aesthetics. From this line of reasoning, then, the aesthetics of environment is ecological.

Our choice is the language of experience, beginning with a commitment to the largest perceptual context, one that the concept of ecology reflects most adequately. This, as we have seen, is not the biological setting alone nor the physical conditions of environment only. Since our reference is to experience, the human perceiver is central, and the condition that binds together all aspects of the context is perceptual experience. When central, such experience is thus aesthetic, and the aesthetic becomes the primary mode of experience. For these reasons, then, environmental aesthetics can be considered ecological aesthetics, and this implies a cultural ecology.

Environmental aesthetics thus translates ecology into experience; it is the human meaning of ecology. This is another way of saying that the concept of ecology is of an environment understood as a complex of interdependent objects and factors. The scope of such an environment is defined by the activity and intensity of such interdependence. As its force begins to fade and other factors become prominent, a different ecosystem begins to emerge. Such boundaries are rarely sharp, but distinctions are nonetheless possible as, for example, between an urban ecosystem and a suburban one or between the city and the countryside. Mountains and valleys are distinguishable even though their precise boundaries cannot be plotted.

The aesthetic experience of environment is thus the perceptual counterpart of ecology. Environmental aesthetics embodies the ecological meaning of environment. This has profound implications for environmental understanding and design and thus for ecological aesthetics.[4] Ecology in this sense requires constant reference to aesthetic experience as a guide and a criterion in environmental design. The work of many environmental artists is important in pointing up the experiential aspect of environments, that is, the awareness that environments do not consist of objects but of experiential relationships. Pioneer work is being done in integrating an aesthetic dimension in ecologically oriented environmental design, and such work is significant for both environmental and ecological aesthetics.[5]

Ecology and Culture

The interplay of humans within the natural world is experienced and understood in sharply different ways in Western and Eastern cultures. An observation such as this would seem to force us into broad and overpowering generalities, and this is invariably misleading when joined with a commitment to the diversity and particularity of experience. Still, recognizing the dangers should not prevent us from recognizing common patterns, despite differences that exist among the many writers and movements that reflect them. And these patterns are revealing.

A full historical analysis would undoubtedly display a richly varied tapestry describing the human world. And a nuanced commentary would reflect their intermingling and divergent strands. But at the same time, and for our purposes here, it is important that this variety and complexity not obscure the broad patterns that emerge. It is these that stand as a potent illustration of the cultural influences on experience. In its bold outline, the characteristic patterns by which experience is understood in Western cultures display a sense of separation of humans from the natural world. Eastern cultures, in contrast, reflect an understanding of the harmonious integration of nature and humans.

Both opposing views have ancient origins. The Western understanding is embodied in early texts that have had a powerful influence. The two most influential intellectual sources are works written down at approximately the same time, that is, the fourth century BCE, and largely middle Eastern in origin. One justifies taking possession of the natural world for human purposes; the other denigrates sensory experience. The first is the Hebrew *Bible*, which establishes a justification for humans appropriating the creatures, objects, and resources of nature for our own interests and uses.[6] The other is Platonic philosophy that ascribes to natural objects a lowly status in the order of things and posits a higher reality that is the refuge of truth and reality itself, an understanding found throughout Plato's dialogues and most famously in *The Republic*.[7] Whitehead's comment that Western civilization is a footnote to Plato testifies to its effect.

These influences have combined to shape the Western view of the natural environment. "Environment" is an idea we have devised to identify our material matrix, commonly defined as "surroundings" in Western languages, giving linguistic credibility to a way of thinking endemic in Western culture.[8] It reflects a tradition that we can trace to the religious beliefs and practices of ancient Greek Orphism that separated the physical world from what is distinctively human.[9] It was an understanding that appeared in various forms during the Golden Age of classic Greek philosophy and continued in religious and philosophical formulations to emerge in the Enlightenment in Descartes's dualistic objectification of the physical world as the full rational reconstruction of human experience.

This historico-cultural development of Western civilization led to understanding the world as an objective condition separate from and independent of humans, and it turned environment into an object for humans to control and manipulate. Thus we speak easily about the relation of person and environment, as if they were two distinct things that can be causally connected. Such a conception fits easily with the growth of early modern science and the technological revolution it generated. This was a development that quickly altered the human environment and led, among much else, to the environment-transforming practices that have reached a crisis level in our time.

In their rapid industrialization, Eastern countries such as China, Japan, and India have compressed Western development into a few short generations, resulting in many of the same environmental problems that the West is confronting. At the same time, the cultural historical influences in Eastern cultures provide the basis for a very different conception of environment that is struggling to assert itself against short-term economic and political interests. Common to the many different strains of Daoism is an understanding grounded in the view of living in harmony with nature. Eastern culture here offers a remarkable parallel with recent Western ecological thought, for it is a way of thinking that we can describe as ecological in character. Of course, the first is a religio-cultural understanding and the other a scientific one. But what is relevant here is not their differing sources but their similar understanding. While originating as a biological theory, ecology offers a compelling theoretical framework that has not only shown its value in the social sciences but has special relevance for the environmental sciences and for environmental philosophy.

What ecology offers is an understanding of environment as an integral whole. Environment thus does not consist of a relation between humans and their environment as distinct and separate entities. Environment rather *includes* the human as an interdependent and engaged constituent. One of the most important lessons we can draw from ecology is that there is no environment apart from and distinct from humans.[10] Humans and environment need to be understood as interdependent constituents of a complex whole that has identifiable contributing factors but not separate parts. This is a way of thinking about the world, and it may help explain the attraction of ecological aesthetics for Chinese environmental aestheticians.[11]

It is interesting to consider whether this cultural matrix is simply an alternative worldview. That would imply a cultural relativism in which the differences are essentially arbitrary. However, there are more or less accurate ways of representing environment, and we can claim that an ecological model better reflects our present knowledge of environment, whether understood in a physicalistic, scientific sense, in an experiential one, or philosophically. This does not imply an "objective," absolute truth but rather a less assumptive understanding that shares the compelling, evidentiary claims of science. The conception of environment as ecological affirms its meaning as a human meaning, its meaning as experienced. As experienced, environment does not stand apart but is always related to humans, to the human world of interest, activity, and use. That is the human meaning of ecology.

On the subject of experience, we encounter a great body of thought. From the physical and social sciences to the literary arts and philosophy, one can consider human experience the most inclusive subject of inquiry. This discussion of environmental aesthetics offers but an endnote to that research. Perhaps, rather than an endnote, it is more of a searchlight that may be directed over the range of scientific and scholarly commentary, since it centers on understanding that experience on which all other inquiry rests.

At the risk of affirming the obvious, it will be useful to call attention to some characteristics of experience that are easily overlooked. The categories into which we pour the molten intangibilities of experience are so engrained in habitual thinking that we are likely to assume them as ontological rather than customary: categories such as emotions, sensations, thoughts, memories, ideas, feelings, imagination, consciousness, cognition, perception, and more. The challenge is how to make the ephemeral tangible, and these categories have long served as convenient receptacles. But like the proverbial emperor's new clothes, though we persist in thinking we see those categories as something (i.e., as ontological), there is nothing there. Moreover, taken alone, whatever meaning content such categories have is informed and constrained by the habits of so-called "common sense," heavily clouded by the multitude of influences that give them conceptual shape and content. Think of the many meanings given to "perception" and of the severely limited vocabulary with which we identify emotions, as well as the metaphors with which we attempt to grasp consciousness, from Locke's atomistic theory of substance and his corpuscular theory of mind to James's "stream" of consciousness.

Thus there are multiple overlays through which we discern and interpret experience. One obvious overlay is cultural, expressed through our natal language, traditional practices, prevalent beliefs, and systems of belief, all infused with regional geographical and climatological conditions as their context of reference. To this cultural overlay must be added a historical one. Our understanding is subtly and not so subtly influenced by historical circumstances: the notable events and conditions of the time, in addition to their influence on the cultural climate. We can identify still other overlays of differing scope, such as professional, avocational, social, and educational, along with the more transitory influences of taste, style, fads, and fashionable ideologies. All of these, moreover, are themselves categories through which we isolate and identify dimensions and perspectives of experience. These observations on the multiple matrices of experience are not intended to obfuscate our attempts at illuminating it. Rather they begin to make more explicit the multidimensional landscape of experience and lead us to recognize the conditions under which we attempt to grasp the human world.

What, one might ask, do these general comments have to do with the aesthetics of environment and how we think and talk about it? In one respect, merely to ask the question is to answer it, for environment is a fundamental category of experience through which we organize our understanding and identify the issues. It is important, however, to make these observations more definite by identifying basic cultural differences in understanding environment, recognizing all the while that large trends mask many variations. These differences, deeply historical and cultural, characterize differing relations of nature and humans that are fundamental in both Western and Eastern thought.

Whether a resolution of these divergences is possible is a difficult question. The answer will not lie in a choice between simple alternatives but requires determinations that are circumstantial and may be complex. Satisfactory resolutions must be decided in relation to the specific context and to the particular points of balance between the options that are available. These will vary with scientific, poetic, and political environments and will reflect the order of values chosen, itself a cultural determination. Is it possible to attain equipoise between the technological capabilities of Western cultures and the cosmic proportionality of the Eastern? The answer to this rests with whether the social and political development of human civilization has attained the capacity for such a resolution.

* * *

This rich array of ideas does not allow for a simple summary. I have tried to reshape the issues so that the relationships between conceptual understanding (ecological aesthetics) and perceptual experience (environmental aesthetics) become clearer. It is important to realize that the former must be seen in the light of the latter. When we recognize that ideas originate in perception and should be translated back into experience, we can then proceed to reshape our world in ways that better meet our interests and fulfill our needs. The possibilities are there, often hidden in a miasma of false constructions and misty assumptions. The question remains whether we will be able to find our way through them clearly enough to survive and prosper.

6

Some Questions for Ecological Aesthetics

The passion for knowledge and control of nature has been a persistent force throughout the course of world history. It led the Greeks to create elaborate mythologies describing divine explanation and influence, as well as to form the earliest speculative natural philosophies. It led to the creation of the great national folk epics by cultures in Asia, Africa, the Americas, and Europe[1] and to fictitious historical narratives that provide a basis for ethnic identity and a justification for ethnic claims. Various rites developed that offered ways of attempting to influence natural events and processes. All these were followed, of course, by the emergence of early modern science and its more recent spectacular theoretical and technological developments that have provided the possibility of greater understanding and more effective control of natural forces and events.

Yet science is replete with concepts and constructions intended to help us grasp the invisible forces and powers at work in nature. Its modes of explanation are imaginative as well as rational. They lead us away from the directness and immediacy of perceptual experience and into the safety and solitude of abstractions and conceptual constructions. The history of modern science documents a remarkable cultural achievement that has transformed both human life and the planet.

In all this, the experience we call aesthetic has not fared well, though it has been recognized and valued, despite official suspicion and discouragement, from Plato to the present. "Aesthetic" is the term generally used to denote the normative perceptual experience associated with the appreciation of art and of beauty in nature. Aesthetics is the study of such experience, a multidisciplinary field that may be philosophical, psychological, sociological, or historical in its orientation. While there is general agreement on the meaning of "aesthetic," the accounts that guide its application to objects and experiences are heavily theoretical, influenced in the West by an almost 2,000-year-old history of cultural thought and theory. So much is encompassed by the term "aesthetics" that some reference works do not include an entry under that term because of the lack of general agreement on conceptual, theoretical, semantic, and empirical grounds.[2] I shall deal here mostly with the philosophical understanding of the aesthetic.

Aesthetic Appreciation

Since early in the course of Western thought, philosophers have recognized the power of people's aesthetic engagement with nature and the arts. The classical Greeks early noted that the experience we call "aesthetic" transcends the rational order. Plato acknowledged this reluctantly; his great suspicion of the arts came from a profound disapproval of the potent influence of this transcendent experience.[3] Aristotle was less condemnatory and developed his theory of catharsis to account for the powerful effect of tragic drama on its audience.[4] Throughout most of the subsequent history of the arts, suspicion and censorship predominated until modern times, although both Church and State readily turned to the arts to provide experiential support for their own purposes. Since the Renaissance, however, the arts have proliferated in variety and popularity, testifying to the fascination they hold and to their distinctive force. And while writers during the Classical period expressed admiration for nature, it wasn't until the seventeenth century that the natural environment was recognized by artists and writers as deserving both aesthetic appreciation and scientific understanding.[5] Interest in the aesthetic value of the arts and of nature continued to grow over succeeding centuries. Why so much interest? Why so much concern for their influence?

While the arts have long been admired for their aesthetic attraction, the aesthetic appreciation of nature has developed more slowly. Natural beauty shares with the arts the appeal of a distinctive kind of pleasure. While aesthetic experiences have long been recognized, it was not until the eighteenth century that aesthetics began to be incorporated into systematic philosophical thought, acknowledging it as an identifiable and important area of philosophic study. The landmark event was the publication of Alexander Baumgarten's *Aesthetica* in 1750, and its definition of aesthetics cast the die for the work that followed. Turning to the Greek term, *aisthēsis*, which literally means perception by the senses, Baumgarten defined aesthetics as "the science of sensory knowledge directed toward beauty" and art as "the perfection of sensory awareness."[6] Kant's turn to aesthetics in the late eighteenth century for the completion of his philosophical system was the founding act of modern Western aesthetics and remains the dominant influence today.[7] The crucial insight in this tradition is that aesthetic appreciation rests on sensory perception.

Yet Plato's suspicion of the aesthetic persists today philosophically as well as politically, and the history of aesthetics is replete with attempts to control the arts by political constraints and to enclose the aesthetic within an acceptable cognitive system. Sometimes this was a theological order that justified constraints on the aesthetic so that it would not exceed the boundaries of theological doctrine. Sometimes it was the social order that imposed conventions of moral propriety on the arts and their experiences. Sometimes the larger sociocultural forces took form in a philosophical order that imposed limits on what was acceptable. Yet the aesthetic has continually broken out of such constraints, dismaying theologians, moralists, and philosophers, too.

It is clear that the dominant intellectual order of the modern world is scientific and, from the mid-twentieth century on, science became the model for much of Western philosophy, including aesthetics. Attempts to enclose aesthetic experience within scientific boundaries have taken different forms. Some use science as a cognitive model and emulate scientific method through careful definition and analysis of concepts and of language, itself. Various scientific disciplines have been taken as models to guide the investigation of aesthetic phenomena. Psychology is a notable example, ranging from experimental investigation in the second half of the nineteenth century (Fechner, Wundt, Helmholtz), and continuing in empirical studies of the arts, to the powerful influence of Freudian psychological theory in explaining creativity and aesthetic experience.[8] And now most recently, the popularity of neuroscience has led to its application to aesthetic phenomena in and the development of the subdiscipline of neuroaesthetics.

A powerful influence on aesthetics in the past half-century and more has been the use of particular scientific theories as a key to understanding aesthetic phenomena. Marxism, with its mixture of science, history, economic theory, and philosophy, is a continuing example. In recent years, evolutionary theory has been prominent in accounting for artistic and aesthetic activity.[9] Other writers make the general claim that scientific knowledge is necessary for the full appreciation of nature.[10] Still others have taken the scientific theory of ecology as a model for the aesthetic appreciation of nature.[11] While there are suggestive insights in many of these efforts, all represent the effort that began with Plato to respond to the distinctive experience of aesthetic appreciation by making it subordinate to an intellectualist standard or model. While the recent turn to scientific explanation may be motivated by different concerns from Plato's, it represents the same effort to somehow subsume the perceptual experience of the aesthetic under the aegis of a cognitive model.

Scientific influence can assume very different forms. Such efforts are misguided when they turn away from the primacy of the phenomena of aesthetic experience by subsuming them under a scientific model. The scientific study of aesthetic phenomena, whether perception, experience more generally, or behavior patterns of individuals and groups, is a legitimate direction for research. It is essential, however, to avoid the misapprehension that such inquiry will explain these phenomena by considering them through the psychology of perception, biological processes, generalizable patterns of behavior, and the like. Another questionable use of science is in applying a credible theory such as evolution, causal determinism, relativity physics, or ecology to define, explain, or account for aesthetic phenomena or experience. The danger that lies throughout these efforts is in attempting to constrain or explain the distinctive power of the aesthetic by the order or model of some form of scientific cognition.

The proposal in this chapter is to qualify the use of science in aesthetics by challenging its hegemony as a universal explanatory model. This is in response to influential efforts to use the dominant prestige of science to account for aesthetic appreciation. It applies to Carlson's imposition of scientific cognitivism on the aesthetic appreciation of nature. It qualifies applying evolutionary and ecological theories to the aesthetics of nature, resulting in aesthetics becoming a subfield of evolutionary or ecological theory. This is not a question of the relevance or usefulness of science in aesthetics but a question of hegemony: Can the aesthetics of nature, for example, become a subfield of evolutionary or ecological theory? The scope of inquiry that this question requires is equally broad, far more than can be pursued in a single essay. Let me, then, select one recent instance of the application of a scientific discipline to aesthetics: the use of ecology in accounting for aesthetic value. This will also allow us to consider the more general and critical question of the relation of scientific cognitivism to aesthetic appreciation.

Ecology and Aesthetics

The tendency to turn to the biological sciences for a model of aesthetic practice is not surprising. Since evolutionary theory loosened the underpinnings of the medieval theocentric and anthropocentric worldviews in the mid-nineteenth century, the sciences have forced us to reshape our intellectual landscape. It is a process that continues, not without its benefits but not without some inherent problems. I should like to discuss here one such influence: ecological theory.

Ecology offers a holistic principle of explanation founded on a biological model by considering the interactions among organisms and their environment as interdependent systems. An ecosystem refers to a community of organisms and environment functioning interdependently as a complex whole. Since its origin in biological science in the mid-nineteenth century, ecology has been a rich and productive biological concept applied to an endless range of scientific and humanistic disciplines: psychology, politics, philosophy, literature, and now aesthetics. Its application in the natural sciences has led to a wide range of scientific studies, not only in biology but in natural resource management, agriculture, and the like, where it lends itself particularly well to environmental sciences. What needs to be considered, however, is how well it applies to the social and human sciences, such as economics and psychology. In some of its uses, ecology has left the study of environmental systems far behind in becoming a generalized principle of explanation. Its application to the aesthetics of nature is one of these, and the question needs to be asked of how suitable ecology is in these nonbiological contexts.

One of the seminal contributions in the recent turn to ecology in aesthetics was made by Jusuck Koh, who developed the idea of an ecological aesthetics in the early 1980s. Koh made a wide-ranging and inclusive case for a holistic conception of environmental design. In a paper entitled "Ecological Aesthetics: A Holistic Evolutionary Paradigm for an Environmental Aesthetics,"[12] Koh articulated three principles of ecological design that he has continued to advocate. The first is inclusive unity as a principle of the creative process. This integrates form with its purpose and context and is, he argues, a necessary condition of the creative process in nature and in humans, and reveals an interrelationship between the creative process and aesthetic experience. Moreover, ecological aesthetics goes beyond the subjectivism of traditional Western aesthetics to rest on the human desire to be in unity with landscape. He associates this with an interactive relationship of persons and contexts, a unity of people and place, similar to my idea of an aesthetic field and Barker's idea of behavioral setting.[13] Ecological design, for Koh, centers on designing human–environment interaction in which architecture is understood as environment and the role of ecological designers is concerned not so much with form and structure of objects or environments as with designing human–environment interactions.

A second principle of the creative process is the inclusive unity of form as a system with its purpose and context, a unity of environment and place, as well as with the users as participants. Inclusive unity, Koh argues, denies distance and separation between subject and object, man and nature. And a third principle is dynamic balance, a qualitative equilibrium that is concerned with ordering creative and developmental processes in and between organic and inorganic forms. Koh associates this with what he calls complementarity, a principle that overcomes the dualities that pervade our thinking about nature and the world. He stresses the indivisibility between subject and object, time and space, solid and void, as well as conceptual divisions of form and content, matter and form, romanticism and classicism, feeling and thought, conscious and unconscious. Complementarity is also an aesthetic principle joining formal order with richness of meaning, inside with outside, eros with beauty.

Koh sees these three principles: inclusive unity, dynamic balance, and complementarity as helpful in understanding both Western and Oriental art, fine and practical art, architecture and landscape design. Ecological aesthetics, he claims, is an inclusive paradigm in that it deals with the total perceptual experience, not just the visual, "and sees human and environment as a system." It is evolutionary because it focuses on processes and change as well as formal order and "regards both the built environment and human perception of it as a creative, evolutionary, adaptive product and process."[14]

The idea of an ecological aesthetics has been taken up by a number of writers since Koh's work in the 1980s. Space and time do not permit me to review this literature, which includes contributions by Allen Carlson, Arnold Berleant, and Fanren Zeng. Let me turn, for contrast, to the recent development of this idea by Xiangzhan Cheng.[15] After a comprehensive review of the development of environmental aesthetics and of ecological aesthetics, Cheng recognizes the distinctive approach of each but insists that the idea of ecological aesthetics be given a strict meaning based on ecological ethics, "treating the natural environment as a dynamic organic ecosystem and holding a respectful attitude towards the natural environment."[16]

In his essay, "On the Four Key Points of Ecological Appreciation,"[17] Cheng emancipates aesthetics from its narrow focus on beauty in order to expand the notion of appreciation to include ecology, an idea he calls "ecological appreciation." Such appreciation joins an ethical dimension to the aesthetic and makes ecological awareness central. It uses ecological knowledge to stimulate imagination and feeling so as to go beyond anthropocentric values and preferences.

In a careful analysis, Cheng ascribes four points to ecological aesthetics. The first is that ecological aesthetics abandons the contrast or opposition between humans and the world, replacing it with aesthetic engagement to encourages their unity. In this Cheng is in full harmony with Koh. "Only through aesthetics of engagement that transcends the subject-object opposition can an intimate relationship between human and the world be established."[18] Cheng's second point predicates ecological aesthetic appreciation on ecological ethics. He claims that ecological consciousness of ethical values is inherent in ecological aesthetic appreciation. This ecohumanism, recognizing the interconnectedness of humans, human institutions, and the nonhuman environment, is in direct contrast to the Western tradition in aesthetics that removes ethical values from the scope of aesthetic appreciation.

The third keystone of ecological aesthetics appreciation that Cheng identifies is the necessity of ecological knowledge for full ecological aesthetic appreciation. This challenges a fundamental issue in the tradition of Western aesthetics, its essential noncognitivism, and it requires fuller consideration. It is well known that Kant claimed that judgments of taste can have universal validity not on cognitive grounds but only subjectively,[19] and Western aesthetics has followed doggedly in his footsteps. Ecological knowledge is fundamentally a scientific discipline claiming general validity on the basis of objective, empirical evidence. The study of natural processes is, to be sure, central to ecological science; the question is whether and how this is relevant for aesthetic appreciation.

It is essential to confront the issue here squarely and directly. Cheng cites Leopold in a telling reference.[20] Of critical significance here is that Leopold emphasized the importance of the perception of natural processes. That is, whatever knowledge we have of natural processes is aesthetically relevant if it affects our perception and not as cognition in itself. Cheng's discussion falters here, for he refers extensively to Callicott's interpretation of Leopold's land aesthetic in which Callicott goes beyond Leopold's restriction of knowledge to its perceptual influence: As Callicott writes, "The experience of a marsh or bog is 'aesthetically satisfying' less for what is literally sensed than for 'what is known or schematically imagined of its ecology.'"[21] Cheng seems to agree to include nonperceptual ecological knowledge in ecological aesthetic appreciation. More on this in a moment.

The fourth and final keystone Cheng identifies in ecological aesthetic appreciation is the principles of biodiversity and ecosystem health. This brings to a point the issue of the relevance of ecological knowledge in aesthetic appreciation. That these principles are at the heart of ecological appreciation is clear and there are dramatic examples of the problems for ecosystem health caused by invasive species, one of which Cheng cites (i.e., *eichhornia* or water hyacinth). Here Cheng's moral concerns become paramount, for he insists that "love for the beautiful has to be founded on the respect for all things equally," which means that to appreciate the beautiful requires ecological awareness.[22] It is not difficult to let one's knowledge of widespread ecological abuse and injustice become dominant, and we can sympathize with Cheng's intent to couple the ethical with the aesthetic, the better to support his moral perception. The question is whether and to what extent such an association is aesthetically relevant.

Critical Questions

It is instructive to compare these two outstanding efforts at establishing an ecological aesthetics, that of Jusuck Koh with that of Xiangzhan Cheng. In joining ecology with aesthetics, Koh emphasizes ecology's holistic, systemic character. The aesthetic character of environment displays a unity of form and purpose, of creativity and aesthetic experience, but it goes beyond subjectivity in recognizing the human need to be in a union with landscape, a unity of people and place.[23] Indeed, such inclusive unity "denies distance and duality between the subject and the object," between man and nature, transcending dualism in recognizing the environmental engagement that is inherent in the dynamic balance of an ecosystem. Koh takes this as an aesthetic principle.[24] And by including the idea of complementarity as an aesthetic principle, Koh recognizes that aesthetic value can be achieved when meaning is integrated in aesthetic experience: "When the beautiful and the meaningful and the form and content are integrated, the aesthetic experiences are likely to be more intense, perhaps because human perception and cognition mutually complement [one another] and are indivisible."[25]

Cheng's use of ecology is quite different. Going beyond Koh's unity and complementarity, Cheng asserts the necessity for ecological knowledge as the basis for aesthetic appreciation.[26] His argument is rich and complex, for it introduces the integral role of morality in ecological aesthetic appreciation.[27] The proper reference for such moral awareness is not humans alone but the entire biosphere, and this distinguishes it from traditional ethics, which is human-centered. He finds this broader scope not only in Leopold's thinking but in the long-standing Chinese tradition of recognizing the essential harmony between humans and nature, which is really an ecologically based humanism.

Cheng goes further to develop at length what he calls "ecological aesthetic appreciation," arguing that ecological knowledge is essential to fully appreciate the natural environment.[28] He acknowledges his divergence from the Western aesthetic tradition that has been heavily influenced by Kant, who claimed that aesthetic appreciation is noncognitive. Cheng derives his argument from Leopold's land aesthetic, observing that Leopold appealed to ecological knowledge to enhance "the perceptive faculty." However, Cheng diverges from Leopold's association of cognition with perception to follow the argument that Carlson uses to justify what he calls "aesthetic cognitivism." Just as background knowledge of art history is necessary for art appreciation, so knowledge of nature is necessary for nature appreciation.

While this analogy may seem plausible at first, it is actually fallacious. Knowledge of art history can, indeed, enhance our appreciation of art, but it does so not by adding cognitive content to our perceptual experience but rather by sensitizing us to perceptual features and details that we may have overlooked or not understood. Thus, understanding the theory of cubism enables us to visually apprehend a cubist painting as presenting multiple views of objects on the same picture plane, thus enhancing our perceptual experience. Similarly, knowing the theory of light and color that guided the Impressionists, and the aesthetic theories of the expressionists, abstract expressionists, color field painters, and other movements, enables our visual apprehension of what might seem chaotic or confusing to the uneducated eye. The point here is that knowledge of painterly techniques and artistic styles can enhance our perceptual sensitivity and thus our aesthetic appreciation. Such information may be satisfying in itself but, if taken alone, it is aesthetically irrelevant.

There are instances, to be sure, in which ecological or evolutionary knowledge can help free our perception from irrelevant considerations. Leopold calls this "the mental eye." Yet at the same time he retains the tie with aesthetic experience by joining such knowledge with perception. Cheng turns to Callicott's interpretation of Leopold's land aesthetic to support his ecological cognitivism. This is regrettable because Callicott is not sensitive to Leopold's careful practice of associating such knowledge with perception, and it is only this tie that validates such an ecological aesthetic. As Cheng relates it, Callicott holds that "the experience of a marsh or bog is 'aesthetically satisfying' less for what is literally sensed than for what is known . . . of its ecology."[29] This leads Cheng to give surpassing importance to biodiversity and ecosystem health, important considerations for ecosystem appraisal but perceptually irrelevant. And it brings Cheng to conclude that "the two guiding principles of ecological value for ecological aesthetic appreciation are biodiversity and ecosystem health."

Unfortunately, Cheng is guided here by ecological and ethical values rather than by aesthetic ones. Yet at the same time he cites Leopold approvingly, Leopold who required sensible perception in environmental aesthetic appreciation. There may well be an equivocation here in determining which is essential and has primacy: ecological knowledge, ethical value, or aesthetic experience. Indeed, it seems that by emphasizing biodiversity and ecosystem health as principles of ecological value, Cheng has entirely overlooked the aesthetic. Indeed, Paul H. Gobster, in his contribution to the same collaborative volume as Cheng's essay, considered various conditions under which conflicts between ecological and aesthetic values may occur. He calls this an "aesthetic-ecological disjuncture" and concludes that "Aesthetic quality and ecological quality are conceptually separate dimensions of landscape quality . . . and it might make more sense to deal with them in separate assessments."[30] I deliberately overlook cases here, such as the effluvium of a festering bog, in which the health of an ecosystem entirely contradicts experiences of beauty and aesthetic delight.

Ecological Values

These issues, in short, suggest the need to recognize values in environment that are important though different: ecological values, ethical values, and aesthetic values. Ideally, we might wish these values to be mutually complementary, for all are important factors in the human world. At the same time, candor requires that we acknowledge their differences, and it does nothing to resolve those differences to simply assert their compatibility in an ecological aesthetics or ecological ethics. There is no *a priori* necessity that these values harmonize with each other. Indeed, the very fact of their frequent conflict raises the issue of their incompatibility.

Appreciation is a valuing experience and, as we have seen, it can be based on different things, such as identifying important ethical considerations, recognizing and valuing the understanding that ecological and other scientific knowledge can provide, or experiencing the aesthetic qualities of a situation. When Cheng speaks of ecological appreciation, he is referring to a cognitive value, not an aesthetic or an ethical one. It is therefore misleading to speak of "ecological aesthetic appreciation" as if these two forms of appreciation are joined or even necessarily compatible. There are instances, not that common, in which both cognitive, ethical, and aesthetic values, though different, can be combined in enlightened land use planning, zoning, or social and environmental policy. There are cases, more common, in which they are in conflict.[31] This points up the confusion in the very idea of a cognitive aesthetics, which Cheng seems to join with Carlson in advocating, for the concept of "cognitive aesthetics" is actually an oxymoron. That is because aesthetic values are grounded in perception and cognitive ones are conceptual, both entirely different, as Kant reminded us. One must hope that by developing an awareness of these values and of their differences, we will encourage the greater collective normative realization.

Perhaps ecology may best serve as a metaphor for the holistic, contextual character of environmental aesthetic experience. Such a sign of the unity of humans and environment in the experience of aesthetic engagement is close to what Koh has consistently urged and, in fact, is in harmony with traditional Chinese thinking. Science can contribute much to our understanding and appreciation of environmental experience and values. To the extent that scientific knowledge sensitizes us perceptually to our environmental transactions, it is aesthetically relevant and can enhance appreciation. To the degree to which ecological and other scientific information enlarge our intellectual appreciation and admiration of nature by expanding our perceptual awareness and acuity, it offers cognitive value that has aesthetic consequences. Thus, for example, relativity physics has transformed our understanding and our perception of the physical universe. Using this knowledge in recognizing the relativity and legitimacy of our spatial experience has enormous aesthetic significance, for it enables us to apprehend environment always in relation to the participating perceiver. Similarly, when our knowledge of evolution sensitizes us to the perceptual details that accompany adaptive changes of fauna and flora to changing environmental conditions of light, wind, climate, and ambient temperature, this may be aesthetically relevant and significant. Moreover, there is important scientific research on perception that has direct implications for aesthetic theory.[32]

This critique of the important theories developed by Koh and Cheng can help us identify the conceptual errors and methodological misapplications that occur in some recent efforts to develop an ecological aesthetics. None of these values—ethical, scientific, or aesthetic—is necessarily dominant in any particular environmental complex. Most often they constitute a normative complex in which their relative importance is determined by the unique character of the situation and by the judgment of those making the assessment. It is more justifiable to argue for a respectful acknowledgment of the important contributions of each, of ethical scientific/ecological, and aesthetic dimensions, in environmental experience and understanding. Environmental appreciation must be understood, I believe, by a philosophically guided study of appreciative, that is, normative experience on its own terms, whether scientific or aesthetic.

I call this "philosophically guided" because philosophical assumptions play a central role here, and uncovering such assumptions is both clarifying and liberating.

I hope that this critique has outlined a broad field of inquiry that needs to be pursued further, both theoretically and in particular environmental complexes. Enthusiasm for the rich possibilities of ecological awareness should be balanced by recognizing its differences with ethical and aesthetic interests and values. A proper application of scientific knowledge in environmental experience must be accompanied by recognizing the ethical values inherent in particular environmental situations, along with their possibilities for aesthetic appreciation, accompanied by a careful consideration of situations in which they are joined. My hope is that this discussion has helped by clarifying how these values may be recognized and how, while different, they may be compatible.

Part IV

Aesthetic Exploitation

7

A Critical Aesthetics of Disney World

It might seem strange to propose an aesthetic consideration of the theme park, that artificial bloom in the garden of popular culture.[1] The aesthetic is often considered a minority interest in the modern world, yet it offers a distinctive perspective even on an activity that has mass appeal, and can provide insights that would otherwise remain undiscovered. Aesthetic description and interpretation can illuminate the theme park in many directions: as architecture, design, theater, landscape architecture and environment. I shall focus on the last of these, environment.

Nominally, a theme park is a combination of amusement park and world's fair, a place where people forget their cares and enjoy leisurely diversion in garden-like surroundings. Its relaxed, secure atmosphere is a marked change from the public places we frequently inhabit, such as the workplace, the market, and the thoroughfare. At the same time, theme parks are complex palaces of delight that offer an extravagant variety of multisensory activities and experiences and even purport to be educational. They are places of mass entertainment, easy to enter and enjoy, whose sounds and sights engulf us as soon as we pass through the gate. The concept of theming is an environmental approach to the concept of place; taken collectively, theme parks constitute a multiplicity of environments, each with its own character.

Disney World collects many of these themes into one enormous "fantasia," a composite of disparate types from various sources—futuristic, ethnic, fantasy, adventure. It is a true anthology of distinctive environments. In its enormous variety, Disney World might be considered a microcosm of America's cultural pluralism. On the contemporary scene it stands as the kitsch of postmodernism. One is reminded of Baudrillard's concept of simulacrum in whose final stage an image or sign is not related to any independent reality but stands on its own as hyperreality.[2]

Yet its meanings do not lie wholly on the surface. Disney World invites a range of interpretations that parallels its postmodern ethos, making it at the same time an endlessly fertile subject for the subtextual elaborations of aesthetic analysis. Like some of its rides whose sights appear abruptly out of the darkness, the rich significance of Disney World's environments appears on levels and in strange juxtapositions. By exploring some of its multiple facets through an aesthetic analysis, I hope to uncover some unusual dimensions of Disney World's character as a postmodern environment. And exposing some of its multiple meanings will not only disclose its powerful normative message but inform a moral judgment as well.

Disney World as an Aesthetic Environment

Theme parks are totally constructed environments whose character is decided largely by their prominent aesthetic features. By aesthetic features I mean the perceptual dimensions through which we experience an environment directly—what we hear, see, and feel with our bodies as we move through it and how these sensory qualities combine with our knowledge and beliefs to create a unified experiential situation.

Part of what determines an environment is the perceptual horizon that defines its boundaries. Disney World achieves this architecturally. Each area is stylistically coherent internally and distinctive externally. The three main divisions of Disney World—Magic Kingdom, Epcot Center, and Disney-MGM Studios, are separated physically from each other and delimited by definite borders punctuated by an entrance gate. Each division, in turn, breaks up into distinct areas defined by architectural style and color. In the Magic Kingdom, for example, the rustic structures of Frontierland are brown, the modernistic buildings of Tomorrowland are pink, while the green of tropical trees and plantings supports the wilderness character of Adventureland. The location and limits of each area, moreover, are clear. Dominant landmarks signal its center, while sharp shifts in the prevailing color and architecture form invisible lines that separate it from neighboring ones. Epcot Center has two major sections, Future World and World Showcase, within each of which are pavilions housing different kinds of scientific technology or distinct national enclaves. Although each of these stands separately, garden pathways connect them, and miniature trains, buses, boats, and a monorail assist travel from one area to another.

Disney-MGM Studios also has two divisions: the studio and production section and the various set locations and entertainment features. In all three parks, each area or building offers us a distinct, individual domain of time, place, or pursuit.

As soon as one passes through the gate, the usual temporal parameters disappear. While a few events are scheduled, reservations are easy to make at electronic stations. Clocks are difficult to find, and the functions by which one usually structures time blend into a constant present. Numerous snack bars, cafeterias, and restaurants provide food for all tastes and pocketbooks on any impulse. Restrooms are everywhere and clean. Opportunities for play, purchase, entertainment, excitement, education, and rest are always within easy reach. One can even live in Disney World, since several themed hotels and resorts are located tangentially, connected by pathways and miniature trains. The stress of time and the rigidity of schedules disappear, and one floats along in a pressureless, though eventful, temporal haze.

As one enters a different domain of time, so one lives in another realm of space. The outside world is quite forgotten. Architectural intimidation, so common in industrial societies, does not exist here. No skyscrapers or structures of overpowering mass oppress the visitor. The scale of buildings is comfortably proportionate to the human body, and garden areas are all about, so that despite the large numbers of people, one never feels claustrophobic. Lines do not seem excessively long. They typically follow a switchback pattern, are hidden by landscaping whenever possible, and are rendered less tedious by settings and backdrops keyed to the upcoming ride or attraction. Because nothing is very high, space is experienced as largely horizontal. Everywhere one has a sense of expansiveness, even without any large, open pedestrian plaza. One's attention is drawn instead to the many local niches and attractions. All this may account for the remarkably benign behavior of its large crowds.

Most people walk everywhere, and this sets the pace of movement. This is not burdensome, for frequent garden enclaves provide places of rest and retreat. While Disney World casts its appeal largely to a juvenile audience, it attracts families and people of all ages. Yet in spite of the nature and diversity of its visitors, the level of stress is remarkably low, and loud voices and fast movement are rare. The leisurely pace and serendipitous atmosphere keep one in a state of relaxed anticipation. Yes, there is canned background music, but it is qualitatively better than the canned goods at other markets and effectively blankets the ambient noise. The sound system, moreover, is of high quality and unobtrusive, with its volume low and its speakers hidden in the garden foliage.

The Multiple Realities of Disney World

Disney World, then, is a comfortable mix of discrete regions, styles, activities, interests. It is interesting to speculate on what makes this mélange successful in luring people there to spend days on end without a feeling of surfeit. The clear division into distinct areas and activities, the gentle pace, the superabundance of easy satisfactions, and an unthreatening atmosphere of fantasy all belie the stresses of ordinary life and encourage feelings of comfort and pleasure. Disney World offers the visitor multiple worlds, from the storybook fantasy of the Magic Kingdom and the futuristic fantasy of Future World to the idealized cultural environments of World Showcase and the fragmented three-dimensional images of the movie world at Disney-MGM Studios. Disney World is, in fact, a pop postmodern environment. With its heterogeneous profusion of brief distractions and fragmentation of attention into three-minute spots, it is a flowering of our electronic entertainment culture.

Although this giant collection offers a seemingly endless variety, there is an underlying logic in its order as well as in its intent. The multitude of worlds resolves into four kinds: fantasy, adventure, futuristic, and national-cultural. The fantasy environments of Disney World are idealized recreations which freely use every cliché in the popular imagination. Mickey Mouse, the Haunted Mansion, the Liberty Bell, the Victorian facades of a turn-of-the-century small town, Cinderella, the Mad Hatter's Tea Party, and Snow White are some of the cultural classics or cliches that populate the park. Another of Disney's worlds appears in the adventure environments, from the American frontier, the Swiss Family Robinson's treehouse, and a Jungle Cruise to Caribbean pirate strongholds, space travel simulations, 3D films, and films with wrap-around screens. Its futuristic environments contain Disney World's euphoric presentation of a benign high-tech future dominated by a space travel scenario. Communication, health, transportation, habitat, food, the sea, energy, creativity—the exhibits and language of Future World sing the ideology of endless technological progress.

Cultural environments are the fourth component of Disney World. Across the central lagoon at Epcot Center is World Showcase: eleven national pavilions or rather ethnic enclaves representing Mexico, Norway, China, Germany, Italy, the United States, Japan, Morocco, France, the United Kingdom, and Canada. Each endeavors to convey a sense of its nation and culture through replicas of famous landmarks and indigenous architectural styles, gardens, local crafts and wares, restaurants serving national cuisine, and live performances of traditional arts. An Aztec pyramid, the Eiffel Tower, Katsura Palace, the Venice campanile, the Temple of Heaven, and a Rocky Mountain landscape make many of the pavilions instantly recognizable. "Illuminations," a high-tech light show, music, and fireworks extravaganza above the central lagoon closes each day at Epcot Center, drawing the darkened pavilions together with laser spotlights and music from different national traditions.

Despite the overwhelming profusion of buildings and events, these many environments share certain characteristics. Most striking to the reflective visitor is the thorough planning, extending to the seemingly spontaneous parades, skits, and other street performances. Visible and invisible controls make these environments so carefree that, despite the crowds and the ceaseless activity, these public spaces never become threatening. We are in a wonderland in which people readily suspend their usual attitude and behavior and where criticism and controversy never occur.

Disney World as a Postmodern Environment

This jostling multiplicity of environments actually turns Disney World into a parody of postmodernism. The most salient feature of postmodern architecture, its imaginative combination of stylistic elements from a variety of traditional sources, here assumes the hyperbole and fluidity of cartoon time and space. Like postmodern architecture, Disney World presents historicality without being itself historical. Despite a content of real and imaginative histories, it is, in fact, actually ahistorical. History here is idealized and fictionalized, its selections taken from a design book for their entertainment value. The historical replicas here did not develop and age, and they show no signs of the processes of time or the wear of use. Everything is changeless, eternally new, bright, and clean. Authenticity becomes irrelevant and is replaced by satisfaction. Indeed, authenticity must be given a different definition in Disney World's postmodern sense of time. When cartoon and movie characters and events come to "life," one joins them in a different order of reality, a fun-loving, carefree world.

Moreover, like so many of the contemporary arts, Disney World is explicitly and intrinsically self-referential, simultaneously referring to itself and its methods as it presents them. Visitors continuously move in and out of both levels, concurrently participating in and learning about them. Some "informational" exhibits are pure fiction, from Mickey Mouse's bed to a tour of the technological future—fantasy about fantasy. Disney World is also culturally self-referential.

It provides visitors with a tour of American beliefs about itself and corporate beliefs about technology. Even more, it embodies them.

Like postmodern architecture, Disney World combines disparate styles with a rich complex of allusions and references and presents them as entertainment. And like postmodern architecture, its order does not lie entirely in its forms but in its meanings and interpretations. Lyotard has argued that the mark of the postmodern lies in putting forward "the unpresentable in presentation itself.... [It] searches for new presentations, not in order to enjoy them but in order to impart a stronger sense of the unpresentable."[3] Disney World epitomizes this conception of the postmodern, for behind its plethora of presentations lie meanings and beliefs that cannot be shown directly. There could be no more apt subject for interpretation than this, for while Disney World is a rich subject, interpretations are multiple and often incompatible, a cognitive analogue of the eclecticism of postmodernism. Yet the very fact that they form an inconclusive order makes Disney World an ideal subject for aesthetic analysis.

Disney World's Multiple Meanings

Although interpretations multiply freely, they are either descriptive or critical. Of the first, the most obvious sees Disney World as an entertainment park where visitors are encouraged to be carefree and spontaneous. People can be guided by impulse alone without fear of unhappy consequences, for fantasy is the overall motif and every outcome is positive. This is a world of happy make-believe, a place in which ordinary limits do not apply and one can do anything. As an entertainment park Disney World succeeds admirably. It is an enormously large and successful business that has made itself into an institution of American culture with a wide and devoted following and has become a major destination for foreign visitors, as well. One can also describe Disney World as an educational institution, and many of its attractions make that appeal: The activities and exhibits in Future World cover a wide range of scientific and technological areas, World Showcase is a three-dimensional travelogue, Disney-MGM Studios offers tours of animation and movie sets and studios, while in Magic Kingdom, Liberty Square provides visitors with lessons in American history. Yet behind its joyful surface lies a highly complex and intricately planned operation, for Disney World is a model of high-tech planning and population control. Everything has been thought of to ease and please its large crowds of visitors. Nothing is allowed to tarnish its brilliant image of cleanliness and order, and no trash is ever in sight. An elaborate network of controls regulates all events and activities, and in a supreme gesture of self-referentiality, there is even a tour of the control center.

Yet this virtuoso technology and manifestly wholesome entertainment and instruction conceal a deep subconscious, metaphorically speaking, which, like its Freudian analogue, is nine-tenths submerged. As a cultural symbol, Disney World is subtly penetrating. Behind its environment of glittering surfaces, its "wilderness of images," to use a phrase of T. S. Eliot, hides disturbing meanings. In numerous ways the park both illustrates and epitomizes kinds of thought and practice that characterize the industrial-commercial culture of our period. One wonders how many visitors note the pervasive identification of the corporations sponsoring the giant pavilions that display and laud technology with technology itself and the kind of life it makes possible. And that kind of life is associated with consumption. Disney World, in fact, openly purveys the culture of consumption. It is easy, convenient, and painless to spend money here, for this is the land of consumerism. The very fact that admission to the park entitles one to enter every building and attraction fosters a sense of free entertainment that easily moves out to include the kiosks and shops that stand at every turn, while purchasing Disney Dollars encourages a sense of monetary make-believe.

Disney World is actually a soft-sell environment. While everything seems designed for ease and pleasure, subtle controls extend in every direction, leading to the total manipulation of its visitors, although with disarming gentleness. In fact, Disney World stands, perhaps more than anything else, as a monument to consumer culture. Everything is converted into matter for consumption: national and ethnic traditions, science, technology, education. Even the family is transformed into a unit of consumption. History, too, of science, of technology, of nations, is just another commodity that can be fashioned to meet the requirements of the situation and sold to the public. Entertainment has become Big Business, and the business of Disney World is entertainment. Its product is pleasure and its production is consumption. Eco considers such a place "at once absolutely realistic and absolutely fantastic. . . . Facades [are] presented to us as toy houses and invite us to enter them, but their interior is always a disguised supermarket, where you buy obsessively believing you are still playing." It is what Morawski has called a "consumerist fairyland. No codes and no norms deserve any serious attention as they cancel each other." Spectacles produce excitement and a pleasant confusion, while their hidden messages, buried in the casual occurrences of mass culture, effectively take over.[4]

What we have here is actually a new colonialism, a corporate colonialism over the consumer, a cultural colonialism of the high-tech nations over the

Third World. The culture of consumption has appropriated the past, ethnic practices, even science, all in the name of corporate interests such as those that designed and operate nearly all the major pavilions in Future World. The social consequences of this are alarming, for despite beneficent, indulgent appearances, Disney World is in practice a totalitarian environment. One encounters no scowling face, no disagreement, no dissent, differences, or alternatives to the omnipresent good nature and good cheer. The Disney Corporation has, moreover, very strict hiring guidelines. Disney World hires only about one in every ten individuals interviewed. Euro Disneyland, outside of Paris, created a good deal of animosity by requiring its employees to display smiling faces, a custom more American than European. The fact that everything is planned so successfully means in practice that everything is controlled, and controlled in the interests of a single optimistic message. Many of the exhibits are badly out of date, seemingly stuck in the 1970s. Most show little environmental consciousness, no questioning of faith in science, and no acknowledgment of alternative lifestyles or of Eastern religion, to name a few absent alternatives.

Moreover, Disney World is no aberrant development. Not only are the Disney parks models for theme parks everywhere, but the model has been extended to entire nations, from considering Mexico as the Third World theme park for Americans, rural England as a theme park for escaping urban dwellers, and Britain as a giant rain theme park, to a proposal to market the entire United States as a theme park for visiting Europeans. Moreover, the theme park can create history by influencing our beliefs about the past.[5] To turn the world into a collection of theme parks, a future some fear, is to conquer the very planet, using the smile as the ultimate weapon to subdue a mass population with good humor.

This is an environment, then, in which nothing is as it appears to be. Spectacular in scale and brilliant in execution, Disney World is a "masterpiece of falsification." "What it sells is, indeed, goods, but genuine merchandise, not reproductions. What is falsified is our will to buy, which we take as real, and in this sense Disneyland is really the quintessence of consumer ideology."[6] Not only does Disney World run its subject matter past a distorting mirror, it actually contains *levels* of falseness, for even when something is itself authentic, its context renders it false. The architectural designs in World Showcase, for example, are accurate replicas of indigenous architectural styles. Yet they are merely surfaces, authentic facades. Behind each is another tourist shop, a snack bar, or nothing at all. What is authenticity in such a setting? Is there such a thing as authenticity any more?[7]

Other purposes hide behind everything. Disney World represents itself as the full flowering of the modernist ethos, with its confidence in a future guided by scientific imagination toward a technological utopia. But the contrast is vivid between the use of that technology and the kind of experience visitors have. As we are pleasantly lulled into accepting the modernist ideology of Disney World, we are subjected to a level of exploitation virtuosic in its sophistication and insidious in its effects: the total co-optation of our beliefs and purposes and their ultimate absorption into the credit card culture of consumption.

The juxtaposition of futuristic visions with historical and fictional experiences actually contradicts and subverts a key modernist element, the idea of steady, limitless scientific progress. Unidirectional time is abandoned. One inhabits a timeless realm in which everything is constantly available and the future lies before us as eternal beneficence. There is no acknowledgment that technology has consequences and that many of the planet's present problems, from acid rain and the depletion of the ozone layer to overpopulation, nuclear waste, and modern warfare, are the largely unplanned or unwanted results of industrial technology. And history, its hard pain painted over by bland romanticism, becomes sentimental entertainment.

Even more, the universal scope of the theme park undermines our grasp of reality. Not only are there multiple realities here of fiction, fantasy, science, geography, history, and nationality, each with its own special claim: The distortion of their content, the blurring of distinctions among them, the deliberate confusion of their modes, and the omission of everyday economic reality ingeniously exploit what Disney World purportedly honors: (i) children, by turning the world into a cartoon; (ii) the family, by promoting social stereotypes and identifying the family with a lifestyle of consumption; (iii) ethnic traditions, by transforming them into consumable curiosities and collectibles instead of genuine practices integral to their cultures; (iv) science, by portraying it as inevitably successful and invariably benevolent; (v) technology, by ascribing to it a limitless capacity for improving life by inventing consumables that are always desirable.

These different realities do not only form a heterogeneous mass; their order is indeterminate. The national enclaves of World Showcase, for example, offer ethnic realities within another reality—Epcot Center, within another reality—Disney World, within yet another reality—themed hotels and resorts, within still another reality—Orlando. Yet does any of these realities predominate? One might be tempted to say the "outer world" of Orlando. Yet we are hardly aware of Orlando at all and most visitors encounter the city only from the super highway or the airport. Furthermore, the immediacy of one's present location is inevitably the most forceful, making it constantly unclear which end is up, as we move from one place to another. This is true not only inside the theme park; we carry such confusion away with us, just as we whistle a tune after the show is over or have uneasy dreams after watching a horror movie. Disney-MGM Studios further epitomizes this jumbled juxtaposition of worlds, this cultural cubism. Its animation studios and movie sets show how film reality is fabricated out of fragments, and the park itself encourages a breakdown of the difference between the movie illusion and actual places and events. Things are equally real and equally hollow. Is there a cultural schizophrenia at work here? This disintegration of reality structure is what Marin has called "a degenerate utopia . . . at once absolutely realistic and absolutely fantastic."[8]

Most of Disney World's multiple meanings, moreover, convincing yet not always compatible, are not delivered directly but gain force precisely through their indirection. Perhaps it is not just that they are not presented immediately but that they cannot be. This is Disney World's postmodernism in Lyotard's sense, its presentation of the unpresentable. What are the hidden meanings, the subliminal forces at work here? Do we begin to discover them as we peel off the smiles? Lyotard claims further that "modern aesthetics is an aesthetic of the sublime, though a nostalgic one. It allows the unpresentable to be put forward only as the missing contents; but the form, because of its recognizable consistency, continues to offer to the reader or viewer matter for solace and pleasure."[9] By presenting the unpresentable on a magnitude hitherto inconceivable and perhaps beyond rational comprehension, Disney World, one could argue, represents the sublime in this postmodern age. The theme park is at the same time the sublimation of commercial culture and the desublimation of the sublime. Disney World has become, in fact, our monument to the sublime, its most salient expression at the culmination of the twentieth century. Yet can magnitude without elevation attain the sublime?

The Normative Significance of Disney World

I had originally thought to end this chapter with an inconclusiveness appropriate to the topic. Yet an aesthetic analysis of Disney World shows that the dilemma of multiple, incompatible interpretations and the impossibility of resolving them do not obliterate normative judgment. On the contrary, this discussion stands as an argument against moral indecisiveness. For normative judgment is built into the very pursuit of understanding and this last critique embodies a powerful moral condemnation. It is true that one can see Disney World as both a fairyland for family entertainment and an enormously complex and sophisticated work of popular art. Surely these mark its positive contribution to popular culture. On the other hand, our analysis reveals the most sophisticated and comprehensive instance in our time of the subversion by corporate interests of personal motives, social institutions, and public values. Disney World stands as a megamonument to the commodification of culture. Can we determine which values in this heterogeneous mix are preeminent? Does an aesthetic analysis carry us beyond the coexistence of multiple, mutually incompatible interpretations to a moral conclusion?

The case for Disney World is obvious. In its favor stands the mass audience of the theme park. For its avid followers, regular visits are a high point of personal and family life, and they happily spend vast sums for what they perceive to be full value. Who could quarrel with family fun and healthy popular art? Yet the positive case can be countered in more than one way. Against the elaborate serendipity of Disney World are the witnesses to the simple, unencumbered life, from the ancient Stoics to E. F. Schumacher, Scott Nearing, and the contemporary rediscoverers of Buddhism in the West. To find the universe in one's backyard, as Thoreau once urged, suggests an economy directed, not toward the consumption of luxuries but toward enlightenment, the cultivation of aesthetic sensibility, and a deepening of moral experience that lead us to recognize the ultimacy of life and the omnipresence of the sacred.

More compelling than this alternative, however, is the unsettling picture that presents itself when we look closely at what the theme park is and what it does. As we begin to detect the falseness and manipulation that underlie its pleasant gloss, we are led to condemn its empty pleasures as soporific and exploitative. The Socratic tradition that forsakes satisfaction for understanding is a perennially sobering influence in matters such as this. While we cannot appeal to a simple hierarchy of values, we do have in this instance a clear choice between the dissatisfactions of a Socrates and the satisfactions of a fool, to recall Mill. The determination of value here lies in having experienced both.[10] Once we recognize the motives and interests that underlie the theme park, can we ever again find satisfaction in its joyful surfaces?

What we approach through postmodernism is a sense of things that has been emerging slowly throughout the long and difficult twentieth century and its successor: the realization that the tradition of clear resolutions and final certainties distorts the facts of irresolvable difference, limited understanding, and a residual pluralism of truths and values. Dewey's recognition that "the quest for certainty" is misdirected helped inaugurate a different sense of knowledge, one not governed by the goal of complete, permanent, and univocal truth but rather of truths in the making, provisional, multiple nodes in a constantly altering web of knowledge governed by changing conditions, needs, and activities.[11] Yet realizing this does not abandon us to intellectual fragmentation and cognitive chaos. It calls rather for a conceptual landscape vastly different from the modernist ideal of an unequivocal order revealed by "the light of reason." We need something akin to what Merleau-Ponty termed "the good dialectic," "capable of differentiating and of integrating into one sole universe double or even multiple meanings . . . because it envisages without restriction the plurality of the relationships and what has been called ambiguity."[12]

It means admitting value, too, into an enlarged cognitive realm. Values cannot be relegated to the shadowy region of the emotive, as the positivists would have it. We have come to realize that the normative pervades all experience, cognitive as much as any other. No human activity, scientific or artistic, can breathe air that is value neutral. Value suffuses the human presence and whatever we touch has a normative dimension. That is why an aesthetic analysis of Disney World that began with an attempt at pure description ends with moral judgment. This does not create an unwelcome complication in the knowledge process; it recognizes that another facet on the complex jewel of human understanding has been glowing all along. We find ourselves returning, in this humanized landscape of understanding, to the insight of our classical forebears that truth and value are inseparable, but we must couple this with the recognition by contemporary science and philosophy that these are invariably contextual and contingent.

Such an approach offers a direction, at the close of the postmodern age, that may rescue us from the morass into which an overly simple epistemology has sunk us. It suggests that multiple interpretations do not all have equal weight, that postmodernism requires aesthetic analysis, and that this leads to a conclusion somewhat less destructive than indefiniteness and less autocratic than "Truth." This aesthetic analysis of Disney's worlds, by showing how realities are created and subverted, confronts us with the pervasiveness of the normative and the inseparability of the moral and the aesthetic. The challenge of our time is to reform knowledge and value in a way that is pluralistic and open-ended and yet provides the basis for both decision and action. Such restructuring is an inevitable consequence of the inadequacies of the old millennium and the necessary precondition for the foundation of a new.

8

The Subversion of Beauty

> *In due time, the theory of aesthetics will have to account not only for the delight in Kantian beauty and the sublime, but for the phenomena like aesthetic violence and the aestheticization of violence, of aesthetic abuse and intrusion, the blunting of sensibility, its perversion, and its poisoning.*[1]

Aesthetics has traditionally been concerned with understanding the experience of beauty in the arts and in nature. In the contemporary world, however, aesthetic values are no longer confined to the museum and the scenic drive where they are honored but isolated and made innocuous. Aesthetic experiences and values have now become increasingly prominent in all areas of modern life, raising conflicts with values in morality, religion, economics, environment, and social life.[2]

Perceptual Experience

Such aesthetic experiences are largely, though not entirely, perceptual and occur in various ways, both directly through sensory engagement and indirectly through sensory imagination. The broad scope of perceptual experience in the contemporary arts and artistic practices has led to the proliferation of sensory engagement in distinctive and sometimes unique ways. This developed capacity has been refined in the arts but it is also diffused in an endless variety of ways and places throughout people's activities and practices.

The concern with perceptual experience pervades the history of philosophical aesthetics. We only need think of Plato's suspicion of the moral influence of music and poetry because of their seductive qualities and enervating influence and their enticing and compelling though irrational appeal. Together with Aristotle's recognition of the cathartic effect of tragic drama, both of these seminal figures recognized the powerful and emotionally compelling force of perceptual experience. This is a theme that continued with greater or lesser force in the development of Western aesthetics, leading, as we have seen, in the mid-eighteenth century to Baumgarten's designation of *aisthēsis*, literally, perception by the senses, as the science of sensory knowledge directed toward beauty and to considering art as the perfection of sensory awareness. We do not sufficiently credit the fact that the origins of aesthetic value lie in sense experience. This is shown not only in the etymology of the term "aesthetics" but also in the dependence of aesthetic appreciation on the sensory content of our encounter with a work of art or a natural landscape. This encounter centers on perceptual experience: acuteness in viewing, listening, touching—the full somatic engagement with the rich world of sensible experience in which we are inextricably embedded.[3]

It is not necessary to review here the subsequent history of aesthetics in order to follow the expanding presence of sense experience through the twentieth century and into the present one. A sensory presence has never been more influential than now, when the expanded scope of sense experience and of subject matter entertains no limit and admits no restraint. We now have aesthetic inquiry that includes the involvement of all the senses, not only the traditional distant ones of sight and hearing but also the bodily, contact senses of touch, smell, taste, kinesthesia, and the like.

At the same time, the range of activities and experiences has broadened so that nothing is excluded from aesthetic uses and participation. Aestheticians now probe the folk and the popular arts, as well as the traditional fine arts, and aesthetic inquiry extends to food, sport, environment, and culture. Along with an unrestricted scope of attention, aesthetic inquiry now explores the entire range of perceptual experience of the body and its social matrix. This enlargement of the scope of aesthetics has flowered in such areas as environmental aesthetics, the aesthetics of everyday life, social aesthetics, and the aesthetics of politics. The enlargement of aesthetic inquiry has increased our awareness of its active, participatory character, a condition I call *aesthetic engagement*. All this has led me to think of aesthetics as the theory of sensibility.

As the theory of sensibility, aesthetics focuses on the range, qualities, and nuances of sensory experience, and on its discrimination, acuteness, and subtlety, its perceptual, experienced significance and its emotional component. Thus from this standpoint, aesthetics embraces the full range of perceptual experience, and cognitive factors (history, information, theory, interpretation, and such) are relevant only insofar as they enhance direct perceptual experience.

This enlargement of aesthetic awareness has had a profound effect on the field of aesthetics. Not only does aesthetic inquiry now embrace the objects, activities, and experiences of human life without constraint; it necessarily implicates other areas of philosophy. When aesthetic inquiry embraces social domains, ethical and even metaphysical concerns cannot be ignored. When eyes sensitive to beauty in art and nature encounter the objects and activities of ordinary life, they see not only their hidden charms[4] but also their failings.[5] Thus aesthetics has come to include a negative domain and become a moral instrument and even a political factor in developing new thought in cultural analysis.[6]

The aesthetics of everyday life offers a fresh perspective on the world of ordinary experience, revealing facets that have long gone unremarked. These experiences may not be spectacular and may even be routine. Aesthetic value is discovered in common objects, conditions, and situations, ranging from the houses, landscaping, and trees encountered during a walk in one's own neighborhood to basking in the spring sunshine; from tossing a ball back and forth and even, one scholar has suggested, to finding a certain aesthetic satisfaction in hanging laundry.[7] As Yuriko Saito has noted, "We are yet to develop an aesthetic discourse regarding artifacts such as utensils, furniture, and other objects with which we interact in everyday environment and activities that we undertake with them, such as cleaning, cooking, and socializing with others."[8] All these offer occasions of delighting in the sensible experience of an ordinary situation and the sheer sensory pleasure of being alive.[9]

We can see, then, that aesthetic experience pervades every society and every aspect of sensibility. Some things that affect that experience are obvious, such as our physical endowments, educational and recreational opportunities, life activities, and previous aesthetic experiences. There are also many hidden influences on sensible experience: unknown physical or perceptual endowments and limitations and, most striking, ethnic background, and the pervasive cultural conditions and forces of one's lifeworld.

The Co-optation of Sensibility

Aesthetic sensibility is profoundly influenced by the experiences and practices that characterize mass consumer culture. While pervasive, many of these are hidden and their influence undetected. An aesthetic critique is uniquely capable of revealing their subtle force. Because of its ubiquity, sensible experience has many manifestations, both overt and hidden. Let us consider some largely covert practices by which aesthetic sensibility has been subtly appropriated and exploited. These practices have resulted in what may be called "the co-optation of sensibility." Their damaging consequences to health, society, and environment are incalculable. Let me explain.

As one cannot help being aware, the developed world has fostered an industrial-commercial culture obsessed with profitability. From schools to public agencies, no institution is immune to the business imperatives of reducing costs and increasing profits. This is dramatically different from the *raison d'être* of service institutions, which is to meet people's needs, assist them in fulfilling their goals, and promote the transmission of culture. These institutions are particularly vulnerable under a business model, since the high labor costs of providing services are a major expense and directly impede the maximization of profit. This model has taken an increasingly firmer hold on schools and universities, on health care, and on public services of every kind. All have been subsumed under the standard of profit-making enterprises. Although my observations make special reference to practices in the United States, they have global relevance wherever these practices are found.

The capability for the experience and appreciation of aesthetic value, which I call here inclusively "beauty," has been subverted. Indeed, those capacities of human sensibility have been deliberately appropriated and distorted in mass consumer culture in at least four distinct ways: by gastronomic co-optation, technological co-optation, emotional co-optation, and psychological co-optation. By appropriating, controlling, and impairing the capacities of human perception, these forms of co-optation undermine the free sensibility that is the heart of aesthetic appreciation, thus subverting the possibilities of aesthetic value.

Commercial and political practices have developed slowly and irresistibly to control and shape the very capacities for perceptual experience, a process that can be called *the co-optation of sensibility*. It consists in the appropriation of the capacity for sensible experience in the interests of mass marketing and corporate profit. Moreover, the political process has itself increasingly come under the influence of this economic model and been dominated directly and indirectly by its interests. Let me offer some examples of four domains in which the co-optation of sensibility in mass consumer culture takes place. These practices have become a global menace to human health, cultural pluralism, and well-being overall. How does mass consumer culture subvert the experience of beauty? Let me mention briefly a few examples of four different kinds of sensible co-optation.

Modes of Sensible Co-optation

Gustatory Co-optation

The first kind of sensible co-optation to consider is gustatory co-optation. One might ask what relevance this has for aesthetics. I have several reasons for beginning with this mode of co-optation. One is that the aesthetics of food has emerged as an interest in aesthetic theory as well as in practice, generating serious discussion in the recent literature. The flagrant abuse of gustatory sensibility is so widespread and deleterious to health that it provides a vivid illustration of the phenomenon of co-optation that I am identifying.

Having a sweet tooth is more than an innocent indulgence; it carries consequences for health. Sugar is associated with what is called the metabolic syndrome: obesity, heart disease, stroke, and diabetes.[10] Moreover, sugar is addictive and plays a part in encouraging the consumption of other addictive substances, including the caffeine in soft drinks such as Coca-Cola and coffee, and alcohol in a range of drinks.[11] Salt is another food substance where a tasteful and necessary substance is often used to excess in most prepared foods and a "taste" for salt is encouraged. At the same time, its influence in raising blood pressure is well-documented. Other gastronomic examples are plentiful, such as the excessive use of fats and oils in deep-fried fast food, a habitual practice that leads to high cholesterol levels and obesity.[12] Junk foods in general use excessive amounts of sugar, salt, and fat, together with chemical preservatives for the producers' convenience. Our very sensibility is being distorted as well as our health affected in order to promote addictive consumption and profitable results.[13]

Technological Co-optation

Technology has assisted in the fabrication of perceptual experiences through chemistry, as well as electronic and digital technology. The conveniences are obvious and the products are widely adopted, but there are some hidden sensory costs that are not generally recognized. Smell, for example, is a sense modality that has been co-opted. False fragrances are infused into a multitude of products, from hand cream and bar soap to laundry and dish detergents, so that it is difficult to know how something actually smells. Fragrant overlays suffuse hotel rooms and emanate from pets and people. A principal source of perceptual information has been lost.

Still another impingement on sensibility lies in the colors used in clothing, home decoration, and, of course, in print advertising and on the internet. Strident and garish colors are widely used to attract attention to signs and clothing on commercial strips so that subtle and muted colors are not noticed or have simply disappeared from the marketplace altogether. Most obvious and pervasive are the cell phone and computer, whose requirements impose enormous demands of time and attention to fully utilize their capabilities.

Auditory Co-optation

Music has a place in nearly every culture and is especially widespread in modern developed societies. Sound is an elusive phenomenon. While we can usually identify its source, sound spreads broadly and, like perfume, tends to envelop others. This is one of the appealing qualities of musical experience, but in some cases this attractive feature is exaggerated so as to become oppressive and inescapable. Extremely high volume is used in some rock concerts to increase the appeal of the music and create a manic audience response. Such high volume is intended to impress the audience by its sheer force, and indeed one can often literally feel the physical pressure of the sound waves. This presumably attracts a large attendance and makes such entertainment highly profitable. Other consequences to auditory sensibility may take a little longer to recognize, such as the hearing loss from damage to the tiny hair-like cells in the cochlea of the inner ear that are the auditory nerve receptors.

Moreover, the auditory environment is not free from pollution. Because sound is intangible and invisible, it is easily imposed on others with impunity. Public space has long been taken over by businesses that sell sound in the form of canned music to fill empty sound-space. Commercial sound saturates transitional public places, such as waiting rooms, bars, restaurants, malls, and even streets and parks. And when canned sound is not present, people cooperate by supplying it through their own headsets. Silence, even relative silence, has become a rarity.

Auditory co-optation can be recognized in poor sound reproduction in speakers and microphones, while electronic sounds have widely displaced those naturally produced. Indeed, the ubiquity of handheld electronic devices, when used to excess, has tended to alter auditory sensibility. It not only usurps perceptual attention but entices people into centering their attention on smart phones, tablets, and laptop computers, seducing them into alternative perceptual worlds at the cost of being unaware of their actual perceptual environments. Obviously, this refers to the perceptual consequences of the abusive overuse of such devices and not to their practical convenience. Another domain of technological co-optation occurs in the false, impaired perception of architectural space and mass through deceptive design. Mirror walls that distort space and confuse the approaching pedestrian, towering masses that intimidate and oppress the body—these are some ways in which architectural design can be used to overpower and subjugate human sensibility.

Emotional Co-optation

Then there are the means by which sensibility is distorted or drugged. One of the most widespread and insidious practices of cultivating sensory pleasure for profit is, of course, cigarette smoking. Few smokers enjoyed their first cigarette: the taste is unpleasant, the smoke choking, the physical effects nauseating. But the appeal of emulating celebrities, the desire to display sophistication, the attraction of transgression, and peer pressure are powerful incentives. Even more are its narcotic effects. The tobacco industry uses these successfully to create a desire in many people so strong that it overcomes their initial distaste, gradually leading to an acquired taste and to nicotine addiction with its deleterious consequences in the high incidence of lung and other forms of cancer.

The use of alcohol has become a regular pastime for many people, reinforced in popular culture, on TV, and in film by romanticizing drinking and appealing to self-indulgence. It is much like the way cigarette smoking was associated with sophistication until its damaging effects on health were shown to be so widespread and costly that legal measures were enacted in some developed countries to restrict smoking in public places and by the young. Alcohol abuse may be somewhat less visible than smoking, but it is a public health problem of epidemic proportions. At the same time, the production and dissemination of alcohol is a major industry for drugging sensibilities. Its manifold forms, from beer, wine, and iced tea to mixed and straight drinks, are widely encouraged on many social and economic levels. The excessive use of alcohol is a major public health menace that carries high personal and social costs.

Another form of emotional co-optation has long been used by religious and political social institutions. This consists in cultivating and playing on people's emotions or religious and patriotic feelings to control behavior for political, social, or commercial purposes. Developed and enhanced by modern techniques of marketing, advertising, propaganda, and other forms of thought control, emotional responses are cultivated to create false consciousness and manipulate behavior whose authentic base lies in the normal complex of natural feeling.[14]

Psychological Co-optation

The present-day obsession with psychedelic and narcotic drugs to induce altered states of consciousness supports a huge illicit industry that encourages a desire for exaggerated and extreme perceptual experience for relief, escape, or adventure, all at the cost of normal functioning and health. The enormous quantity of prescription and nonprescription drugs consumed in the United States has reached the proportions of an epidemic.

A related instance in which sensibility has been co-opted is pornography. Erotic sensibility is easily co-opted, and the pornography industry profits enormously from appropriating people's normal erotic desires by removing feelings of caring and the richness of complex human relationships, narrowing erotic sensibility into pure titillation, and exaggerating it by excess in order to stimulate an erotic response.

The Meaning of Co-optation

These forms of co-optation offer only a partial descriptive account of the most obvious forms of sensory intrusion, sensory manipulation, sensory alteration, and sensory numbing, and at times they may overlap or merge. The word "co-optation" is not common but it has a powerful meaning for a social and political critique. It means something like "appropriation," "taking something over."[15] Marcuse spoke of "the social and psychological mechanisms at work in society that make the proletariat complicit in their own domination."[16] The appropriation is hidden so that the "victim" is entirely unaware that it is happening. Moreover, the meaning here is that the appropriation is not just hidden; it is embedded in the person.

It is essential here to acknowledge the forces identified in the analyses by Jean Baudrillard of simulacra, simulation, and hyperreality that add a further dimension to this analysis. Baudrillard's accounts of hyperreality and simulacra disclose the cognitive manipulation of reality in which its basic structures and content are fabricated or altered; the co-optation of sensibility I have been describing is perceptual. Our very perception is appropriated and put to the purposes of others. It is, one might say, an appropriation on the most basic level.

It is a perceptual manipulation that distorts perceptual experience on the most basic level of apprehension.[17]

How is this an issue for aesthetics? It follows from understanding aesthetics as the theory of sensibility that aesthetics is concerned not only with how such sensory experience is enhanced but also with how it is abused. This supports a critical aesthetics, an aesthetics of social and political critique.

I am claiming that it is a principal characteristic of our contemporary mass, corporate culture to exploit people's sensibilities, first, by dwelling on certain sensory satisfactions, second, by overemphasizing and exaggerating them in order to entice people to purchase products and services, products that are often unhealthy, harmful, addictive, or simply unnecessary, and third, by taking "normal" sensory experiences and turning them into false needs, needs that are exaggerated and excessive. Mass corporate culture turns humans into consumers, not only by propaganda in the form of sophisticated advertising designed to create and intensify desires but by restructuring their very capacity for sensible experience, the substance of human life.

We can see how an aesthetic analysis of the mechanisms of mass culture can reveal many of the hidden ways in which sensibility is appropriated and controlled. It may not be too far-fetched to recall Aristotle's definition of a slave as a living tool. How else should we think of a person whose sensibility has been so taken over that one's very perception of the world is controlled by others. This is more than physical domination, more than thought control; it is control over the very substance of experience. Would it be too strong to call this total enslavement? Through such an analysis as this chapter proposes, aesthetics is empowered to become an instrument of emancipation.[18,19]

Part V

Negative Aesthetics

9

Art, Terrorism, and the Negative Sublime*

It has become increasingly clear that the arts, and the aesthetic, more generally, occupy no hallowed ground but live on the everyday earth of our lives. Recognition is growing that the aesthetic is a pervasive dimension of the objects and activities of daily life.[1] Perceptual experiences that possess the characteristics of aesthetic appreciation are marked by a focused sensibility we enjoy for its intrinsic perceptual satisfaction. We typically have such experiences with works of art and with nature, but they are equally possible in other occasions and with other kinds of objects. Such experiences engage us in an intensely sensory field in which we participate wholly and without reservation, as we customarily do with works of art. The objects and occasions, however, may be ordinary ones, such as eating, hanging laundry, engaging in social relations, or operating a perfectly functioning automobile or other mechanism. The range of such occasions is limitless, and this adds to the significance of the aesthetics of the everyday.

Such an expansion of the aesthetic has important consequences. Perhaps the most striking is acknowledging that the range of aesthetic experience includes more than the appreciative engagement with art and nature. But not only does the aesthetic extend to the uncustomary; it encompasses the full range of normative human experience. Experiences of the aesthetic include not only the elevated and noble but the reprehensible, degrading, and destructive. This is so not as the result of an arbitrary decision to include them but from actual experience and practice. The aesthetic offers a full and direct grasp of the human world. That it may include violence and depravity is not the fault of aesthetics but of that world.

---

* This chapter first appeared in *Contemporary Aesthetics*, Vol. 7 (2009). I would like to thank the anonymous reviewers of *Contemporary Aesthetics* for their helpful comments on this chapter.

Terrorism as Symptom of the Malaise of the Human World

A salient symptom of the malaise of that world is terrorism. Its wanton violence and uncontrolled destruction are appalling. But easy moral outrage offers no understanding, and only by grasping the meanings and significance of terrorism can we hope to deal with it effectively. Let me begin with the Happening, for the Happening can provide a forceful illumination of the aesthetic of terrorism.

Not that Happenings took negative form. A syncretic, visual-theatrical artistic development of the 1960s, Happenings were a deliberate artistic innovation intent on transgressing all the hard boundaries that protected the arts and made them safe. In Happenings audiences became the performers, no clearly circumscribed object could be identified as the work of art, aesthetic distance was relinquished to the active engagement of the audience, artistic genres were fused into unrecognizable combinations, and, most significantly, the boundary between art and life disappeared. Happenings were often playful, even festive occasions that danced over the pieties of conventional artistic axioms.

Some commentators quickly recognized that the importance of the Happening lay beyond its iconoclasm and entertainment value. One of them was Régis Debray, a young French radical intellectual, who "regarded a revolution as a coordinated series of guerrilla Happenings. Some of his admirers, in fact, took part in Happenings as training for future Happenings when they would use guns and grenades."[2] What many had considered a bizarre exaggeration following the dismissal of traditional artistic forms turns out to have been an uncanny prevision of the world half a century later. The net of terrorism in which the world is now enmeshed is all-enclosing. But how can terrorism be considered in the same sense as art? The question itself seems outrageous.

Happenings made a radical break from the aesthetic tradition by denying that art occupies its own exclusive realm separate from the world outside. Yet it was not only Happenings that rejected this tradition; many other artistic developments in the twentieth century deliberately crossed that boundary. The presumptive difference between the world of art and the world of daily life lies at the source of such perennial problems in aesthetics as the status of truth and illusion in art, the moral effects of art works, and the nature of artistic representation. Such continuing issues, all of which can be traced back to Plato, find in artistic autonomy the domain of human freedom, as Kant had claimed.[3] Yet at the same time, separating the arts from daily life establishes an autonomy that, by philosophic decree, vitiates the force of the arts and ignores their power.

The tradition of restricting and removing art from the world of daily life dates from Plato's suspicion that the arts can have a morally degenerating influence. Expressed most famously in *The Republic*, it led him to advocate strict controls on the use of the arts in education and to propose censorship.[4] This, of course, was related to Plato's mistrust of sense experience, which he considered the source of illusion and false belief. These views were reinforced and enlarged by Kant, who claimed early in the modern period that the autonomy of judgments of taste is entirely independent of the existence of the object of our satisfaction and is not bound up with practical interest.[5]

The effect of these ideas on the history of philosophy has been profound. Plato's mistrust of the senses and artistic independence, and his failure to recognize the imaginative contribution that the arts can make to education and moral development, joined with Kant's denial of full aesthetic satisfaction to the interests of daily life. Together they functioned effectively to muzzle the power of the arts. Yet once we recognize the active interplay that occurs between art objects and activities and the world in which they exist, we find vast new opportunities for power and influence.

The force inherent in this relation has not been lost on the modern state. For philosophical aesthetics deliberately to ignore the political potential and use of the arts is to hand that power over to others whose values, standards, and behavior are often ignorant, manipulative, and self-aggrandizing. The traditional separation of aesthetics from daily life has freely allowed the political appropriation, often the misappropriation, of the arts. That is why governments practice "news management" and other forms of censorship, why they "stage" conferences, rallies, and other political events, why they promote "official" art, and why they persecute artists who do not conform to their purposes and destroy their works. Art is dangerous, and Kant got it backward when he placed morality and art in separate domains.

In the interpenetration of art and the human world are the grounds for a new aesthetic vision and the need to articulate it.[6] When Happenings fused art with the everyday world, they did so as art. But what about presumably nonart objects that are directly perceived as art? There is, of course, *found art*, where an object is extrapolated from the everyday world, segregated, and framed: a piece of driftwood, a bouquet of field flowers, and, of course, the perennial urinal. Art is claimed where none was intended. Some instances of found art are benign, some provocative, others deliberately inflammatory. They say nothing about the motives of those who did the making and for whom the idea of art was probably far from mind. What found art does do is center our attention on an object or event in a way that resembles the intense focus we give to things designated *as* art by an artist, an institution, or the art world. Like Happenings, found art places art squarely in the ordinary world. Can this apply to acts of terrorism?

Some of the most striking claims of art for things outside the art world were responses to the terrorist attacks of 9/11. The avant-garde composer Karlheinz Stockhausen called them "the greatest work of art ever. . . . the greatest work of art for the whole cosmos," "a jump out of security, the everyday." And the British artist Damien Hirst excluded art from all moral judgment, arguing that the violence, horror, and death associated with Ground Zero (the name given to the site of the demolished New York World Trade Center) do not rule out the possibility that film footage of the attack could be "visually stunning" and resemble works of art.[7] Indeed, perceiving that footage as art may be the ultimate act of framing. Whether these events can be considered found art can be debated, but the label we give them is incidental. Of more concern here is the claim that they *are* art or *like* art.

Terrorism as Art

Attributing artistic achievement to the perpetrators may seem revolting, but it would be arrogant and myopic to blithely dismiss statements like Hirst's and Stockhausen's. For we must take care not to confound the aesthetic with art or to consider either of these necessarily positive. To call the film footage of the attack visually stunning acknowledges its aesthetic impact. Many art works could be described in similar terms but yet reflect different content and moral meaning. Frederick Edwin Church's "The Icebergs" (1861) is visually stunning; so are Turner's "The Burning of the Houses of Lords and Commons" (1834) and Mathias Grünewald's "Crucifixion" (1515).

But so also are many natural events: sunsets, the full moon in the night sky, the sea in a great storm. Perceptual force alone, while aesthetic, does not make art. It may lie in the subject matter of an art work, but as part of the whole, it is something different. There is a sense in which Stockhausen's comment can be taken literally by regarding the 9/11 terrorist attacks as theater. Stockhausen himself composed musical works with dramatic venues and enormous scale, so his calling the attacks "the biggest work of art there has ever been" was not entirely unpredictable or out of character.

But how can we respond to these comments? Is it possible to disentangle the aesthetic from the moral in such a highly charged situation or does the moral issue entirely overpower the aesthetic one? There are no unequivocal answers and perhaps the consideration of Happenings, transgression, and violence can help us make these assertions understandable. They may suggest a way of grasping them that is not immediately obvious. But first, however, is the matter of terrorism, itself.

Simply to list the definitions of "terrorism" would take pages. What they have in common is the use of violence or the threat of violence.[8] Most often added to the definition is that terrorism focuses on a civilian population with the intention of creating widespread fear, and that it is motivated by political or ideological objectives. Terrorism also carries an element of the unexpected. An element of chance enters into its choice (if we may call it that) of victims and sometimes in the determination of specific time and location, and this adds greatly to the fear that acts of terrorism evoke.

It is interesting to consider that this combination of elements that define terrorism—violence, civilian victims, fear—does not specify the perpetrators. These may be indifferently radical groups of the right or left, military, paramilitary, governmental, or nongovernmental organizations. The media unquestionably play a central role in promoting such fear. When fearmongering is deliberate, the media that practice it could themselves be considered terrorist organizations, just as could other fomenting organizations, such as government bureaus (what Badiou calls "bureaucratic terrorism"[9]) and *ad hoc* groups of individuals who may be the perpetrators, as in the Oklahoma City bombing. It is important to recognize the scope of terrorism, since labeling organizations as "terrorist" because they use or threaten violence toward a civilian population, regardless of their place in the social order, is revealing and sobering: they are not necessarily marginal. Recognizing the wide range of sources of terrorism helps avoid self-righteous exclusions.

It is important to realize that the use of terror is not confined to Asia or the Middle East. Terror, in fact, has become a standard practice at the present stage of world history. Totalitarian states know well that terrorizing a population is the most effective way of controlling it, far more potent than overt force. We can recognize the climate of fear and terror that has spread not only throughout regions in the African, Asian, and South American continents; it is being deliberately implemented in Western industrialized nations, as well, by the use of so-called national security measures. Indeed, if state terror were made visible, it would obscure the individual acts of terror that have achieved such notoriety today.[10]

Acts of terrorism are appallingly inventive and their range is extreme. They extend from suicide bombers in the Middle East and the release of the nerve gas sarin in the Tokyo subway by the religious cult Aum Shinrikyo and its attempts at biological terrorism, to the 9/11 suicide plane crashes perpetrated by Al Qaida. But we cannot exclude state terrorism in this portrayal: the use of overt police action and military force to control social activities, gangs dispatched to foment social violence, and secret police to instill fear. And there is also the increasingly sophisticated propagandistic use of the media—magazines and newspapers, TV talk shows, and news broadcasts—to proliferate false information, obscure and distort current events, and instill insecurity. This is no reign of terror; we are living in an age of terror.

Can Terrorism Be Justified?

The scope of terrorism is, then, surprisingly large and its definition surprisingly inclusive. At the same time, it is important to recognize the difference between terrorism and terror and not to confuse the two. Terrorism is, as we have seen, the calculated use of violence or threat of violence against a civilian population with the intent of causing widespread fear for political purposes. Terror, on the other hand, is the overpowering *emotion* of intense fear. More about this later. What I am concerned with just now is terrorism, not terror, as such.

Can terrorism ever be justified? What makes terrorism so morally appalling is that its victims are circumstantial, uninvolved, and oblivious of what is happening. It is a vicious lottery with equal opportunity to lose. The devastating results of terrorist acts are not much different from the so-called "collateral damage" suffered by civilian populations throughout the whole history of warfare. Violence visited deliberately on an innocent, circumstantial population condemns it as one of the most heinous social wrongs, irrespective of any self-justifying motives. For this reason terrorism can never be vindicated, and terrorism practiced by a state is no more exempt from moral condemnation than when used as a tactic by a political or religious group.

But apart from the question of whether terrorism is ever justifiable, it must nonetheless be recognized and understood. Visible and bold acts of terrorism force us to acknowledge that such acts of violence are not aberrations committed by deluded individuals but social actions deliberately perpetrated by groups and for clear reasons. They may be the arms of state oppression or they may represent political opposition to what is perceived as correlative injustice. Terrorist acts are often committed in response to the social violence of exploitation or oppression of one population group by another. Yet one form of violence cannot be selectively justified over against another. By being directed against unwitting victims, all such actions are morally flawed. A violent act committed in response to other acts of violence is not thereby exonerated: both are equally condemnable. Can terrorism be considered morally justifiable if it is the only available means to a political or ideological end when there is no alternative way to redress an injustice? This is the critical moral question and central to understanding terrorism.

The question of the justifiability of terrorism does not, however, answer the *aesthetic* question:

> Are aesthetic values present in terrorist acts? Is there an aesthetics of terrorism? What, indeed, has terrorism to do with aesthetics at all? It is necessary to confront these questions because acts of terrorism make effective use of the techniques and skills of art and possess aesthetic force. Yet how can we speak of political acts such as terrorism in the same breath as art and the aesthetic? Must art that uses violence to convey a moral message and make a moral judgment be condemned when that message could not be made in any other way? We arrive again at the same moral dilemma. This is a question that must be faced by any argument for true democracy, the political form that claims to provide means for peaceful social change.[11] Democracy or terrorism?

The use of terrorism as a political act thus raises difficult aesthetic as well as moral issues, and it is important to understand terrorism, not just to condemn it. Indeed, considering terrorism from an aesthetic vantage point can cast considerable light on such acts. For these events are perceptually powerful, engaging not only the visual but all the senses. They are aesthetic because of their sensory force. These are desperate acts committed in order to make a moral and political statement through their aesthetic, that is, their sensory impact. Moreover, their inherent political import is a dramatic rejection of the traditional difference between art and reality, a feature they have in common with the modern arts.

Since aesthetics centers on direct sensory perception, it is clear that acts of terrorism have powerful aesthetic force. All those who experience the effects of terrorism—its chance victims, their relatives and associates, the organizations and institutions that are damaged, the general public, the social order—can attest to its aesthetic impact. Human values—and the value of humans—are at stake, but we cannot measure such value quantitatively. How is it possible to compare or judge experience? Is a physical act of terrorism such as a suicide bombing worse than the repression of a whole population by a government policy instituted in the name of security, causing widespread fear and requiring overt acts of brutality to enforce it? Is a deliberately planned riot designed to manipulate a population less terrifying than, say, an attempt to poison a public water supply? Here, I think, differences in conditions, means, and consequences need to be identified and each situation appraised on its own terms and not by some general formula. At the same time and more important, such alternatives are morally unacceptable as well as rationally irresolvable. There is no choice between Hitler and Pol Pot.

Unlike acts of sabotage, acts of terrorism have no direct military target. Perhaps it can be said that in this respect they mirror the largely self-contained character of art. And what sort of aesthetic value can terrorism have? "[T]he tragic in real life will necessarily have an aesthetic dimension as long as the sensibility of the subject comes into play by judging something as being 'tragic.'"[12] Is there art in terrorism? It cannot be denied that much of the political effectiveness of terrorist acts comes from their carefully planned aesthetic impact. Indeed, their effect is primarily, often spectacularly theatrical. We can in fact say that such actions are deliberately designed to be high drama. In this sense, then, is theater any less appropriate a way to describe a spectacular act of terrorism than it is to designate military activities? Perhaps it now becomes understandable how an artist could consider a terrorist act a work of art.

Can terrorism have positive moral value? Simple ascriptions of positive and negative value no longer fit. Such morally complex situations demand a different kind of analysis. If a terrorist act contributes to achieving social justice, can we even ask whether it is morally positive or negative? A Kantian analysis would find it negative, for such actions cannot be universalized. A utilitarian analysis might find it positive to the extent it contributes to political or social reform, if it does indeed have that consequence, rather than the redoubled use of state terror. But can we even presume to balance immediate pain, death, and destruction against possible future benefits?

Neither of these analyses resolves the issue. Universalizability is an ethical principle and a logical desideratum, but it is not axiomatic and exempt from critical reflection. And to consider consequences only selectively is effectively to disregard their wide-ranging fallout. Moreover, failing to acknowledge the full scope of consequences continues the common practice of hiding behind moral principles at human cost. Most important is the further consideration that means and ends are never separable. What kind of society can emerge from terror-induced change? Though the intent of terrorist action may be the goal of human liberation, the short-term effects are unavoidably negative. And its possible long-term effects?

It is clear that the moral issues terrorism raises are complex. In traditional terms the judgment may seem clear, but under full consideration it becomes ambiguous. As in warfare where everyone claims right, justice is on every side—and so, too, is injustice. The pain of an enemy is no less great than one's own. Life lost is lost life, no matter whose life it is.

Is a spectacular terrorist act aesthetically negative or positive? It must be considered positive because of its dramatic force. If, however, fear and terror overpower perceptual experience, not only in its unwilling "participants" but also in its larger "audience" so that they feel in actual danger, a terrorist act exceeds the possibility of aesthetic experience and so is aesthetically negative.[13] So aesthetically, too, terrorism is indeterminate. Such situations seem, then, to be ambiguous both morally and aesthetically.

How a terrorist act can be morally positive in any sense may be difficult to see. We must acknowledge that the strategy of the acts and the motives of the actors may be guided by the goals of liberation, of a more just social order, of an end to oppression and exploitation, and other humane objectives. But they may also be guided by the intent to preserve power and the social and economic privileges that accompany it. Do any ends ever justify terrorist means? Their morally reprehensible effects are so blatant that it seems inconceivable that any goal, however noble, could exonerate them. One cannot choose between two incommensurable wrongs. At the same time, even if a terrorist act could claim to be morally positive—which I do not believe is possible—does this justify its aesthetic negativity? Morality and aesthetics are not easily distinguished here. Pain and delight are both inherently moral and aesthetic: The same act can be both morally and aesthetically positive or negative, for the moral and the aesthetic may be fully interdependent, inseparably fused. The very perpetration of a terrorist act is at the same time both aesthetic and moral, spectacularly destructive in both respects.

Generalities pale before the intense particularity of terrorist acts. Every incident has its unique conditions and no logical decision procedure seems possible. Does the sheer scope and force of a terrorist act place it in a new and different category? Just as we cannot measure aesthetic pleasure or grade works of art, fear and terror are not truly quantifiable. Nor are consequences fully determinable. And because both their scope and their intensity cannot be specified precisely, they are truly inconceivable. There is a concept in aesthetics that denotes experience so overwhelming that it exceeds comprehension—the sublime, and it is worth considering whether the sublime could conceivably be applied to acts of terrorism.

The Negative Sublime

The sublime is a theory that reflects on a distinctive kind of aesthetic experience. While the sublime became prominent in the eighteenth century as a key dimension in the development of aesthetic theory, it has become increasingly important in recent aesthetic discourse. The starting point is usually Kant's account, although Kant was not the first to elaborate a theory of this distinctive mode of aesthetic apprehension. Burke's discussion of the sublime had come half a century before,[14] and while Kant's formulation has dominated subsequent discussions, Burke's observations are particularly germane to the present one. For according to Burke, the central feature of the sublime is terror. The most powerful passion caused by the sublime in nature, he states, is astonishment, a state of mind with an element of horror in which all other thoughts are suspended. Fear at the prospect of pain or danger freezes the capacity to reason and act and evokes the overpowering feeling of terror. As "the strongest emotion which the mind is capable of feeling," Burke maintained that the feeling of terror is a principal source of the sublime: "[W]hatever is qualified to cause terror, is a foundation capable of the sublime."[15] And, "Indeed, terror is in all cases whatsoever, either more openly or latently the ruling principle of the sublime."[16] Burke described many emotions associated with the sublime and the conditions under which the sublime may be experienced, and he cited many instances of terror incited by fear. His analysis, however, did not proceed beyond such descriptions.

Kant, too, recognized fear as a feature of the (dynamical) sublime.[17] In contrast with Burke, Kant developed an elaborate theory illuminated by a distinction between the mathematical and the dynamical sublime. In the first, the magnitude of the absolutely great is a measure that the mind cannot wholly encompass.[18] Applied to a terrorist act, its effects and consequences cannot be fully described or even mentally encompassed and are incommensurable. Its material consequences in the form of physical destruction and social disruption, the scope of the human anguish inflicted, and the protective measures and reciprocal violence wreaked upon society in reaction can never be fully enumerated. Its human consequences are immeasurable because they are incalculable. We may indeed say that we cannot quantify the destructive force of a terrorist attack: it evokes the mathematical sublime.

The second, Kant's dynamical sublime, concerns the fear we feel in response to the enormous might of nature, although we must nonetheless feel personally secure and unthreatened, able to rise above that fear and not be subject to it.

Ironically, even war, Kant avers, has something sublime in it if carried on with order and respect for citizens' rights,[19] presumably by protecting noncombatants. In the place of might in Kant's dynamical sublime, the sublime in terrorism is present in the intensity of physical force, in its engulfing emotional power, in the overwhelming psychological pressure of the situation.

Like Kant's dynamical sublime, the effectiveness of terrorism lies in its potential threat to safety and in the very insecurity and social instability that result. In terrorism safety is especially equivocal: while there may be noncombatants, everyone is vulnerable. The actual victims are but sacrificial lambs for their effect on the larger population. Another important similarity is in the fact that, like the quantitative forms of the Kantian sublime in which both magnitude and might (as force) seem to be immeasurable, the intensity of the terrorist sublime is also immeasurable and its dimensions indeterminate. And it results in consequences that are qualitatively indeterminable and thus incomparable. Only in their circumstances and means are the acts and effects of terrorism distinguishable. Since both the scope and the intensity of terrorist attacks are beyond conception, both morally and aesthetically, we need a new concept, the "negative sublime," as their truest and most eloquent identification.

Because acts of terrorism elude meaningful quantitative determination, we must further acknowledge their *moral* and *aesthetic* incommensurability, indeed, their very inconceivability. Perhaps the only concept that can adequately categorize them is the negative sublime. Like the aesthetic, the sublime is not necessarily a positive determination but a mode of experience. Hence to consider acts of terrorism instances of the negative sublime is not an oxymoron but the recognition of negativity whose enormity cannot be encompassed in either magnitude or force. The uniqueness of such extreme actions renders them capable of description only. One might claim that an act of terrorism exemplifies the postmodern sublime, as Lyotard described it, in making the unpresentable perceptible.[20] And because the moral and the aesthetic are inseparable here, the negative sublime incurs identical aesthetic and moral value. That the moral is also aesthetic makes it even more intolerable. Death is the ultimate human loss, and body counts and statistics are deceptively specific and impersonal. Such qualitative consequences as the human suffering from extreme acts of terrorism are beyond measure. As Dylan Thomas mourns, every death is final.[21]

Acknowledging that there may be an aesthetic in acts of terrorism, even a positive aesthetic, does not condone or justify such action, for in terrorism the aesthetic never stands alone. Recognizing its presence may help us understand the peculiar fascination that the public has with such events of world theater.

These are indeed acts of high drama that fascinate us by their very sublimity.[22] But the theatrical forcefulness that impresses us with their image is indissolubly bound up with their moral negativity, and identifying them as the negative sublime is to condemn them beyond all measure. As an agent here in the social sphere, art affects the world directly. Indeed, "by attacking reality, art *becomes* reality."[23]

Terrorism dramatically exposes the inseparability of the moral and the aesthetic, yet this is an extreme form of what is always the case. Utopian thought, to turn to the other side of the normative ledger, also has a strong aesthetic component. Utopianism is pervaded by moral values of social and environmental harmony and fulfilment. Its goal of facilitating living that is deeply satisfying through the fruitful exercise of human capacities is as aesthetic as it is moral.[24] The tradition that separates the aesthetic from the moral mirrors its segregation from everyday life and constricts its force. Let us see the picture whole and not in parts.

10

Reflections on the Aesthetics of Violence

The words "aesthetic" and "aesthetics" are often used casually to refer to the arts, to the pleasurable experience we have with them, and to beauty as the distinctive mark of that experience. In its most general import aesthetics concerns sensible experience, experience centering around perceptual events and the elaboration and refinement of sensory awareness. This is reflected in the etymology of the word "aesthetics," which, as we have noted earlier, derives from the Greek *aisthēsis*, perception by the senses. Such experience is not purely sensory but is colored by culture, education, and personal history. Developing a sensitivity to perceptual experiences is one of the gratifications of living: delight in the subtle signs of seasonal change, in the curved volume of a Chinese vase, in the imaginative unfolding of the intricate plot of a Dickens novel, in the spontaneous expression of a child's response. But at the same time as this perceptual capacity is enhanced, it becomes more vulnerable to abuse and to pain.

All these possibilities derive from the philosophical sense of those terms, which identify the aesthetic as the value we recognize in the largely perceptual experience we have in appreciating the arts and natural phenomena. Often those experiences and the value we find in them are called "beautiful" and "beauty," and philosophical aesthetics is the study concerned with identifying and exploring them. However, we must recognize that not only are some experiences of art and nature not beautiful in the positive sense of the word, but they may be disappointing, demeaning, offensive, or even hurtful. Thus the aesthetic value of an object or experience may be negative as well as positive, and this requires us to recognize the range of aesthetic value in its various degrees and modes. We can call an aesthetic experience negative, then, when the aesthetic value in such experiences lies beyond being merely neutral, that is, insipid, bland, or unmoving, but rather is offensive, demeaning, repugnant, or even painful.[1]

Aesthetic Negativity

It is important not to confuse negative aesthetics with aesthetic failure, that is, bad art, bland architecture, formulaic writing. Failure occurs when an artistic attempt does not succeed in creating the direct perceptual participation of aesthetic engagement that is the mark of successful art. Of course, here, too, there are degrees of failure as there are degrees of success, but in all such cases the value we call aesthetic is more or less inadequately realized. Recognizing aesthetic failure is important in extending the range of aesthetic perception. My concern here, however, is not so much with failure as with its contradiction.

Aesthetic negativity is widespread in daily life but its presence is often obscure and hidden in part because it is commonplace and unremarked. I want to explore here one of the manifestations of such negativity: the conjunction of the aesthetic with violence. This critique does not oppose the artistic appropriation of violence. It condemns its social acceptance through turning the presentation of violence into an object of disinterested appreciation. When aesthetic appreciation of violence is engaged, however, it can become a humanizing force testifying to the moral influence of aesthetic experience.

Negative aesthetic experience occurs in many guises, from the offensive environmental conditions that shadow daily life to the drama of terrorist attacks, but perhaps the most egregious instances of negative experience are those that inflict physical or emotional pain. A distinctive feature of pain is the difference between the experience of one's own pain and the pain of others. We blindly avoid the first, whereas the pain of others seems to exert a strange fascination. How is such pain experienced? Wherein lies the fascination with the pain of others? Our understanding of aesthetic experience may help reveal some of the contours of these questions.

Rather than aesthetic failure, the issue here concerns the relation of aesthetics to violence. This discussion, however, does not honor the aestheticization of violence; that is, I am not concerned here with the motives, significance, or consequences of efforts to idealize violence by turning it into an object for delectation.[2] Violence has often been made appealing by prettifying, romanticizing, or sentimentalizing its appearances, so to speak by aestheticizing it. The present discussion, however, centers not on how or why violence may be given a positive cast but on ways of understanding the aesthetic experience of violence as it occurs in the arts.

Aesthetic Violence

The practice of joining aesthetic values with violent content is found in most societies, and its frequency in recent times suggests that it has become a dominant theme. Because violence so permeates the popular media, it is easy to overlook the fact that the fascination with violence has ancient origins. Not only are prehistoric images of hunting scenes found on Paleolithic cave walls; ritual sacrifice was practiced in the early history of many cultures. National art museums feature paintings that depict famous historic battles. Uccello's fifteenth-century depiction of *The Battle of San Romano* is a classic example,[3] as is J. M. W. Turner's dramatic painting of *The Battle of Trafalgar*.[4] Many other artists turned to the drama inherent in violent events for their inspiration and embodied them in graphic scenes of the chaos and horror of massacres and battlegrounds, the most famous modern example of war-borne violence undoubtedly being Picasso's *Guernica*.[5] Paintings of the crucifixion of Jesus constitute a genre in their own right and extend from the beautified portrayal of Rubens[6] to Grünewald's grisly depiction.[7] It is easily overlooked that the prevalence of the cross in Christian iconology idealizes an instrument of torture, turning the cross into a symbol and an ornament. Nor is literature far behind in its dramatization of violence, from the bloody battles in the *Iliad* and the murders that inform the tragedies of Aeschylus, Sophocles, and Euripides to the dramatic accounts of Shakespeare and Tolstoy. The violence of battle has been romanticized for English-language schoolchildren, who are taught to admire Tennyson's Crimean War poem, "The Charge of the Light Brigade."[8] And from war slogans to the titles of laws that by legal strictures and oppression terrorize the lives of refugees, immigrants, and simply poor citizens, rhetoric is regularly put to the purpose of sanitizing legal violence.

All of this is familiar to those who find in the arts distinctively rich occasions of experience and recognize the prevalence of violence in art. Indeed, we can easily trace the fascination with violence in multiple aspects of contemporary popular culture. Ranging from deadly chases to full-fledged battles in space, violence is as vividly depicted today in film, television, and video games as it was in the past in painting and theater. Moreover, this pattern continues in sports and in contemporary ritual and performance art. Here the vision has changed from paintings that recall past violence to enjoying and even participating in actual violence in the process of occurring. What kind of aesthetic pleasure is found here? What kind of aesthetic is at work when the perceptual experience leads not only to the enhancement of awareness that is one of the marks of aesthetic appreciation but also to dismay, pain, and the mortification of moral feeling?

Violence and Art

This brings us to the crux of the issue. A concern with the aesthetics of violence is a matter quite separate from the perpetration of violence that, in its many forms, so imbues the world of the present. The ubiquitous association of violence with the arts has special significance, not only as an issue in philosophical aesthetics but as a problem in its relation to ethics. The larger question, of course, concerns the appeal of violence in human social behavior, an attraction that encourages commercial as well as political exploitation in addition to its artistic appropriation. My discussion here centers on one aspect of this issue: the influence of aesthetic appreciation on the acceptance and promotion of violence. For questions of aesthetic appreciation are not only about the distinctive experience of art and nature *eo ipso*: appreciative practice also carries moral implications and social consequences.

Human violence has changed in form and extent over the course of human history and, as I noted earlier, it is obvious that acts of violence are experienced differently by the perpetrator and the victim. But what of the spectator? Institutionalized exhibitions of violence have long-standing popularity. There was a large Roman audience for gladiatorial combat in the Coliseum, and jousting was a frequent martial entertainment in Europe in the Middle Ages. Many sports are combative, even if not as overtly as football and fencing. Violence has proliferated in ways other than by direct physical harm. Many social critics are devoted to exposing the subtle and ingenious forms of institutional violence and structural violence that infuse modern societies, and they urge peaceful alternatives.[9]

I am concerned here, however, only with the aesthetics of violence, violence that assumes various forms of perceptual experience in art and culture. This is far from a purely theoretical philosophical fancy. Not only a subject matter, the arts are regularly used to contribute to war frenzy and have long played a role in romanticizing violent events. I have noted how the history of painting is replete with renderings of violence, from crucifixions to battles and executions. Think of the many versions of Judith with the head of Holofernes, a favorite subject in Italian Renaissance painting.[10] Where would Elizabethan drama be without murders? Where would film be without chases, fights, and war scenes? Not only is violence widespread in human societies, it has long been reflected as a subject in the arts. The history of the arts displays no evolution toward moderation and benevolence but, on the contrary, shows increasingly imaginative exhibitions of violence. Consider Kovalcik and Ryynänen's account of the contemporary Viennese actionists:

> Their Orgies-Mysteries Theater (1970–) at Schloss Prinzdorf has included a large number of performers and spectators who have performed Dionysiac orgies of blood and gore. The activities of this group performance included ritual disembowelment of different animals (bulls, sheep), the act of stuffing entrails back into hacked-open carcasses, pouring blood on actors representing Christ and Oedipus, and night-time processions around Prinzdorf with goats, pigs, horses, sheep dogs and cattle, not to mention actors who bore flaming torches. One member of the group, Günter Brus, drank his own urine, and sang the Austrian National Anthem while masturbating in another performance, and Hans Cibulka posed with a sliced open fish covering his groin.[11]

Vienna is not alone in attracting artistic expressions of violence. Violence in art has become a reflection of the ever-increasing social violence of the present world. Witness the continuing popularity of the quasi-documentary (mondo) horror film, *Faces of Death*, and its sequels. Performance art that disfigures the body, temporarily or permanently, is common, and self-mutilation is a frequent feature. Marina Abramović is an early and major exponent of such performances, and some of her work involves audience participation in body deformation. Sites of natural as well as human violence have a grisly attraction, and disaster tourism has become a profitable commercial enterprise. The popularity of the American crime drama, *The Sopranos*, in which murder is as casual as eating breakfast, confirms the observation of the rock musician who commented, "Violence is as American as apple pie."[12] Violence takes imaginative forms with different degrees of subtlety in the various genres of art. It is an easy matter to document the prevalence of violence in the arts, not to mention in the larger society, and those I have cited are but a small sample. But it is as a philosophical issue that the role of the aesthetic appreciation of violence has evaded critical analysis.

Violence and Aesthetic Satisfaction

The aesthetic enjoyment of violent spectacles may seem sadistic; yet, as we have seen, it has a long history. Violence has had an eager audience, from the throngs that filled the Roman Coliseum to the onlookers at public hangings or lynchings. Some people attend boxing and wrestling matches or football and hockey games from similar motives. These spectacles are ritualized performances, and the dynamics of such displays are not unlike those of theater.

Yet what is their aesthetic? The question calls to be asked, how can witnessing violence be satisfying? How can violence, with its attendant brutality and pain, provide aesthetic pleasure? When art romanticizes, idealizes, or glorifies violence, does it mean that it is being used to sanitize and justify such acts? Is this what Henry R. Giroux calls an aesthetics of depravity, "an aesthetics that traffics in images of human suffering that are subordinated to the formal properties of beauty, design and taste–thus serving in the main to 'bleach out a moral response to what is shown'"? Giroux mourns the growth of a "culture of cruelty" in which people find aesthetic satisfaction in images of violence.[13] These may be ethical concerns more than aesthetic ones, yet they demand attention here since moral issues are embedded in the aesthetic on which the enjoyment of violence rests. As an ethical phenomenon, such enjoyment may confound the moralist more than the aesthetician, who has been told to keep aesthetics clear of ethical interests.

Psychological questions are intimately involved, as well. Theodor Adorno put the key issue squarely: "The inability to identify with others was unquestionably the most important psychological condition for the fact that something like Auschwitz could have occurred in the midst of more or less civilized and innocent people."[14] The incapability of empathizing is a crucial question for social psychology, yet it also has an intimate bearing on the aesthetics of appreciation. But while the enjoyment of violence clearly implicates ethical and psychological issues, the attraction it holds also has social and political dimensions, as Benjamin recognized when he identified violence as central to a fascist aesthetic.[15] However, the question for us here is not psychological or political but aesthetic, and it concerns the aesthetics of appreciation: how is the appreciation of violence possible and what are its implications? And I return to the issue with which I began, the philosophical issue lurking behind this question: what kind of aesthetic is at work here? For this is an aesthetic issue as well as a moral one.

Aesthetic appreciation follows many forms and occurs under many conditions, not only in the arts but in the informal experiences of daily life: the passing delight in the color and texture of a piece of fabric, the momentary illumination of a shaft of light, the play of shadows on winter snow, the panoramic view of a landscape. And the many forms of the popular arts evoke appreciative responses, from boisterous enthusiasm to maudlin emotion.

When aesthetic satisfaction is sought deliberately, different patterns may prevail. One pattern is exemplified by the spectator disinterestedly contemplating a painting in a gallery or witnessing a theatrical performance. This pattern incorporates the "official" aesthetic conventionally employed by critics and scholars and embodied in formal exhibitions in museums and traditional performances. It is grounded on an ontology of objects separated by use, function, and interest. This is the pattern of most inquiry, scientific as well as practical problem-solving: the pattern of an observer regarding a distinct and separate object. It takes a special form in the disinterested contemplation of art as object or spectacle. And it enables the aesthetic enjoyment of violence.

Violence and Aesthetic Engagement

There is another pattern of aesthetic enjoyment, one that reflects a distinctive sense of the world of human experience. It is found in many places and situations that exhibit a particular sense of involvement, of a connection and participation with an object and the occasion. It can be found in the wild enthusiasm of the audience at a rock concert but also in the imaginative participation of the viewer of a film, the engagement of the reader in the world of a novel, and in the absorption of the listener at a musical performance. We easily experience appreciative engagement with drama in film, theater, and the novel, as well as in dance. Sometimes this perceptual engagement is spoken of as empathy; sometimes the experience is described as being "caught up" or "carried away." It is important to make clear that this is not just a state of consciousness, a psychological condition, but an act of full bodily engagement. There may be overt physical participation in foot tapping, head nodding, muscular tension, tears, perspiration, an increased heart rate, and other signs of physical involvement. But it may also be restrained, intense, internalized participation, though no less engaged. Vastly different from the distancing of disinterested contemplation, engagement in an aesthetic process is familiar to both the creative artist and the performing artist. Such experience embodies a different worldview from the contemplative aesthetic usually assigned to the spectator. Engaged appreciation is more familiar to Eastern cultures that have been deeply influenced by Taoism and Buddhism, worldviews that emphasize a continuity of humans and nature and that embrace the particularity of perceptual experience.[16] When manifested in the aesthetic appreciation of art and nature, this aesthetic is known as aesthetic engagement.

What kind of aesthetic theory supports the satisfaction in regarding violence? I suggest that there is indeed an aesthetic that underlies the benign appreciation of violence. It is an aesthetic that turns the focus of aesthetic experience into an object of contemplation, that separates aesthetic satisfaction from personal interests and regards aesthetic pleasure as disinterested. This is the familiar aesthetic of Western cultures, first developed by British theorists early in the eighteenth century and later given theoretical formulation by Kant. It identifies aesthetic enjoyment as a contemplative state of consciousness directed toward an external object. This is an aesthetic in which "taste in the beautiful is alone a disinterested and free satisfaction . . . The object of such satisfaction is called *beautiful*."[17] Kantian aesthetic pleasure projects a distanced spectator and enables aesthetic gratification without concern for uses or consequences and without incurring moral judgment. It recognizes aesthetic satisfaction but interprets its condition as the disinterested contemplation of a perceptual object. It is an aesthetic that abets the representation of violence.

An aesthetic of disinterested satisfaction tolerates and even encourages the appetite for violence of an uninvolved voyeur. It objectifies the material of aesthetic gratification and insulates the subjective enjoyment from any misgivings or moral qualms.[18] An aesthetic of distance allows violence to be tolerable, acceptable, even pleasurable because it projects appreciative experience as the enjoyment of a disinterested spectator toward an object insulated from any moral or practical interest.[19]

An aesthetics of engagement, by contrast, identifies a different kind of aesthetic sensibility, one that rests on an interpenetration of subject and object. Indeed, it transcends that dualism in a continuity of perceptual experience and concern. Moral interests are not foreign to an engaged aesthetics. Such an aesthetics recognizes that the inhumanity of violence is germane to aesthetic engagement and is not reluctant to recognize the moral concerns inherent in negative aesthetic experience. Far from the aestheticized paintings of Uccello and Turner, paintings that encourage disinterestedness by muting the violence in their representations through painterly grace and sensory delectation, an aesthetics of engagement leads to a quite different experience. It is the direct encounter with violence that is the aesthetic force in Grünewald's Isenheim Altarpiece[20] and Pieter Brueghel the Elder's "Triumph of Death."[21] An aesthetics of engagement encourages empathetic human feeling. It recognizes the inseparability of the moral and the aesthetic in the confrontation with violence in the arts. Moral interest is inescapably present; it is inherent in the encounter with the image. To exclude or ignore the moral content in such depictions of violence is to eviscerate the image, to render it lifeless. By the standard of such experience, the aesthetics of violence is unqualifiedly negative: It is not contemplatively benign or complaisant but appalling. The engaged aesthetic of violent occasions produces experiences that are never pleasant but are genuinely distressing emotionally and repugnant morally. It is a direct encounter with negativity.

Violence and Terrorism

In our age of widespread violence, perhaps its most egregious manifestation is the proliferation of acts of terrorism. Terrorism is an especially vicious expression of violence. Acts of terrorism, by their very nature, have dramatic impact; this, indeed, may be their larger purpose. The aesthetic character of terrorism lies largely in its bizarre drama, its deliberately staged theatricality. Thus we may speak of an aesthetics of terrorism.[22] Through their aesthetic impact, acts of terror overpower the boundaries of objectivity. Their audience, the public, is not disinterested; it feels threatened and vulnerable. The perpetrators of terror may themselves be disinterested, their specific effects arbitrary, and their victims impersonal and abstract—an ethnic group, a nationality, a race, a religious community. However, the experience of the onlooker or witness is personal and compelling—an engaged aesthetic.

This critique does not oppose the artistic appropriation of violence; it condemns its benign or tolerant appreciative acceptance. Turning the presentation of violence into an object of disinterested appreciation acts as a vindication of violence. An aesthetic that promotes the distancing of violent acts and events reinforces acquiescence in the public and private violence that pervade the world of the twenty-first century. By contrast, engaging with violence aesthetically can sensitize and chasten those who encounter it. Disinterested appreciation has the effect of condoning violence, whereas when aesthetic appreciation is engaged, it can become a humanizing force, a testimony to the moral significance of aesthetic experience. The aesthetics of violence is a decisive test for aesthetic theory.[23]

Part VI

Aesthetics as Cultural Critique

11

The Sublime Troubles of Postmodernism[*]

Postmodernism refers to a phase in Western intellectual culture that became prominent during the final decades of the twentieth century. As a complex period with distinctive cognitive traits, it could be called, to use Foucault's language, an *episteme*.[1] A number of influential though disparate writers contributed to identifying a cultural trend they called postmodernism. They differed from one another so much that commentators named them as a group by their temporal period in intellectual history—coming after modernism—rather than by a shared principle or style. What seemed common to all was a skepticism toward the basic tenets of high modernism and a critique of its articles of faith. Postmodernist writers questioned, in particular, the social stabilities and values, primarily identified with rational order in material and cultural progress through science, that had governed the post–Second World War period. This was a time that saw the rebuilding of Europe and the flood of technological innovation, especially information technology, and commercial expansion into a global economy.

Morawski's Critique of Postmodernism

In a small book written in English, the Polish Marxist aesthetician Stefan Morawski developed a broad yet detailed critique of this diffuse movement.[2] He was able to reflect the complexity and vagaries of a large literature without reducing postmodernism to a simplistic formula. For many cogent reasons, he cast doubt on the value, even the identity, of a movement that encompassed a large number of disparate artistic and cultural forms and practices exemplified in the work of a wide range of influential figures. At this late phase of

---

[*] This essay was written for a Festschrift commemorating the centenary of the birth of Professor Stefan Morawski and was published in *Cultural Studies Review* (*Przeglad Kulturoznawczy*). The author wishes to acknowledge the contributions of Professor Riva Berleant-Schiller to the development of the argument and the insightful comments of Michael Alpert.

postmodernist thought, it will be useful to review his findings and consider his insistently negative assessment of postmodernism. What stands firm and clear in Morawski's far-reaching survey of its expressions and tendencies is his steady commitment to humane values and the honor that he accords the noblest achievements of the arts, a regard unqualified by the vagaries of fashion. Given the scope and diffuseness of postmodernism, we may ask what insights reside in Morawski's reflections on the culture of these times.

How does Morawski characterize postmodernism? He begins by recognizing that modernism, itself, embraces a diversity of meanings and practices in art and culture. Juxtaposing modernism and postmodernism, Morawski notes that, despite their sharp differences, both end in disaster. Postmodernism is distinctive, however, in abandoning any claim to the autonomy of art. He finds that architects such as Michael Graves and James Stirling, and artists like Jeff Koons and David Salle, exemplify the consummation of pop art. Their work exploits, in every imaginable way, the gleam and glitter of glib conventions derived from consumer culture.[3] Morawski also singles out for disapproval Rob Scholte, whose voluminous work co-opts images from art history and the media, and Haim Steinbach, who appropriates and displays found objects on small shelves.[4] Postmodernism was not confined to pictorial art, and Morawski considers film at length, noting its imitative use of parody and a pastiche of styles, plots, and characters. Other arts can easily be included, such as the postmodern dance of Yvonne Rainer and the minimal music of Steve Reich and Terry Riley.

Throughout Morawski's litany of postmodern artists and works, no grounding principles and values are identified. That is largely because postmodernism, both in philosophy and in art, displays a fascination with the consumerism, opportunism, and vacillations of mass culture. In a telling phrase, Morawski sees as its basis the "commodification of the whole social fabric because the rule of obsolescence has become dominant."[5] One could easily confirm this analysis by using a search engine to document the profusion of artists and works he cites. Cleverness, ingenuity, imagination, gloss, and glitz are used to full effect in flooding the fickle marketplace of cocktail party art.

The suffocating influence of mass culture deeply troubles Morawski, constituted, as it is, of sometimes degenerate myths and easily influenced by managers who control taste by market standards. He is particularly disturbed by the myth-making capabilities of mass culture, which he condemns for parodying and degrading the ideas and values found in great art and philosophical conceptions. Film, of course, is the mass art *par excellence* and stands as a ready object of Morawski's postmodern analysis. He recognizes its contribution to popular culture, but what he adamantly opposes is turning film into "the paragon of culture."[6]

It is as a philosopher, however, that Morawski is most troubled by postmodernism. Here the clarity with which he began his critique is quickly obscured in the intricacies of the many scholars he surveys. For they represent a movement that is not a school of thought but a cultural tendency, or perhaps only a cognitive mood. His antipathy to this tendency is swept along in a deluge of words, names, and works. To clarify and sharpen the issues, let me center on one concern to which Morawski pays particular attention, the postmodern sublime.

Lyotard on Postmodernism

Jean-François Lyotard was instrumental in bringing the term "postmodernism" into circulation. Inaugurated in his 1979 book, *The Postmodern Condition: A Report on Knowledge,* the concept of postmodernism soon gained currency, being taken up by many different cultural critics and applied in a profusion of contexts.[7] In introducing his work, Lyotard provided a key to the motivation behind the movement as well as to its signal achievement: "Postmodern knowledge is not simply a tool of the authorities; it refines our sensibility to differences and reinforces our ability to tolerate the incommensurable."[8] This statement contains the inflammatory spark of postmodernism as a cultural movement as well as its profound value, for it is in Lyotard's discussion of the sublime that the incommensurable is revealed most sharply.

"Modernity, in whatever age it appears, cannot exist without a shattering of belief and without discovery of the 'lack of reality' of reality, together with the invention of other realities."[9] While "lack of reality" is reminiscent of Nietzsche, Lyotard sees an intimation of this earlier in the Kantian sublime. "I think . . . that it is in the aesthetic of the sublime that modern art (including literature) finds its impetus and the logic of avant-gardes finds its axioms."[10] Lyotard recalls Kant, who regarded the sublime as "a strong and equivocal emotion" combining both pleasure and pain, which we have in response to chaos or in perceiving its size and might "in its wildest or most irregular disorder and desolation."[11] Kant developed this feeling as a conflict between the faculty to conceive of something and the faculty to present something, which, when conceived in a reflective judgment, is pleasurable. Lyotard's analysis of the postmodern follows the direction of the Kantian sublime. From this conflict between taste and reason, it is in the presentable that exceeds reason that the sublime appears. However, the sublime, in Lyotard's formulation, occurs "when the imagination fails to present an object which might, if only in principle, come to match a concept. . . . Those are ideas of which no presentation is possible."[12]

Moreover, while Kant finds the sublime in "our attitude of thought" that we assign to nature, Lyotard finds it in the postmodern.[13] In further associating the postmodern with the unpresentable, Lyotard seems to find the postmodern sublime in "the pleasure that reason should exceed all presentation, the pain that imagination or sensibility should not be equal to the concept."[14] Thus the postmodern sublime lies in the presentation of the unpresentable. "The postmodern would be that which . . . puts forward the unpresentable in presentation itself."[15]

Herein lies Morawski's deep dismay over the postmodern and over Lyotard as its principal protagonist. For it is in culture (and art) that the postmodern is encountered, and Morawski locates Lyotard's postmodern sublime in "the black hole of Being, the immaterial," the avant-garde's "vain attempts to embody the sublime."[16] Morawski, moreover, characterizes postmodernism as "the cultural logic of late capitalism." In his own penetrating formulation, "what most probably distinguishes the new cultural mutation in its permanent functional interconnecting of political and socio-economic and cultural transfigurations is the prevalence of the circulation of cultural goods and the emergence of a special class of intermediaries involved in the management of this type of commodity society."[17] It is not easy to grasp the core of Morawski's disapproval of postmodernism by wading through his flood of references and allusions. He seemed to regard postmodernism as fundamentally conformist. It does not embrace the avant-garde but rather favors commodity art, which it confounds with high, "and it glories in eclecticism." Morawski most vehemently decries mass art, while he sees the avant-garde as preserving the genuine search for aesthetic insight. Postmodernism he regards as the climax of the cultural crisis at the close of the twentieth century.[18] In its mistrust of theory, even philosophy cannot escape the scalpel of deconstruction, and aesthetics degenerates along with it. Morawski turns, in the end, to Aristotle's concept of *phronesis*, practical wisdom, for the proper balance of philosophy and politics as a guide against any reliance on the modern autonomy of art, aesthetics, and philosophy.[19] And he concludes the intricacies of his analysis with a question: "Does not postmodernism stand as an alarming sign of a cultural crisis in which not only the ultimate answers but also the ultimate questions cease to be self-evident?"[20]

In their polemical presentations, both Morawski and Lyotard not only reflect on postmodernism but also seem to exemplify it. Through an array of names, ideas, and works without clear logical sequence or coherence and in a torrent of words and citations, both cultural commentators endeavored vainly to present the unpresentable. Is there anything that one can conclude from Lyotard's identification of the postmodern phenomenon and Morawski's relentless diatribe against it?

The Postmodern Sublime

One may conjecture that Lyotard's reformulation of the sublime in postmodern terms characterizes the unconstrained permissiveness of postmodern society, and Morawski provides a brilliant documentation of its excesses. Does not a culture in which anything is possible and everything is permitted stand as the presentation of the unpresentable, the postmodern sublime? This is even more the case than in 1996, when Morawski's critique appeared. Perhaps a revived and enlarged conception of the sublime can offer a key to the postmodern condition. I suggest that the postmodern sublime is a dramatic yet incisive characterization of the unfathomable negativity of the postmodern age.

This is what I have come to call "the negative sublime."[21] We have left behind the Kantian sublime, which is unpresentable because no concept can embrace the indeterminable magnitude of the starry heavens or the overwhelming might of natural forces.[22] Postmodernism replaces the boundless immensity of Kant's mathematical sublime[23] with the information society, which entangles everyone in its all-enclosing electronic web. It exceeds every concept of enormity in the proliferation and extent of the personal information it amasses, encompassing identity, location, thought, and behavior. The detail and completeness of the pervasive global web dwarfs the magnitude of the starry sky. This is the ultimate elaboration of the information society, whose excess of data overwhelms the astronomical magnitude of the mathematical sublime, entrapping paltry individuals in an electronic net whose controllers are hidden.

The postmodern sublime also dwarfs Kant's projection of the dynamical sublime by the presentation of the unpresentable embodied in the ominous presence of arsenals of nuclear warheads stockpiled around the globe. This condition establishes the permanent possibility of universal destruction, the inestimable magnitude of whose force renders puny the thundercloud, the overhanging rock cliff, and the hurricane-roiled ocean. Unlike Kant, for whom our mind maintains its superiority over nature, there is no way of separating ourselves by an act of cognitive consciousness from the overwhelming arc of destruction lurking in the widespread distribution of nuclear arsenals.[24] The postmodern sublime is a negative fate we humans have contrived for ourselves.

The postmodern sublime further magnifies the complexity of the more benign traditional conception. Interestingly, both Kant and Burke before him recognized that an element of terror from a sense of threat is inherent in the experience of the sublime. Burke, in 1757, called terror "the ruling principle of the sublime," while Kant, three decades later, recognized the presence of "a delightful horror" in the experience of the aesthetical sublime.[25] For both, an element of terror not only accommodates but amplifies the disturbing features of the classic conception. In the postmodern sublime, the enormity of terror cannot be encompassed by the intellect.

Postmodernism, moreover, moves the sublime to a new level in the omniscient yet indeterminable insinuations of its immateriality. This may be seen in the unpresentable of the so-called "information age," the unpresentable that lies in the digital technology of the global information net, the indeterminable web in which we humans are enmeshed like hapless flies, buzzing futilely into our computer screens. Here resides another mode of the postmodern sublime. Unlike its classic predecessor, the postmodern sublime is neither edifying nor ennobling but humanly demeaning and cognitively terrifying. It reduces persons to faceless units serving the insatiable avarice of distant administrative and mercantile agents.

The postmodern sublime is, then, both a negative dynamical sublime, whose force exceeds conception, and a negative mathematical sublime, whose quantitative enormity defies calculation. In its scope and power, the postmodern sublime evokes boundless terror. Unlike Kant, our minds cannot stand superior over these immensities; thus the postmodern sublime asserts its negativity.

It is, then, ironically appropriate to characterize this late postmodern age in which we find ourselves by Lyotard's formulation of the postmodern sublime as "the presentation of the unpresentable" in a negative mode. The foundation of civil society is overwhelmed nationally and internationally by the magnitude of corporate and political autocracy and greed. The controllers have furthered their interests, manipulating mob mentality to overwhelm the last vestiges of Enlightenment rationality and humanism. This is expressed in the breakdown of the safeguards of conventional distinctions in the name of liberation by an aesthetic glorification of the mundane in objects (postmodern assemblage and sculpture), movement (postmodern dance), sound (ambient sound and minimal music), visual art that trivializes its history and its materials by the repetition of the commonplace in pop art, decontextualized stylistic features in architecture, and commercialized objects, and glitzy forms in sculpture. The art world is buried under variations on the postmodern theme, from Andy Warhol's obsessive iterations of the mundane images of pop culture, Sherri Levine's appropriations and Cindy Sherman's self-portraits, to Philip Glass's repetitions of simplistic harmonic progressions and postmodern dance choreography of pedestrian movements.

At the same time, postmodern culture has had a powerful influence by undermining the conventional pieties of high art and expanding the scope of aesthetic experience. While this has enlarged the range of appreciative experience, it is important to free ourselves from the glitzy permissiveness, eclecticism, and brash arrogance of pop culture. At the same time, we should recognize the startling expansion of the objects and scope of aesthetic awareness in the postmodern period, from the land aesthetic to the resurrection of found objects and debris.

So it is that postmodernism has vastly enlarged the range and the influence of the aesthetic. It may be here where its lasting significance lies. Postmodern dance has elevated the mundane into spectacle. In theater, the novel, music, and performance art, the conventional divisions in the aesthetic field of artist and performer, and object and appreciator, have been overcome in the sharing of artistic and aesthetic functions with the transformation of the audience into performers and the artist's body into the art object. Traditionally distinct functions of artist, work, performer, and audience have amalgamated into an enlarged, integrated aesthetic field of perceptual activity. What has always been the case experientially has now become manifest. At the same time, not all art of this period is on the flat plane of mundane sensibility. There is little in the art of any period that exceeds the aesthetic richness of abstract expressionism, the profundity of Mark Rothko, the intricate energy of Jackson Pollack, the tangible strength of Karel Appel, and the dark power of Anselm Kiefer. The tradition of high art lives on.

Postmodernism and the Aesthetic

As an art and cultural period, then, the postmodernism episteme has vastly expanded the aesthetic.[26] Postmodern art exemplifies the eclecticism and permissiveness of our time. Traditional conventions and proprieties have faded.

The objectivity of truth has fallen before the irrationality of partisan slogans and paranoid explanations. Centralized control of the media has undermined the independence and objectivity of fact. Novels have exposed the multiple experiences of the same events.[27] And the objectivity of fact is obscured by opposed cultural traditions and political organizations vying for hegemony, as well as by countercultural forces on the right and the left.

Further, the widespread influence of the esoteric has proliferated: Eastern cultures and the exotic in Buddhism and Zen, mysticism, and the propagation of contrived mystery and deliberate irrationality in questioning science and truth, more generally. While these have led to vastly enlarging the scope of the aesthetic, at the same time they have been exploited and trivialized by publicity- and profit-seeking innovations. In the aesthetic of pop culture is postmodernism's confirmation of its own criticism of modernism's claim of endless progress.

We could not do better than to characterize the late postmodern period than by using Lyotard's formulation of the postmodern sublime as the presentation of the unpresentable. In this ironic conversion of the traditional sublime, we encounter the romantic's dilemma in dealing with the failure of the ideal of human perfectibility in the face of human imperfection.

We live in the Anthropocene age where the malfunction of societies nationally and internationally is exposed in the magnitude of individual and corporate greed and in governmental corruption. The last vestiges of Enlightenment humanism have disappeared with the decline of rationality in civil society. The overpowering negativity of the postmodern sublime makes manifest this presentation of the unpresentable. Postmodernism is the proof of its own criticism of modernism's claim of endless progress. This is the tragic condition of the sublime world humans have constructed. The postmodern sublime does not elevate us: it is our epitaph.

Part VII

Aesthetic Community

12

Getting along Beautifully
Ideas for a Social Aesthetics*

If want compels man to unite with man in social relations: if reason develops social maxims in his mind, beauty alone imparts to him a social character. Taste alone introduces harmony into society, because it develops harmony in the individual. All the other forms of social action disintegrate man's nature, because they are exclusively founded even upon the physical or spiritual portions of his being; the conception of a beautiful form combines these elements into one, because both the spiritual and the physical natures are necessary to effect that result.
                    Friedrich Schiller, *On the Aesthetic Education of Man*[1]

Grounds for Social Aesthetics

In this chapter I want to sketch out the case for a social aesthetics. Relating the theory of the arts to social thought is not common. Indeed, apart from Schiller's tantalizing insights, it has rarely been attempted. True, there are tangential associations of the aesthetic with the social, as in the growing interest in aesthetic education. And of course, the intersection of art and morality, which has increasingly entered into aesthetic reflection, brings the two together, since morality always implicates human relations. Probing this connection more directly and explicitly will be illuminating in surprising ways. Even more, it might contribute to a philosophy of culture. Let us see how this is possible.

---

* This chapter is revised from "On Getting Along Beautifully: Ideas for a Social Aesthetics," first published in *Aesthetics in the Human Environment*, ed. Pauline von Bonsdorff and Arto Haapala (Lahti: International Institute of Applied Aesthetics, 1999), 12–29, and is reprinted by kind permission of the editors.

It may seem rather strange at first to speak of a social aesthetic. After all, aesthetics has long concerned itself with relations of appreciation and normative judgment in experiencing the arts, with the theory of the arts, and understanding beauty in nature. And such understanding, as Baumgarten, the originator of modern aesthetics, thought of it, lies in the perfection of sensory awareness.[2] It is easy to see how this can relate to the various arts and to our appreciation of nature. These are preeminently sensory, embracing the full range of perceptual experience in all its modalities, not only by means of the senses but also in the sensory aspects of imaginative experience that involves recollection. So understood, perception is broad, indeed, and necessarily so, since it is important to recognize how thoroughly and completely sensation pervades all experience. This domain of perception, especially in the arts, seems to have little to do, at least directly, with the social world. Aesthetics as theory, then, has been seen as the province of the arts, in that attempts to understand the arts lead us to aesthetics. Or, more strictly speaking, the arts and certain aspects of nature appreciation are the province of aesthetics, and our experience of them is commonly regarded as intensely personal.

This is the heart of the traditional view, and it is essentially true of the course of its long and respectable history. But if aesthetic theory is to reflect the meaning of the arts in an unprejudicial fashion, we must be prepared to look further. For the arts and their practices suggest the expansion of aesthetics in both interesting and important ways. To show how this is so, how an aesthetics of the arts leads us beyond the arts, let me turn again to the customary account of the aesthetic situation.

According to the usual description, the distinctive pleasure we associate with the arts involves an aesthetic of objects—of art objects and sometimes of objects in nature. These stand at the theoretical center, and most discussion concerns the distinctive characteristics of such objects: their properties, qualities, and other features, their form and order, the ways in which they may relate to the world beyond, and how these objects are aesthetically enjoyable. Complementing this aesthetics of objects is a distinctive way of appreciating them. Once these art objects have been singled out and identified as paintings, sculptures, musical works, theatrical productions, dance performances, and the like, the need arises for a distinctive response, a way of appreciating them that matches their special character with an equally special reception. Balancing this aesthetics of objects, then, is traditionally an attention that is essentially passive and contemplative, a response that delights in those objects for their own sake without any concomitant application or other purpose—in the usual terminology, *disinterestedly*.

Curiously enough, this traditional account, this aesthetic of objects and their passive reception, itself leads to the possibility of a social aesthetics. One can develop a sequence of arts that proceeds from a simple, delimited art object with its correlative response to a condition that transcends that divided order to become, instead, an integral aesthetic-social situation. To begin, a painting, as the paradigm of a single, delimited object, can easily be circumscribed by two dimensions. Enclosed by a frame, this art of the surface is clearly set off from what is around it and offers a clear and convenient focus for the appreciative eye. To these two dimensions, the related art of sculpture adds another. Yet sculpture resembles painting only superficially, for it does not simply thicken the surface and bend it around to achieve a third dimension. Depth, which nearly all painting possesses perceptually, is more than thickness. Sculpture, in contrast, incorporates mass, and mass takes its position among other things in the world. Sculpture is unlike painting in still another respect: It not only fills the space as mass, it charges the space around it, creating an aura into which the beholder steps in the act of appreciation.

When we turn to architecture, we find this enlarged space extended inward as well as farther outward. Mass opens within to enclose space, and this interior volume is designed for inhabitants and invites them to occupy it. At the same time, architecture reaches out into the surrounding space far beyond the aura of sculpture, incorporating that space into an ensemble with the physical structure. Such an influence may extend beyond the site and adjoining grounds to contiguous or nearby structures. Artists who construct environments that we can enter and inhabit for a brief time render the enlargement of art more explicit yet. Such environments add to the two dimensions of painting and the third dimension of sculptural mass and architectural space a fourth, temporal dimension. For time enters into the art work as the appreciative observer, who is obliged to become a participant in this art, activates the environment by moving through it.

Despite the theoretical and perceptual constraints of traditional aesthetics, then, we find ourselves well on the way to a social aesthetics, for it is but a short step in this sequence of arts to the social environment. An environment devised by an artist is a fabricated perceptual construct that concentrates features found in every environment. Yet even if a human environment does not originate specifically with an artist, it is a culturally constructed context. And since people are implicated in all experienced places, we end with situated human relationships, that is, with a social environment. Within the structure of traditional theory, then, we can see how an aesthetics of art objects leads to the possibility of a social aesthetics. We arrive at the same point, moreover, if we start from the correlative of the art object, that is, from the appreciator. For appreciative experience is actually not passive at all but demands, at the very least, attention that is alert and focused. So by introducing a human presence, aesthetics has indeed acquired a social dimension.

These brief observations certainly need to be elaborated further.[3] But it is interesting to observe at this point that a traditional aesthetic of circumscribed objects and disinterested appreciators leads eventually to the social domain. When aesthetic theory is developed contextually, however, the social relevance of the aesthetic is still more pronounced. Let us see how this is.

Aesthetics as Contextual

Unlike the traditional account, no single or dominant feature establishes an aesthetic situation in a contextual theory: It has no essence. Instead, a number of factors combine to make it distinctive. A contextual theory integrates these features into an inclusive situation.

Acceptance

In the aesthetic encounter, appreciation involves an openness to experience while judgment is suspended. It takes deliberate effort to set aside selective, restricted attention, the tunnel vision of ordinary life, which centers on specific objects and particular goals. This kind of attention is easily transferred to works of art, setting them apart from other objects and activities. Even Kant retained the teleological form of practical interest, but without a practical object, in his famous "purposiveness without purpose."[4]

The twentieth century fought for the expansion of art against such a limitation and largely established its point. Given the appropriate conditions, anything whatever can now become art. At the same time as the realm of art has expanded, so too has the range of aesthetic appreciation. Nothing is excluded *a priori*, and we must be willing to enter into appreciation with an open mind. This applies to the situation as much as to the object, especially since the art object has proved dispensable and has sometimes been replaced by concepts, programs, found objects, and even philosophy.

Perception

Perception is basic in all experience. What makes it important here is its predominance in aesthetic appreciation. We have already noted that Baumgarten established this when he adapted the Greek word *aisthēsis,* perception through the senses, as the name of this new discipline, defining aesthetics as the science of sensory knowledge directed toward beauty.[5] Sensory experience is never pure sensation, however, as the psychology of perception and social psychology have long known. Many factors shape our sensory awareness, from the physiology of the brain and other organic functions to the formative influences of education and the other cultural institutions and practices that construct our belief system, affect our responses, and contribute to the many-layered complexity of perception.

Sensation, nonetheless, lies at the center of this perceptual depth, and it differs from other modes of awareness with different emphases, such as intellectual cognition, mystical bliss, and intense physical activity. Aesthetic perception, ordinarily thought of as peculiar to the arts, has always been at the heart of our appreciation of nature, from small objects of special beauty, such as a blossom or a stone, to monumental ones in the form of a waterfall, a chasm, or an entire landscape. Nothing in the nature of aesthetic perception precludes its appropriateness for objects and situations other than art. Perceptual experience may also dominate certain social occasions, such as moments of affection between parents and children or between friends or lovers, at times of quarrel or hatred, and in other highly qualitative social settings.

Sensuousness

The senses lie at the heart of perceptual experience, and the pleasure they provide gives them special importance here. Traditional aesthetics has been constrained by intellectualist premises from accepting the full scope of sensory experience. From Plato to Hegel, sight and hearing were declared the sole aesthetic senses, in large part because they are distance receptors and so conform to the contemplative model of knowledge that separates its object and sets it at a distance.[6] Yet all the senses can provide aesthetic satisfaction, including the proximal receptors of tactual, olfactory, gustatory, and subcutaneous kinesthetic perception. Moreover, the common belief that experience flows through separate sensory channels distorts their actual synthesis in perception. In perceptual experience the senses fuse inseparably, a phenomenon called synesthesia that is especially pronounced in aesthetic appreciation.[7]

Discovery

From the central place accorded perceptual awareness, aesthetic experience is, at least in principle, unconstrained by preconceptions about what can be taken aesthetically. Ordinary experience is guided by signs or cues that often reduce its perceptual content to a mere vestige, sufficient only for recognition, and when experience becomes habitual or routine, it loses its aesthetic character. In aesthetic experience, however, the usual order of significance is inverted. Perceptual qualities and experienced meanings become the center of attention, and those features that were once unnoticed or ignored become important. This opens the field of aesthetic experience to unexpected objects and events. And because aesthetic perception is focused and selective, creative and novel ideas and relationships may emerge.

Uniqueness

Because every experience is perceptually unique, different in some respects from every other, this takes on special importance in aesthetic appreciation. Even repetitive objects or events never actually duplicate each other, since each repetition resonates with its predecessors, while at the same time projecting its influence on the repetitions that follow. These changes may be small and subtle, but aesthetic awareness is nothing if not discerning.

Reciprocity

The interplay that develops among the factors in an aesthetic situation is sometimes overlooked, yet this invariably occurs in an intense engagement with art. The experience of an art object is deeply affected by the knowledge and attitude of the person who joins with it.[8] At the same time, the object acts on the beholder and subtly alters the character and quality of awareness. Such reciprocity is highly desirable, for why would we enter the aesthetic if not to engage in such an exchange?

This interplay between art and its appreciator overlaps with similar exchanges involving the other active factors in the aesthetic situation or field, such as the artist and the performer. These may sometimes be different persons but often is simply the recreative, activating attention of the audience. All these factors may contribute information, interpretive judgment, and other kinds of cognitive content, yet in the experiential context of appreciation they always assume a perceptual mode. The recent interest in interactive art is a difference in degree but not in kind. It makes the dynamic exchange of object, audience, artist, and performer explicit and prominent.[9]

Continuity

Not only do these participating factors interact and overlap, but in the living experience of an aesthetic situation they blend into one another. The distinctions between the constituent elements of the aesthetic field that we draw from a reflective distance fade away, and the divisions and separations that we impose on experience to help us grasp and control it melt into continuities. This is the primary milieu of aesthetic experience and secures its contextual character.

Engagement

The concept of engagement encapsulates these features of a contextual aesthetic. Aesthetic engagement renounces the traditional separations between the appreciator and the art object, between the artist and the viewer, and between the performer and these others. The psychological distance that traditional aesthetics imposes between the appreciator and the object of art is a barrier that obstructs the participatory involvement that art encourages. Similarly, the divisions we are in the habit of making among the other factors introduce constraints and oppositions. In contrast with this, boundaries fade away in aesthetic engagement and we experience continuity directly and intimately. Those who can set aside the preconceptions of aesthetic distance and the dichotomizing metaphysics underlying traditional aesthetic theory may discover that the fullest and most intense experiences of art and natural beauty reveal an intimate absorption in the wonder and vulnerability of the aesthetic.

Multiplicity

Because the aesthetic concerns the character of experience itself and is not confined to a particular kind of object or place, it knows no external or *a priori* restrictions. The occasions on which aesthetic appreciation can develop are unlimited and can involve any objects whatsoever. Further, aesthetic involvement need not be rare or restricted. It is limited mainly by our perceptual capabilities and our willingness to participate. At the same time, aesthetic experience does not dominate every situation. Often an aesthetic character is subordinate to other demands and interests, such as religious, practical, technological, or cognitive ones. Sometimes, however, the aesthetic supervenes on our usual expectations, as when *The Bible* is appreciated for its literary art and not its religious significance or when the design of a sewer facility becomes the opportunity for creating a tidal sculpture, recreating a habitat for endangered species and establishing a public-access bay walk, as in Patricia Johanson's "Endangered Garden" in San

Francisco. And the practice of a craft may fuse aesthetic values inseparably with functional needs, as in throwing a clay bowl, building a wooden cabinet, or designing a sailboat or an airplane. In such ways, aesthetic values pervade the entire range of human culture.

These features of the aesthetic situation both establish and reflect its contextual character. Discussions about art often center on a single factor, most often the art object but sometimes the appreciator or the artist. Yet they err by synecdoche, taking part of the situation as if it were the entire domain. Even when the appreciator and the object are regarded as related to each other in appreciative experience, they are usually still considered basically self-contained. Furthermore, if we do not also include the creative, recreative, and performative aspects of such experience, the same error of partiality occurs and the account remains fragmentary. For this reason, discussions about expression, representation, formalism, and feeling are likely to misrepresent art. The concept of the aesthetic field is useful here because it reflects, in an inclusive and convenient way, the interweaving, indeed the fusion, of the objective, perceptual, creative, and performative dimensions of what is actually experienced as integral.[10]

Social Aesthetics

Although this account of the contextual character of the aesthetic has considered mainly objects of art and nature, human relations bear a remarkable resemblance to its situational character. At the same time, they reveal the social significance of the aesthetic. How can this be?

Some of the arts suggest this possibility. Consider architecture. To regard architecture merely as the art of building distorts the way in which it actually organizes an entire environment. That is because the design of a building determines not just its own features; it also affects the site on which the building rests and our perception of the structures that stand nearby. Sometimes, in fact, a building casts its character over an entire neighborhood. For buildings are not self-sufficient objects but are places for human activity, determining the patterns of movement toward, into, and out of them, as well as within them. This fact transforms architecture from an art of physical structures into an art of complex social and environmental organization.

Theater also embodies a social aesthetic. The heart of theater does not lie in its physical properties, although theater design, sets, and costumes obviously exert a strong influence. Nor does it lie in the script, although the text is clearly a central factor. But it is in theater's embodied depiction of social situations and, in particular, of particular human relations that theater's special contribution emerges most vividly. Because of this, theater creates an environment that is predominately social, and the aesthetics of theater must build on this base. Film and television harrow the same field, though with different textures, for the nature of these media determines and shapes the qualitative character of the experiences they generate. Film genres and styles vary enormously, to be sure, yet cinema tends, in general, to focus on personal situations with a visual range and intensity that replace the bodily presence from which so much of theater's special power derives. As the eyes of the mind, the camera can become a virtuoso performer in its own right, invisibly directing both conscious and subliminal awareness. Television exhibits a similar process, but it tends to work best in small-scale situations, where its proximity to the viewer and frequent close-ups combine with the intimacy of quiet speech to make it possible to create social situations that have their own distinctive quality.

Each of these preeminently situational arts—architecture, theater, film, and television—exemplifies a distinguishable mode of aesthetic engagement. Together they constitute a sequence of aesthetic situations that are essentially social. Each implicates and relies on human participants in a different way, and each contributes to our understanding of how aesthetic perception carries social significance. To give an adequate account of this, the usual categories and principles, especially those that focus on the aesthetic object and its properties, will not do. In their place we need a social aesthetics.

If we enlarge the field of aesthetic experience and change our focus to allow for an aesthetics of the social situation, what will this look like? Perhaps it would resemble the aesthetics of environment, where many contributing factors come together to establish its aesthetic character and give it a distinctive identity: participants, physical setting, social conditions, along with time, history, and the powerful influence of culture and tradition, all joined in the perceptual character of aesthetic experience. Social aesthetics may, in fact, *be* a kind of environmental aesthetics, for it is both needless and false to restrict environment to its physical aspects. No environment that we can know and speak about is without a human presence; such a thing, in fact, is empirically impossible.[11]

Social aesthetics is, then, an aesthetics of the situation. But what identifies this particular kind of situation? Like every aesthetic situation, social aesthetics is contextual. Furthermore, it is highly perceptual, for intense perceptual awareness is the foundation of the aesthetic. At work in social aesthetics are factors similar to those in any aesthetic field, although their specific identity may be different. While there is no artist, as such, creative processes are at work in its participants, who emphasize and shape the perceptual features and supply meaning and interpretation. There is no art object here, of course, but the situation itself becomes the focus of perceptual attention, as it does in conceptual sculpture or in environments. And at the same time as its participants contribute to creating the aesthetic character of the situation, they may recognize with appreciative delight its special qualities and perhaps work, as a performer would, at increasing and enhancing them. In such a way, a social situation, embodying human relationships, may become aesthetic.

When Schiller attributed the source of social character in human beings to beauty, he found in such experience the ability to harmonize the disparate qualities that, especially in Western culture, compete and conflict with each other. The usual opposition that Schiller identified as the source of this is psychophysical, "the sensuous [part]" and "the spiritual part of [our] being," as he called it. Social harmony is achieved through taste, by which he meant a developed aesthetic sensibility. This is not just a state of mind. A harmony of the sensuous and the spiritual demands full participation of all aspects of human perception, since the sensory is as much body as the spiritual is consciousness. A social aesthetic, then, is full integration, integration equally of the personal and the social, a goal as much social as it is aesthetic.

A social situation, then, displays aesthetic characteristics when its perceptual and other characteristic features predominate: full acceptance of the other(s), heightened perception, particularly of sensory qualities, the freshness and excitement of discovery, recognition of the uniqueness of the person and the situation, mutual responsiveness, an occasion experienced as connected and integrated, abandonment of separateness for full personal involvement, and the relinquishing of any restrictions and exclusivity that obstruct appreciation.

It is important not to leave this argument in the abstract, for many common social occurrences lend themselves to aesthetic experience and analysis. Each of these invites a fuller discussion of how it may take on a predominately aesthetic character. Nor is that character exclusive, for these settings also fuse moral and social values with aesthetic ones.

Aesthetic-Social Situations

Proper etiquette is ordinarily interpreted as rule-governed behavior, conventions that are devoid of any real content but that serve to facilitate social interaction by establishing regular patterns. Yet there are occasions when the cultivation of such behavior assumes a certain grace, when the participants delight in the skills involved and at the same time manage to introduce genuine human content into what is usually empty ritual. When this occurs, discovery, perception, reciprocity, and the other aesthetic features overcome the sterile formalism often associated with etiquette. In much the same way, other rituals, whether religious or social, may turn into aesthetic situations. Religious rituals sometimes become full-fledged theater, and living drama often occurs at celebrations and festivals.

There are entire societies that seem to possess the harmony Schiller talked about. One such culture is the Foi, a tribe living in Papua New Guinea. Foi society is constituted aesthetically, with close connections between language and movement, both in relation to dwelling and to its territory overall. No boundaries exist between mind and body or the being of life and the being of death, a continuity that Foi sung poetry reveals as the basic conditions of spatial and temporal life. Furthermore, this poetry is fundamental in the discursive life of their communally lived world.[12]

Such aesthetically integrated societies are undoubtedly rare, but many kinds of social situations exist in less favored societies that at times exhibit the qualities of an aesthetic situation. Relations with small children, for example, often take on an aesthetic character when our judgment of bodily presence is suspended and perception becomes heightened by a special delight in sensory qualities such as freshness, delicacy, fragility of expression, coloration—qualities of the sort Rubens depicted in the drawing of his son, Nicholas, as a child. On such occasions one can easily discern other aesthetic features: discovery, uniqueness, reciprocity, continuity, engagement, and the possibility of multiple occurrences of the same sort. These traits of an aesthetic situation occur in much the same way in close friendships where, as Aristotle noted, perfect friendship rests on mutual trust, provides for the good of the other, and is a situation in which the friend's good is inseparable from one's own.[13]

It may be, however, that the deepest and most intense occasions of a social aesthetic occur in the many forms that love may take. Indeed, Aristotle's account of perfect friendship leaves little to distinguish it from love. "Love" is an overused word in human relations, but until recently it has been uncommon in philosophy. On the other hand, "beauty" is a common term in philosophy but not in describing human relations. Can we pair their rarities and write a philosophy of love about beautiful relationships and, perhaps at the same time, a philosophy of beauty about the relationships of love? For both beauty and love are relational ideas and not formal features of objects. Better still, they are characteristics of a situation.

Of the many ways to pursue their connection, little has been said of how love can be illuminated through the traits of an aesthetic situation.[14] But it is equally important to show how love is at the same time a manifestation of beauty. Although there is much to explore here, let me comment on only one feature of that situation, perhaps its key feature and the one that implies the others, as well: aesthetic engagement.

Shakespeare is probably the best known but hardly the first to recognize that music may be an aphrodisiac. Long before, Plato had observed its seductive power with distress.[15] Yet whether sustenance or stimulus, music—or any art, for that matter—can do more than excite amorous passions. Art goes far beyond being only a cause or an accompaniment here. To treat it in these ways is to think of art as if it were separate from love, related yet distinct and apart. Isn't there a more intimate association that holds among the arts and the passions, more precisely between art and love, a relationship that involves more than one being simply an occasion or condition of the other?

I think that there is, but it is no thread joining externals, no curious connection of separates. It resembles, rather, a relationship of consanguinity and one of siblings rather than parent and child. For, I suggest, art and love have in common the characteristics we associate with the aesthetic. What is different is more the participants than the occurrence, more the kind of activity that is involved than the kind of experience we enter into. The one concerns human relationships, although, like Thoreau, a person may love a landscape, a place, a home, or an object.[16] The other involves a fusion of appreciator, object, artist, and activator. Surely some kinds of love reflect a similar experience.

Although art and love show clear differences, their resemblances are striking. Whatever else may be involved in art, dwelling on the features of the object occupies a central place. In the full appreciative engagement of art, what often develops is a sense of personal exchange with the image in the painting or with its pictorial qualities; a sharing of the dynamic progression of the work, as in the unfolding of a musical composition; an intimate involvement in the sequence of movement in a dance and the dramatic raveling and unraveling of a play or a novel; and in theater, the presence of a human situation or condition that may take the form of a momentary awareness or a shocking realization, as in an epiphany, or a feeling of kinship or human empathy.

Yet these are the very signs of love, the common strand in its multitude of forms and instances: a personal exchange, a sharing of dynamic progression, perhaps a sense of dramatic development, the awareness of a rare human situation, a feeling of empathy or kinship. In both art and love we may have a sense of being in place, of a dissolution of barriers and boundaries, of communion. And in both an intimate connection can develop. Such connectedness, such continuity, such engagement lie at the very center of the aesthetic, occurring with great intensity on the most notable occasions, and paler on the lesser, more usual ones.

Others have corroborated such a bond. In her essay on "Human Personality," Simone Weil speaks of "a type of attention, converging upon love, that enables the attender to commune with an object (or person) at the level of the impersonal—seeing it with acuity, understanding, and affection."[17] Communing with an object characterizes aesthetic engagement, while the impersonal here refers to the loss of a discrete, separate sense of self. In an oddly parallel fashion Thoreau likened the aesthetic relation with nature to a loving friendship: "As I love nature, as I love singing birds, and gleaming stubble, and flowing rivers, and morning and evening, and summer and winter, I love thee my Friend."[18] But most important by far are the general resemblances of love to aesthetic contact, continuity, participation, and engagement. These suggest a structural similarity, an isomorphism, so to say, between these two most human of experiences. We might, indeed, describe art and love equally as aesthetic situations. Both involve acceptance without judgment and, at their best, both exhibit free value. After we excise the negative elements of possessiveness, exploitation, insecurity, egoism, jealousy, and power, much of what is left in human relationships is its aesthetic character. This is found in the many forms that love takes with friends, with children, with partners. A lesson for morality lies in recognizing the importance of free value, rare and fleeting though it be.[19] Both love and art dwell, too, in the perceptual domains of sense, imagination, and memory, and both are attentive to the sensory qualities of the situation. A rich love relation, like good art, holds new and surprising awareness, cognition, and re-cognition. The peculiar individual features of the art or love object become the focus of attention: It is ultimate particularity.[20]

Further, both art and love evoke mutuality among the factors and forces in the aesthetic situation. The various arts and the different modes of love exhibit reciprocity in ways that are similar, the participating factors coming to blend into each other.[21] Divisions and separations disappear and are replaced by a sense of empathy. These connections are personal ones, for both art and love evoke a sense of shared living, a certain continuity and oneness, an intimacy in which divisions disappear. Love, indeed, is a binding force that melts boundaries. Empedocles knew this in the fifth century BCE when he described love as the attracting and unifying force in the universe.[22] Finally, both possess uniqueness without exclusivity, for various and diverse occasions and relationships are possible. This is not love *of* the beautiful or love as the *path* to the beautiful, which Plato's Socrates learns from Diotima in *The Symposium*. It is rather love *as* beauty, together both manifold and irreducible.[23]

The Politics of Social Aesthetics

This confluence of the aesthetic and the social carries us eventually to that domain in which the social formalizes itself in political patterns. Here a social aesthetics has significant and powerful implications. Schiller again points the way:

> No privilege, no autocracy of any kind, is tolerated where taste rules, and the realm of aesthetic semblance expends its sway.... In the Aesthetic State everything—even the tool which serves—is a free citizen, having equal rights with the noblest.... Here, in the realm of Aesthetic Semblance, we find that ideal of equality fulfilled which the Enthusiast would fain see realized in substance.[24]

Is "the aesthetic state" merely a metaphor for the aesthetic situation? Or does it, in fact, have genuinely political implications?[25] Could it perhaps be both? If it is in some sense political, then what is equal in the aesthetic state? Does the aesthetic suggest a different sense of equality from the many meanings and practices that have been urged since the Stoics and early Christians? There is a special contribution that the aesthetic can make to this most fundamental of ethical and political concepts. We can explore this best by untangling some of the implications that an aesthetic model holds for political order and, in a similar way, for other social institutions.[26]

The social equivalent of the willing acceptance in an aesthetic situation lies in recognizing the intrinsic value of every person. Like the readiness to engage aesthetically in all kinds of experience, the fundamental acceptance of each person is the precondition of a social ethics. No one is excluded *a priori*. No classification stands between a person and his or her inherent worth: not race, religion, ethnicity, private history, level of cultivation, or any other category by which we lose the person in the generality. This accords with the ethical ideal that holds all people as morally equal, irrespective of all other differences.

The aesthetic emphasis on perception suggests that judgments of worth, whether they apply to actions, practices, laws, people, or institutions, be based on the immediacy of the experience to which they lead, on their empirical manifestations and not on rules, principles, or other substitutes for experience. The sensory character of aesthetic awareness has its parallel in the fact of human embodiment in the political order. People are flesh, blood, sensing, and feeling, not statistics, blocs, classes, districts, or votes. The political equivalent of discovery lies in an openness to new ideas and to change that comes from wide participation in social decision-making. The idea of aesthetic uniqueness provides a special meaning. Equality is not exhausted by the notion of a common moral standing, crucial though this be. It suggests, in addition, that human beings are ultimately never commensurable, and that whatever generic endowments they may exhibit, individual people possess ultimate and irreducible particularity.

Reciprocity lies at the heart of the democratic process, for it takes the essential interplay and fusion that develop in aesthetic experience as a model for social and political order. This means that an aesthetic state must be non-authoritarian and non-hierarchical, and that the imposition of force or power in any form must be rejected in the social dynamic. Genuine reciprocity transforms all parties to the process, as difficult to achieve as it is desirable. Yet how else can true reconciliation and collaboration take place? This turns aesthetic continuity into aesthetic community, a social ideal that promotes cooperation, not conflict, and it dissolves the class divisions and other such separations that impede continuity. By reconciling oppositions and promoting humane connections within a social group, the social equivalent of aesthetic engagement encourages intimacy in personal relations and rejects formalized structures that separate people and form them into oppositions. And we find in the openness and readiness to enter into multiple aesthetic occasions a basis for the social pluralism to which free association freely leads.[27]

We may ask, finally, what claim the aesthetic can make as a social model. It is easy to dismiss the aesthetic state for being as naive as it is noble. Perhaps it does exceed the grasp of our faulty institutions and the flawed people who run them. Yet maybe its rarity has more to do with cynicism, narrow purposes, and an ignoble spirit than with impossibility. For such an aesthetic community does in fact exist in more limited forms, imperfectly and impermanently, perhaps, but nonetheless actually, in art, in love, in societies like the Foi, in some families, and in many small, intentional groups and communities throughout the world. It may be that a modest scope is the precondition for an aesthetic-social order.

However one judges the possibility of attaining it, a social aesthetic remains a distinctive, fresh, and illuminating approach to human relations, whether as friendship, family, or state. It is flexible and adaptable to different kinds of situations. It takes a positive approach to social order, replacing the pattern of conflict—a repressive standard that rests on a social dynamic of power and is really a model of violence, however masked in benign language or pious ideology—with a model of mutuality and support, which is really a model of love. Ultimately and best, in giving new meaning to tolerance, reciprocity, and equality, a social aesthetic offers the basis for a truly humane community. Isn't this what Schiller was leading us to see?

13

Aesthetics and Community[*]

"Man is an animal that lives in a polis," Aristotle long ago observed. Yet the forms of human sociality far exceed those found in his collection of Greek constitutions. Any attempt to find some kind of order among such diversity is bound to overlook the differences and unique adaptations that cumulatively determine the character of a community of people. Moreover, the patterns that are distilled from this variety cannot help reflect the interests of the time. Aristotle's classification of constitutions into kingship, aristocracy, and polity mirrors his concern with the distribution of political power, and this continues to be a central issue in the science of politics.

Ordering Human Experience

Central as this is to any discussion of social organization, one of the guiding beacons of our time is the character of human experience. This is the final touchstone of the success of any political structure, and there is no necessary correlation of one with the other. Contentment of some sort may occur under autocratic rule and pervasive fear may fester in a political democracy. Our time has seen both. Still, these characterizations of social atmosphere are crude at best, for the modern fascination—one might say obsession—with psychology and with consciousness has led to the refined discernment of many states of being.

Yet an account of human sociality is not exhausted by politics or psychology. Not only are these not separate domains, they are not all. The forms of transaction in social institutions and economic frameworks include other strands essential in the complex weave of social life, and other patterns, shapes, and meanings of

---

[*] Revised from "Aesthetics and Community," Arnold Berleant, *Living in the Landscape: Toward an Aesthetics of Environment* (Lawrence: University Press of Kansas, 1997).

personal associations, of body movement, of diet are inseparable from political order and state of mind. We cannot search, then, in Aristotelian fashion, for a single essential property that defines society. Rather we must deal in complexities, complexes that can be arranged and sorted in many different ways and on many different levels.

How such complexes can be elaborated coherently from a metaphysical perspective has been demonstrated with striking originality by Justus Buchler, whose theory of natural complexes offers a comprehensive account.[1] My interest here, however, is rather different. It is partly reportorial, partly classificatory, partly projective. While some might decry a utopian element, it is not literally utopian, for cases of what I shall call the aesthetic community have occurred in the past and do now exist. While I want to give this a dominant place, the aesthetic community is elusive to structural analysis, however, for it concerns the very condition and quality of experience.

Although the aesthetic community may be difficult to define, it is perhaps the poet who can help us recognize the ineffable character of such experience, not just its passing moods. Philosophers can, on rare occasions, be poets of the human condition, too, working with evocation as well as statement to locate its various forms. Surprisingly many have their moments of poetic perception and not just the few who, like Plato and Santayana, lift the body of their work on the wings of art. In modest emulation of this tradition, I should like to proceed in such a direction. This is not to avoid the rigors of hard analysis, for I intend that a firm armature support the equipoise of statement.

Political science and political theory possess a parallel appeal for understanding human society, the one presumably grounded on fact, the other on ideas. "Presumably," of course, is an essential qualifier since, as in religious and moral thought, it is especially difficult to separate facts from ideas and both of these from ideological presuppositions. Political theory and science, moreover, can be said to have had a parallel origin in Western thought, the first in Plato's writings on the state, in which the idea of practice was never absent; the second in the political philosophy of Aristotle, which combined classification and judgment with its descriptions. This tells us something, moreover, about the complementarity, perhaps the inseparability of theory and science.

Yet neither political science nor political theory seems to entirely satisfy our desire to understand the structure and workings of human society. This is in part because the forms and conditions of societies have varied as widely as assessments of their success, and generalization is precarious. Moreover, dissatisfaction and disapproval, both from within the social order and from without, have regularly led to efforts at change, some of them transformative. Given such discontent, it is little wonder that, since classical times, philosophers and political theorists have attempted to envision what a truly satisfactory human order would be like, a moral order, a state of social happiness. Sometimes these proposals have been ameliorative, sometimes utopian, but always significant.

Political Order

The usual approach to social order is a political one, classification by governmental form, by the pattern in which power is distributed. Hence the common contrast of such forms as monarchy, aristocracy, oligarchy, republic, democracy, and state communism. But political order is not the most basic level of analysis. It rests on several assumptions, assumptions about what people are like, including beliefs about human nature and, indeed, that there is such a thing as human nature; about people's motives and goals; about power as an isolable quantity; and about the nature of society. In contrast, I should like to propose a somewhat novel grouping of communities, an order based instead on the character and quality of human relations, on the nature of social experience. Although social experience is not something either simple in structure or quantifiable, it has the virtue of being directly accessible, certainly to the participants and, in one form or another, to everyone, and it can be described in some fashion, literally to a degree and figuratively in ways that can assist our understanding.

What I should like to offer here is a preliminary sketch, but one that I hope makes a significant statement about community. Beginning with some observations about individual and community, surely central factors in social philosophy, I shall propose a convenient schema within which to place many of the endlessly varied instances of human association. This is not an exercise in typology, for the rational, the moral, and the aesthetic communities, the forms I shall identify, are not pure nor are they logically exclusive. They do, however, distinguish different kinds of social experience and understanding, and they are useful for characterizing actually existing societies. Most important, they represent real alternatives in social choice. Since theoretical ideas and moral criteria underlie every conception of community, and since normative experience is the basis on which we must evaluate social forms, let me begin with some observations about ethics.

Ethical Order

The rich history of ethical thought contains a wide range of views on issues too different to be presented accurately along a single continuum. These vary sharply in conception and in what considerations are taken as basic. The most common contrast is likely that between utilitarianism, or what may be called the ethics of prudence, and Kantian ethics, or what we may term the morality of conscience. These are not, as is sometimes thought, true opposites, since they do not differ on the same points but rather diverge sharply in approach. Utilitarianism is an ethic of action, endorsing the careful consideration of means and consequences with the object of obtaining maximum satisfaction. And since satisfaction is always a matter of personal experience, the seat of value and the touchstone for judgment lie wholly in the individual. Kantian ethics, in contrast, focuses on motive, on intent, and carries out the moral process as the decision of an autonomous will through an introspective consideration of whether it can be universalized. While all this is well known, it is important to recognize that both utilitarian and Kantian ethics are essentially theories whose moral center lies in the individual: It is the individual whose satisfaction or will decides moral character of an action. And while both theories take social considerations into account, the one by calculating the extent of satisfaction or suffering and the other by the criterion of universalizability, it is important to recognize that these extensions to a wider venue are secondary additions to what is at heart a private ethic.

Both the ethics of prudence and the morality of conscience rest, moreover, on assumptions that are actually articles of faith: the ultimacy of the individual, a distinct and separate being located in a rational universe, a rational being whose intelligence is largely calculative. Mill's introduction of qualitative experience is a futile attempt to correct the private nature of quantitative judgments of pleasure, futile because it attempts to reconcile two antithetical factors: the personal character of experience with cultural standards of value. These are incompatible in practice as well as theory, as social conflict and political controversy in our own day show only too well.

Kantian ethics has its own share of presuppositions, for it inherits the unhappy baggage of the dualistic tradition, locating the will in a hidden, noumenal realm and denying the possibility of knowledge there, as Kant bravely affirmed, "in order to make room for faith." Although he had thought to provide an adequate grounding for morality, Kant mistook the uneasiness of his dogmatic slumber for an awakening, as Dewey wryly observed. For seen in the way just described, both the morality of conscience and the ethics of prudence are dogmatic philosophies: They make untoward assumptions about experience, about knowledge, and about values, assumptions we now recognize to be fraught with difficulty and infused with error.

The last century and a half has seen important developments in ethical and social thought that have moved beyond the dogmas that burden the classic accounts. Attempting to overcome their difficulties, many of the later proposals appear to have taken sharply different directions, although ironically the earlier assumptions often seem to reappear in new guises. In Nietzsche's case, the refreshing transvaluation of values onto a naturalistic plane nonetheless preserves elements of the individualism and deliberate irrationality of Kant. Although pragmatism expanded utilitarianism's range of consequences and recognized the inseparability of ends from the means for reaching them, it has had difficulty finding a place for modes of rationality that are noncalculative and for modes of thought that are nonrational. And in existential freedom one can even find a radical Kantianism, with its puzzling juxtaposition of subjectivity and universality.

While these traditions in ethical thought engage many issues and concerns, it is nonetheless important to recognize that they have not succeeded in providing a satisfactory grounding for social ethics. And people, desperate for direction, have seized on elements of self-transcendence and mysticism in Eastern religion or have translated morality into technologies of thought control and behavior.[2]

Restructuring Moral Thought

Is it possible to restructure moral thought in a way that not only avoids the dogmatic pitfalls of traditional ethics but also provides a theory less constrained by self-serving assumptions? I should like to explore some alternatives to see how far they can take us in a fresh direction and, in addition, to determine whether they can offer support for a different approach to the problems of political philosophy. This requires not just reconsidering the assumptions of traditional ethics but also grounding ethics on what by now we understand far better about human thought, society, and culture.

Foremost in this rethinking of ethics is our understanding of the essential sociality of human being. Philosophy lags far behind what the human sciences have established to a compelling degree. In both direct and subtle ways, ethical theory struggles with problems involving egoism, conscience, self, moral autonomy, and responsibility, problems structured in forms that preserve in one way or another the discreteness, the separateness, of the moral individual. Reconstructing social thought on the basis of the social human forces us to rethink these problems in radical ways, ways that follow the long-established tradition in philosophy, not of solving such "problems" but of completely recasting them or even rejecting them entirely.

Consider some of the issues centering around moral responsibility. The traditional construction of the moral universe is one in which motives, decisions, and obligations rest at heart in the autonomous individual. The self must freely make its own decisions and be judged by them, based either on its intent or its actions. What happens to this ordering of the moral situation if we discard the notion of the self-sufficient moral individual and recognize that the self is a social construct and even a social product? We cannot, then, speak of a single person, since persons do not come singly. Conflicts between egoism and altruism, self and other, are transformed into alternative social complexes in which personal and social factors are variously intermingled. The very notion of a moral universal, itself the product of an individualistic ethic as the sum of all individuals, must be transformed into degrees of generality that rest on social groups, not quantitative collections of selves. What this means, then, is that morality is no individual matter but always a social one, that no values exist in isolation, and that moral issues arise in social situations and their resolution is a social process.

Ethical egoism and its contrary, an altruistic ethic, are difficult to overcome. An eloquent illustration of their persistence is the feminist alternative to the theory of rights, the ethics of care. Care appears to be a welcome corrective to the self-preservative notion of rights. Indeed, it replaces the litigious focus of rights with motives of concern for others and benevolent actions. Instead of calculating personal benefit, it directs our regard toward others. Care is not only in sharp contrast to narrow self-interest but it also makes a notable addition to a tradition of generosity and selfless service. Another form of altruism, care stands by way of contrast to the masculinist ethic of self-aggrandizement. Yet at the same time the ethic of care remains within an individualistic frame. It informs personal decisions, motivates private acts, and centers on particular cases.[3]

There are alternatives to this egoistic frame. In discussing the inescapability of self-reference in the form of personal satisfaction in any presumably benevolent act, John Dewey drew a critical distinction between acting *as* a self and acting *for* a self.[4] While ethical egoism conflates these, they are actually quite different. Whatever action one performs, one cannot help acting in some sense as a self, since that is the condition of any deliberate action. In any action, a self acts: There can be no action without someone performing it. This is quite different from performing an action directed to one's personal benefit, that is, acting *for* oneself. The fallacy in ethical egoism lies in regarding all cases in which one acts as a self as instances of acting for oneself, whereas the latter is only a special case of the former. Ethical egoism is, therefore, not a universal condition but a particular one.

Another example of a non-egocentric ethic is Erich Fromm's distinction between selfishness, self-love, and self-interest.[5] From a psychotherapeutic perspective, these are quite different, Fromm claims. Selfishness is a form of self-aggrandizement, feeding one's weakness in a futile effort to overcome what is actually a kind of self-hatred. This is futile, since no quantity of personal gain can fill a lack that is of an entirely different sort, a lack of genuine self-regard. Self-love, on the other hand, is the precondition to loving others, not opposed to it. It reaches out from strength, not weakness, and draws people together toward a common fulfillment. One's true self-interest does not lie in private satisfactions but in the ability to conjoin one's personal value with that of others so that instead of these interests being opposed, we recognize them as actually interdependent.

What these two cases show is that resolving the problem of ethical egoism does not require endorsing one form of the egoism-altruism alternative or the other but rather lies in surpassing both, that is, in restructuring the ethical problem in such a way as to transcend the conflict. We begin to realize that self and other are not moral alternatives because there is no separate self and no distinct other. Each is mutually implicated to such a degree that they cannot be thought apart. Self is truly other, other truly self.

Not only, then, is ethics social ethics and morality social morality, but any attempt to rest ethics on the distinct and separate individual is fictitious, albeit a conventional and time-honored fiction. On the other hand, it is equally important to recognize that rejecting a self-centered ethic does not mean endorsing the disappearance of the person into an anonymous social mass and relinquishing self-direction and responsibility. The dialectical opposition of individual and society is itself a product of the very ethical individualism we are questioning. In its place emerges the social human, a new concept for moral philosophy but an old reality of moral life.

Three different directions are possible, then: one that centers on the individual, one on the group, and a third that joins them, not in the form of a synthesis, which is a consequent stage, but as a prior, first condition of being human—the social human. With some of the issues and ideas now before us, let us see how they are reflected in different conceptions of community. While these characterizations may not often appear in clear form, they nonetheless represent the dominant tone of many of the societies we find ourselves part of, a social condition that is rarely chosen and often not clearly grasped.

The Rational Community

The rational community is a community of individuals that sees society as an artificial construct and the state, as Hobbes characterized it, as a leviathan, a monster to be feared, opposed, and tolerated as an unwelcome necessity, at best. The philosophy of this community is utilitarianism in one form or another, from Bentham's classic mode to Rawls's more recent adaptation. Central to the rational community is the individual, motivated by self-interest, guided by reason, and protected by rights. It is the model assumed by political liberalism and economic individualism. Habermas's defense of rationality belongs here, too, for even though the ego may be formed in social relations, the social order consists in the relations of subjective selves with other such selves. In the rational community, the essential antinomy of self and other underlies social experience and the two remain irreconcilable.

What guides individual action in the rational community are prudential motives, a careful calculation of costs and benefits in which nothing is done spontaneously or gratuitously. When collaborative action occurs, it is because people identify common interests. Common interest, in fact, is the vehicle of social action, whether in government, in law, or in the many interest groups that form and dissolve as the occasion demands. Acts of spontaneous generosity may occur in the rational community when people are moved by tragedy, great personal need, enthusiasm, or a powerful common threat, as in war. These, however, are exceptions to the rule and are always accompanied by opportunists on the prowl for ways to turn every circumstance to personal gain. Yet increasingly complex economic dependencies and increasingly sophisticated technologies require collaborative action and drive people together. And while the rational community continues to characterize the modern industrial nation-state, it is coming now to justify internationalism, whether in the form of trading zones, corporate organization, or political union, all these, however, devised for personal, private benefit.

The rational community is more a social order than a community, for whatever is common is so merely by the circumstantial concurrence of private interests. Its principles infiltrate every deliberate action and each social domain. Economically, the rational community justifies a pattern of activity in which every individual pursues his or her self-interest. Because interests rest on need and desire, and desire is never satiated, and because in an economy of scarcity there is never enough to satisfy everyone, competition is pervasive. Opposition characterizes all economic relations, those among the producers and suppliers of services, those among the purchasers of goods and services, and those between both groups. Politically, too, a society of individuals pursuing separate and opposed interests means that political decisions are made with the view to satisfying special interests. Such interests are represented formally by the electoral mechanisms of political democracy in which everyone expresses his or her interests by casting a single vote and informally by lobbies, pressure groups, and powerful economic and political forces that promote their own interests by soliciting and manipulating blocs of "individual" votes by ethnic, racial, and monetary appeals and promises.

Although the rational society is best known in its political and economic expressions, it is actually pervasive. It informs social thought in the belief in individual autonomy, the idea that we exist as persons separate and apart from society, which is considered an artificial construction. And it persists in the belief that personal freedom is secured only through watchful opposition to social action. As the adversarial system in law, it is central to the judicial process. As the belief in free will, which endows each person with moral autonomy, it stands at the center of conventional morality. Even the goals of psychotherapy—emotional independence, wholeness, self-sufficiency, and freedom—reflect this individualistic social ideal. Moreover, the fixation of the therapeutic process on the "self," on self-development and the cultivation of self-confidence and assertiveness, reflects the same individualistic bent, although viewed from an alternative perspective, the "self" appears more like a folk category than the entity it is usually taken to be. And, of course, such a psychology encourages and rationalizes aggressiveness, its common and characteristic behavioral form. Finally, there is a whole philosophical industry at work supporting the *status quo* of the rational society. In addition to utilitarian philosophy, there is the preeminent concept of the ego, expressed in various forms of subjectivism, intersubjectivity, and the correlative "problem" of "the other."

Any alternative to this interplay of interests is difficult to envision, so deeply has it become rooted in the modern mentality. Yet signs have begun to appear with increasing frequency, signs of changes and of forces that undermine the premises of the rational community. First among these is the growing recognition that self-sufficiency, one of the dominant cultural myths of Western societies, is a false ideal. It has, in fact, always been an exaggeration, since wherever it has appeared it has rested on a social bedrock. Embracing the model of economic self-sufficiency, the homesteader or pioneer not only brings along equipment and supplies but, more important still, utilizes a vast body of knowledge and technology developed and accumulated by hundreds of generations of hardship and trial. This exposes the fallacy in economic self-interest: that interests are fundamentally private and opposed, and that the independent, conflicting pursuit of those interests, which we call competition, is the best mechanism for their greatest fulfillment. Even that arch individualist, Hobbes, recognized that benefits beyond mere survival require social order and collaborative action. It is undeniable that individualism rests on a social foundation.

It helps in rethinking the ideas that center around the rational society to draw a distinction between weak and strong dependence. Weak dependence is what we usually mean when we speak of dependence, and it is pervasive. In its sexual form, it is found both in taking the other and in giving oneself up to the other. In marriage, it is monogamy imposed from without through legal stricture and social convention. In social groups, it appears as hierarchical organization and as the persecution of minorities and the weak. It takes political form in the need for power over others and in the cult of the leader. Psychologically, it is found equally in selfish behavior and in selflessness, as Fromm pointed out, the one intended to strengthen a separate self, the other to evade one's personhood. All these express weak dependence because they derive their force from some external source and their application lies wholly beyond the person. One does not gain strength from weak dependence: On the contrary, it reinforces weakness by focusing energies elsewhere and leaving the person essentially untouched.

Strong dependence, on the other hand, is not a sign of emotional or psychological insufficiency; rather, it recognizes the fundamental incompleteness of the human person. Seen in this way, dependence is not a weakness or a defect. Fulfillment is rather achieved through harmonious connections with others, with social forms, and with environment, connections that implicate and change a person. Strong dependence takes equally many forms. Biologically, it consists in promoting life through the family and whatever other forms mutual domestic support may take. Psychologically, it recognizes the manifold ways in which one develops character and personhood through relations with other people. Socially, strong dependence finds in voluntary forms of social order a condition for personal growth, each inseparable from the other. Even environment must be reconceptualized from surroundings separate from oneself to a matrix continuous with and inclusive of ourselves, a constant process of reciprocity among all the active factors. Environment becomes that interrelated system of dependencies we call an ecosystem.[6]

Among nations, too, there is a slowly increasing awareness of interdependence, not in alliances and the various forms of collective political force, all of which express weak dependency, but in legal relations and forms, such as international law, the United Nations, the World Court, and the gradual realization that national sovereignty is a political myth that has lost its usefulness. Economically, too, strong dependence appears in recognizing ways in which mutual interests can be served by carefully expanding trade relations, removing barriers, and replacing economic exploitation with forms of assistance that benefit both the donor and the receiver of aid. Strong dependence even assumes a cosmic scale as we begin to realize that pollution does not observe national boundaries and that industrial practices and commercial policies and products have planetary consequences. All these expressions of strong dependence rest on the premise, a fact rather than an assumption, that our fulfillment as persons and as societies is part of a single process and a single condition, a process and a condition that involve multiple factors. "Person," indeed, becomes a social category, the node of intersecting connections.

The Moral Community

Let me speak more briefly of another social form, the moral community. Unlike the community of self-interested individuals, the moral community rests on the insight that multiple bonds connect people with each other. It recognizes that people are interdependent and the relationships among them reciprocal. The ethical foundation of the moral community is the morality of conscience and its classic formulation can be found in the philosophy of Kant. For him, moral obligation is the binding force that holds beyond choice or desire. An inner self ultimately stands alone with its moral choices. We may not desire its demands and we may choose to disregard them, but this has no effect on its moral authority. The will must determine its guiding principle for itself, yet in doing so it represents every rational being. In this way, the morality of the individual becomes at the same time the force that unites humankind.

This version of the moral community shares two essential features with the community we have just discussed—its rationality and its ultimate individualism. Qualifying the individualism of the moral community, however, are internal forces that press toward a larger order, embracing and joining together morally separate beings into an uneasy confederation of the private and the social. For Kant this is the powerful stipulation of universalization, which frames the moral demand so that it can extend to everyone. In authoritarian societies, the ethic of hierarchy binds individuals into a rigid pyramid of power. As this amalgam becomes more complete, it may reach a point at which the members not only identify with the community but become utterly absorbed into it, relinquishing independent judgment and personal decision-making. When it so overwhelms and suppresses individual volition, the moral community has turned into the organic community.

The Organic Community

The organic community can assume a variety of forms. In a rigidly structured hierarchical order, power filters downward from its pinnacle, from level to increasingly broader level, each deriving a lesser degree of power than the one above until little remains at the bottom. In an autocratic society, a single leader exercises dominant power and its members are subsumed by the whole, achieving their identity, their very being, as part of that whole. While institutional good is the binding concern and the ethos of the group glorifies the social process, an authoritarian center of power and privilege wields influence and dispenses goods. To varying degrees and in distinctive ways, most religious groups, quasi-religious cults, corporations, and military organizations exemplify the organic community. At its most extreme form, the organic community absorbs its members into the corporate body, withholding the ability for any independent action, any autonomy of will, any vestige of personal identity apart from the group, all in the interests of devotion to a "higher" call. The organic community achieves its most complete development in the fascist state or fanatic movement, where the moral imperative of "blood and soil," ethnic purity, national destiny, or religious election sucks up all separate wills into the irrepressible force of an exclusive group. This, of course, is the ethos of fascism.

These modes of community—the rational, the moral and its derivative, the organic—are limited, for the quality of human relations they engender lacks a genuine continuity of individual and social. Coolly calculating one's rational self-interest, bravely standing true in moral isolation, futilely seeking society through intersubjectivity, lost in the endless depths of a searching conscience or the anonymity of a faceless group, these forms do not succeed in developing the condition for genuine community—a unity of individual and social in which neither dimension dominates but each enhances the possibilities of the other.

The Aesthetic Community

It is this condition to which the aesthetic community aspires. This form moves beyond customary ways of thinking about community and, while it has certain resemblances to the other modes, it is important to avoid the temptation to assimilate it to them. The aesthetic community is not an order of individuals, either in the rational sense or the moral one, nor is it a community whose participants relinquish their individuality and deliver themselves into the hands of a leader or become absorbed into a corporate identity. Its fundamental features are distinctive, and to grasp the aesthetic community, we must stand outside the convenient conventional categories by which we usually order our understanding of human relations and social groups. Every community proclaims some kind of unity, sometimes more in word than in fact. Organic unity, in which the parts have no separate existence but are bound to and subsumed under a whole, is often taken as the paradigmatic sense of the term. These parts may have a distinct identity but they lack independence. Like the limbs and organs of a living creature, its underlying metaphor, they function within a whole from which they gain their value and meaning. Although organic unity is sometimes ascribed to a work of art, the aesthetic bond is quite different. Art carries a more subtle sense of connection that illuminates the aesthetic significance of community, a bond best described by the similar though not cognate word, "continuity."

Continuity is not absorption or assimilation, nor is it an external relation between separate things. It suggests, instead, connectedness within a whole rather than a link between discrete parts. Much as William James argued that relations are not external connections but have an immediacy that is directly present and real to experience, relationships in a fulfilled community are not imposed from without but are inherent in the situation in ways that are concrete and operative.[7] The aesthetic community exemplifies this. Internal relations are, in fact, one expression of continuity. The connections among the members of an aesthetic community are as real, as much a part of the community, as the people, themselves. Not only are there no sharp boundaries; there are no divisions. Nor is there any sense in which the society or state is separate from the people who comprise it. Their relation does rest on internalized control (the moral model), on independence and self-sufficiency (the rational model), on isolation (both the moral and rational models), or on domination (the organic model). Relationships of reciprocity and strong dependence among the participants in an aesthetic community replace the barriers and separations that mark the other social modes.

Continuity, moreover, allows for differences, although these are usually not marked by abrupt changes but by gradations, as between the colors in a spectrum. Sharp contrasts may occur, but these are part of a larger harmony. This sense of continuity is not vacuous, however. It denotes a merging that joins things already bound together rather than an assemblage of distinct and separate elements. As the motivic features of a large symphonic movement contribute to the character of the total auditory experience by their contrasts as much as their resemblances, human continuities denote a bond that overrides differences.

One sense of continuity is perceptual and material, as in the sense of one's body, which at the same time incorporates, in a literal sense, the food one ingests, the air one breathes, the clothes one wears, the objects one uses, the place one inhabits, the activities in which one engages. Consciousness is also part of this perceptual continuity, for whether we describe ourselves as an embodied consciousness or as a reflective organism, multidimensional continuities unite our cognitive, volitional, and physical dimensions. Humans have continuity, too, with nature. Nature as we live it is environment, and environment is no external surrounding but the material context with its order of meanings of which we are a contributing and dependent part.[8] But it is in the continuities that unify people that community arises. Here are the connections of place, of human association, of language. Here too are the connections of time as history, tradition, and personal experience. What makes continuity aesthetic is the kind of unity it describes: a continuum of body, of awareness, of context, all joined in the pervasive continuity of perception. In a germinal sense, we can discover the aesthetic community in the relationship between close companions or friends, where a bond may evolve that leads people to surpass the conventional limits of the self to attain what Aristotle considered perfect friendship. This is friendship between those who are good and who so desire the good of each other that one is able to feel the other's experience as in some way coincident with one's own.[9] In the community of friends, the self expands to include the friend and cannot be fully known apart. The thought of the one is always inhabited by the presence of the other.

The erotic community may have more persistence. The community of lovers joins people in a multidimensional unity conventionally described as physical, emotional, and spiritual. What is important here is that the erotic community involves a connection that transcends the customary boundaries that isolate people. It is the closest many people come to the aesthetic sense of community, not a loss of self in sexual ecstasy but the dissolution of protective barriers that separate and isolate, and a heightened sense of self-with-other. This is clearly an entirely different matter from purely sexual release, whose satisfaction is brief and may even narrow into self-indulgent isolation. The various communities I have identified—the rational, the moral, the organic, the erotic—may not be continuous over long duration and are likely to be circumstantial.

Still other occasions offer an intimation of the aesthetic community. One is the dissolution of the discrete self that may occur in meditation and the bonding within the aura of the sacred that sometimes accompanies religious experience. In the feelings of sisterhood and brotherhood, of love and charity, the religious community may dissolve the boundaries that separate people and approach the aesthetic. In its elements of transcendence and its tendency toward the mystical, however, the religious differs markedly from the aesthetic, which is rooted in the world we call natural. Another experience of unity occurs in the intimacy of our association with art, from which the aesthetic community derives its essential character. In our engagement with art, a sense of connectedness can develop that is the prototype of the aesthetic community. At its most generous and powerful, our engagement with art creates a unity of experience that joins artist, appreciator, art object, and performer into a heterogeneous field of continuous forces. This is the qualitative source of the aesthetic community.[10]

In the past some philosophers have recognized forms of bonding that anticipate the aesthetic sense of community. Locke claimed that society exists in a state of nature under the sway of natural law and before any agreement to organize. Nietzsche had the insight that the unifying aesthetic experience, exemplified by Greek tragedy, offers the ground for life in society, for communality. Husserl's idea that everything must be seen in context and within the horizon of the world in which it is presented led him to the notion that the lifeworld is made up of communities that exist in a social and historical setting.[11]

What, then, is an aesthetic community? What kind of phenomenon does the term describe, or is it but an assumption, a construct, a fiction, an ideal? Does the aesthetic community realize continuity through certain kinds and networks of relationships? Like all language that does not wholly create its object, the concept is an approximation, an attempt to locate and identify something apprehended more or less dimly yet with the force of significant reality.

The difference between the perception of a social situation by an observer and the perception by a participant may lead to a clearer sense of the aesthetic community. What to the observer is clearly demarcated and structured by being objectified may, to the participant, not be clearly bounded but fluid and responsive. Because both the rational community and the moral community are, at bottom, communities of individuals, they often reflect an ironic contrast between observer and participant. One can think of oneself as an American individualist and yet be enclosed in a stifling corporation, have an overbearing spouse yet feel comfortably married, be politically powerless yet be an ardent patriot. One can be part of a close family or other intimate group and yet feel alienated from it, insecure, lost, helpless, a stranger in a familiar land.

Forms of control are understood somewhat better now than in the past, and we can see how this split between the world of the participant and that of the observer may be fostered by state—organized societies that are inimical to community. People often experience realities falsely, and political bodies often deliberately foster false consciousness. From thought control and news management to outright censorship and calculated propaganda, the state, whatever its ideological persuasion, has long been adept at manipulating its citizenry, managing its citizen participants from the standpoint of an observer. In all such cases, observer and participant occupy different orders; they speak foreign languages not easily translated and communicated.

In the aesthetic community, the contrast between observer and participant develops more subtly. These two stances do not occupy different realities, each of which may be false to the other, as in the other modes of community. Rather, they rest on the same level and, when the awareness of an experience becomes yet another dimension of that very experience, they inform one another. Because the participant is, as such, actively engaged in community, this engagement becomes the primary mode and the self-awareness of observation secondary and dependent. The observer who is not a participant cannot truly grasp an aesthetic community: both observer and participant must inhabit the same harmonious reality.

The aesthetic community is a community in and of experience. Its resemblance to the situation in which we experience art suggests its name. In art when the potential of the aesthetic field is fulfilled, a rich reciprocity develops among the artist's creative force, the object on which that force is focused, its appreciator, and the performer or activator of the work. Contemplative distancing and the presumed objectification of the knowledge process are foreign to this situation. Aesthetic engagement defines its character instead. The same reciprocity of constituent parts, the multiplicity of interrelated functions, the assimilation of observer into participant, the salience of qualitative experience—all these distinguish the aesthetic community, as well.[12]

In a compelling passage in *I and Thou*, Martin Buber describes the personal encounter that establishes what he calls the world of relation.[13] The intimacy of this world joins what are ordinarily considered quite disparate things, and the kinds of things with which we can engage in this way, Buber shows, are perhaps surprising: first nature, then people, and, ultimately, the creative engagement of art.

We regard nature as the exemplary object of the sciences. Its philosophical ramifications excite the foundational questions of metaphysics and particularly of ontology—questions of order, of purpose, and ultimately of the very meaning and being of reality. Yet the usual way of understanding nature, both for science and for philosophy, rests on objectification and analysis. Furthermore, over the past century and a half, the social and behavioral sciences have dominated the field in their examination of human orders and institutions. The philosophical dimensions of this are nearly as ancient in their origins as ontology, for the quest for an ethical grounding of human relationships has preoccupied thinkers since Socrates and K'ung-fu-tsu (Confucius), and the authors of the Hebrew Bible were concerned with such matters long before that. Here, too, the cognitive process has, until recent times, followed the same scientific and philosophical model of disinterested objectivity and rational analysis.

Yet both our relations with nature and with people can transcend the objectification with which we ordinarily think to distance them. In what Buber called "life with nature," we join in a relation of undivided reciprocity with things. In what he termed "life with men," we do not separate ourselves from others but experience a personal bond that joins us. But it is in the third order, "life with spiritual beings," that the transformative process of intimacy reveals itself most compellingly. It may seem strange for Buber to place art here, but once we recognize in it the act of origination, the discovery that had not found its tongue before, we realize how art epitomizes so fully this high human accomplishment. Yet this kind of life appears not only in the objects and occasions we fashion by our art; they are still more pervasive in that kind of experience that we associate with art objects and by which we identify them as such—aesthetic experience. Such experience, moreover, is not the exclusive province of art but can be extended to embrace nature, as well. And more to our point, it also encompasses the human.

In Buber's world of relation, then, we do not objectify, rationalize, order, and control things but rather enter into an intimate association with them. The analytic model does not work here. All three modes of relation exemplify an association that does not join together discrete entities but involves a kind of giving in which we establish a deep connection. Carrying this farther, we can see in it more than a connection but a continuity and, eventually even more, a community, an aesthetic community.

A social aesthetic here joins an aesthetic of art and an aesthetic of nature with an aesthetic of humans. All three of Buber's worlds—nature, humans, and art—are domains in the same aesthetic realm, a remarkable coalescence of diverse orders into a single, embracing unity of experience. What science has divided into the natural world, the human world, and the mythological world; what philosophy has separated into metaphysics, ethics, and the philosophy of art—all regain their primal unity in the region of the aesthetic. The aesthetic community is a social aesthetic joining humans and environment in multidimensional reciprocity. As the human environment consists not just of places and buildings but of their complex connections with human uses and human participants, an aesthetic community recognizes the social dimension of environment and the aesthetic conditions of human fulfillment.[14]

These forms of community—the rational, the moral and its offspring, the organic, and the aesthetic—are abstract forms but not unrealizable ideals, for they may occur in different spheres and in a variety of ways. By identifying instances of such communities and by learning how to guide them, we can know better how to live with and in them. Understanding the alternative forms of community also enables us to make deliberate choices of which to pursue. What stands here as a study in social aesthetics and philosophy is, at the same time, a matter for political science and practice, and perhaps the cardinal occasion of applied aesthetics. At this stage in social evolution and at this millennial point in human history, is any task of philosophy more compelling?

Appendix

Publications in Social and Political Aesthetics by Arnold Berleant

"The Aesthetics of Politics" DOI: http://dx.doi.org/10.17613/7t9e-hw54 *Sensibility and Sense: The Aesthetic Transformation of the Human World* (Imprint Academic, 2010), 213–24. ISBN: 978-1845401733

Illuminating the pervasiveness and importance of the aesthetic presence was the task I undertook in my book, *Sensibility and Sense: The Aesthetic Transformation of the Human World*, and this essay develops the final chapter of that book. It carries that process still further, most particularly into the regions of political theory. For the energies of the artistic process invariably engage the social world, and the implications of artistic practice and aesthetic experience are necessarily political.

"An Exchange on Disinterestedness" DOI: http://dx.doi.org/10.17613/M6FT8DJ6H
A dialogue with Ronald Hepburn, *Contemporary Aesthetics*, 1 (2003).

The idea of aesthetic disinterestedness has been a central concept in aesthetics since the late eighteenth century. This exchange offers a contemporary reconsideration of disinterestedness from different sides of the question.

"Beyond Disinterestedness" DOI: http://dx.doi.org/10.17613/M69C6S12X *The British Journal of Aesthetics*, 34/3 (July 1994).

The notion of disinterestedness became, during the eighteenth century, the central term in modern aesthetics. Developments in the arts since that time, however, have led to its loss of relevance, although it has continued its preeminence in theory. While rejecting disinterestedness and its kindred concepts of contemplation, distance, and universality, their continuing insights lie in perceptual directness and receptivity and in focused attention. These can be retained in an aesthetics of engagement that reflects the collaboration with artist and art object that is central in appreciation.

"Ethics and Science: Some Normative Facts and a Conclusion," *Journal of Value Inquiry* XI (1977), Winter 1977, 244–58.

The assessment of normative issues must begin by examining basic human needs. Judgments do not create values but only recognize them. Such factual knowledge enables us to determine policy and guide actions, and the human sciences can contribute by identifying such structural universals. This can underlie efforts to establish moral beliefs and practices in addition to social institutions that promote fulfilling those needs.

"The Experience and Criticism of Art," *Sarah Lawrence Journal* (Winter 1967), 55–64.

It is to the world of art that we should look to see how critical judgments work, the actual examining the conduct of criticism by considering it in the context of a situation in which it collaborates with the creative, appreciative, and performative activities. Here we see that the criticism of art instructs the audience in attaining fuller perceptual awareness and contributes to a common body of aesthetic judgment.

"The Experience and Judgment of Values," *The Journal of Value Inquiry*, I, 1 (Spring 1967), 24–37. Reprinted in *Value Theory in Philosophy and Social Science*, ed. Laszlo and Wilbur (New York: Gordon & Breach, 1973).

Difficulties in dealing with values follow from the failure to distinguish clearly between values as characteristic kinds of human experiences and value judgments as statements about such kinds of experiences. Values originate in the basic conditions under which human beings conduct their lives at different times and places. Value judgments are cognitive statements about such experience and must be grounded on such experiences. The failure to distinguish clearly between the existential field of human normative experience and the analysis by which we develop our knowledge of that field is a principal source of difficulty in forming adequate value judgments. An ethical theory that draws from the experiences of persons can then be applied back to these experiences in order to guide human action is capable of fruitful and progressive development.

"The Human Touch and the Beauty of Nature" DOI: http://dx.doi.org/10.17613/M6VH5CH83 Arnold Berleant, *Living in the Landscape: Toward an Aesthetics of Environment* (Lawrence: University Press of Kansas, 1997).

The human presence is unavoidable, not only in the natural world but on the very occasion of beauty. There is little or nothing on this planet that has not been influenced by human action. Not only have people radically altered the earth's surface, but human practices have affected the atmosphere, the seas, the very climate. Moreover, the awareness of beauty and the aesthetic satisfaction this affords are grounded in perceptual experience, a human occurrence. Our recognition and participation are essential in recognizing beauty's presence and indeed for its very possibility. Nature untouched, then, is a state found exclusively in prehuman history and about which we can only conjecture. It exists now merely as a speculative idea, for a person's awareness is the filter through which both nature's meanings and its beauties are necessarily apprehended. The title of this essay is therefore not a conflict of opposites but somewhat ironic, since nature, as we know it, and human action, as we have just seen, are not different realms but the same. They are cited as the subject of this discussion and not as an implied contrast.

"Mothering and Metaphor," *Journal of Aesthetics and Art Criticism*, 57/3 (Summer 1999), 363–5.

This is a comment on Marcia Eaton's article interpreting Joseph Brodsky's claim that "aesthetics is the mother of ethics." Eaton challenges this claiming that they are conceptually interdependent, neither coming first. While Eaton wishes to retain the metaphor, this essay argues in favor of Brodsky's position, giving ethics priority.

"Multinationals, Local Practice, and the Problem of Ethical *Consistency*" DOI: http://dx.doi.org/10.17613/M6PK3B

Ethics and Management, Proceedings of the Fifteenth Conference on Value Inquiry (Brockport, NY, 1981). Reprinted in the *Journal of Business Ethics*, 1 (1982), 185–93 and in *The Ethical Factor in Business Decisions*.

The business practices of multinational corporations raise many provocative moral issues and offer a touchstone for some fundamental ethical concepts. This essay identifies a wide range of problems but centers on the matter of consistency in corporate policy between foreign and domestic practices and the kind of generality of standards that is required to achieve consistency. Two considerations are singled out for illustrative discussion: wage scales and bribes. Proposals are offered for achieving consistency and generality in each case, the principle of contextual generality for the first and the notion of structural universals for the second.

"Negative Aesthetics and Everyday Life" DOI: http://dx.doi.org/10.17613/M6CJ87K6H
  Aesthetic Pathways, 1, 2 (June 2011), pp. 75–91.

The discipline of aesthetics is generally associated with art, and the word "aesthetics" is often taken to connote art that is valued as good or great. What that value is and how to assess it are central questions for aesthetic theory. Despite common usage, however, the word "aesthetic" is not synonymous with "beauty" and has applications far wider than to art alone. The etymology of "aesthetic" emphasizes its central meaning of sense perception, and the word is used to emphasize that core meaning. However, sensory experience, and hence aesthetic experience, is not always positive, and when it is offensive, distressing, or has harmful or damaging consequences, the aesthetic leads us to the realm of the negative. This essay identifies some of the conditions when aesthetic value is present but in unsatisfying, painful, perverse, or even destructive ways. It focuses on the human environment and show how the aesthetic fuses with the moral. We can give a name to sensory experience that has no clear positive value, the underside of beauty, so to say, and call it negative aesthetics.

"Perceptual Politics"   DOI: http://dx.doi.org/10.17613/g2td-pg12 Arnold Berleant, *Sensibility and Sense: The Aesthetic Transformation of the Human World* (Exeter: Imprint Academic, 2010), 274–306. ISBN: 978-1845401733

Moved by the pervasiveness and insistence of political forces in social life, many scholars have been drawn increasingly to recognize the strands of the aesthetic that are woven into its texture. They have gone beyond dealing with the ways that the arts are used in political propaganda and for arousing patriotic feeling. The aesthetic has come to be recognized as a perceptual domain of considerable power and influence, and some analysts have assigned it a crucial place in political theory. Making the aesthetic central in political theory may be surprising, for two such dissimilar domains of thought and experience might seem, at first, difficult to reconcile. Yet the association of aesthetics with politics has been made, and it will be illuminating to look at some applications that assign the aesthetic dimension a critical place in social and political thought. Let me then trace some of the appeals to the aesthetic in founding political theory, first considering Friedrich Schiller before moving into contemporary proposals.

"The Persistence of Dogma in Aesthetics," *The Journal of Aesthetics and Art Criticism*, 52/2 (Spring 1994).

Dogma persists in aesthetic discourse in the assumptions that art consists primarily of objects, that these objects possess a special status, and that they must be regarded in a unique way. This essay claims that they are assumptive and misleading, while Carlson opposes this by supporting the dogmas. I argue that Carlson begs the question (the relevance of the dogmas) by assuming them in his criticism of my challenge.

"Re-thinking Aesthetics" DOI: http://dx.doi.org/10.17613/M6F47GT55 *Filozofski vestnik*, XX (2/1999 - XIV ICA), Proceedings of the XIV International Congress of Aesthetics "Aesthetics as Philosophy" (Ljubljana, Slovenia), 25–33.

This essay proposes a radical reexamination of the foundations of modern aesthetics. This kind of exploration is at the same time a profoundly philosophical act, for philosophical premises lie at the base of modern aesthetics. Exploring these premises, indeed challenging them, can lead us to a new basis for aesthetics derived from aesthetic inquiry itself and not as the afterthought of a philosophical tradition whose origins were quite independent of the aesthetic domain. Conversely, rethinking aesthetics may suggest new ways of doing philosophy.

"The Sensuous and the Sensual in Aesthetics," *The Journal of Aesthetics and Art Criticism*, XXIII, 2 (Winter 1964), 185–92.

The sensuousness of perception leads us to recognize the role of the senses in aesthetic experience. Aesthetics has traditionally admitted the sensuous through sight and hearing but has excluded the contact senses of taste, smell, and especially touch. These contact senses challenge the place in traditional aesthetics of distance and disinterestedness by overcoming their depersonalizing effect and introducing the sensual through direct physical involvement. These senses, however, do enter into the arts and thus are aesthetically important. The distinction that traditional theory maintains between the sensuous experience of the distant senses and the sensual appeal of the contact senses is untenable. With the aesthetic relevance of sensual experience comes an acknowledgment of tactility, the body, and the erotic as legitimate parts of aesthetic experience at its fullest and richest.

"The Social Evaluation of Art" DOI: http://dx.doi.org/10.17613/gd8h-y966 Arnold Berleant, *Aesthetics and Environment, Theme and Variations on Art and Culture* (Aldershot: Ashgate, 2005), 186–99. ISBN: 978-0754650775

How can art and artist be both autonomous and inseparable from the network of social processes? Aren't these incompatible conditions? Not exactly, for while the arts are an integral part of the social order, their social value, this essay argues, rests on the preservation of artistic freedom. Under such a condition the arts not only make their unique contribution and demonstrate their distinctive value, but this curious circumstance provides a basis on which to evaluate the individual work of art. We arrive, then, at an unanticipated consequence: The more completely art is encouraged to pursue its own course, to follow its inherent direction, the more successfully will the arts be able to make their distinctive contribution to social life. The rest of this essay is an elaboration and defense of that claim.

"The Social Postulate of Theoretical Ethics," *Journal of Value Inquiry*, IV, 1 (January 1970), 1–16.

Traditional attempts to ground ethics may be seen to be governed by the intent to preserve established values even when they seem to be most rational and critical. This essay probes the connections of some of the most prominent justifications of ethical theories to the prevailing morality of the dominant social order. This claim is examined in relation to the ethics of Aristotle, Kant, G. E. Moore, and emotivist ethics represented by A. J. Ayer. Even the descriptive account of ethics offered by Toulmin reveals its social premises, as does the approach of ordinary language philosophy (H. D. Aiken). The way out of this theoretical impasse lies in turning to the empirical knowledge of human well-being as informed by the behavioral and natural sciences.

"Subsidization of Art as Social Policy" DOI: http://dx.doi.org/10.17613/M63T9D61W *Journal of Behavioral Economics*, VIII, 1 (Summer, 1979), 23–37.

The arts have always been integrated into their larger culture, responding to shifts in taste and fashion and to changes in the social uses to which they have been put, as much as they have promoted those same changes. Even their alienation reflects a social influence. When this relation between society and the arts is recognized and affirmed, it can enhance both by rediscovering the human locus of perceptual meaning and by encouraging fuller social consciousness. An enlightened and imaginative program of subsidies would promote cultural evolution. And an inclusive conception of art and its social role can lead to their distinctive contribution to the physical and social shape of our environment.

"Surrogate Theories of Art" DOI: http://dx.doi.org/10.17613/M6958P *Philosophy and Phenomenological Research*, XXX, 2 (December 1969), 163–83.

Many explanations have been offered to account for our experiences of the arts. Notable among them is that art is the representation of ideal beauty, that it expresses emotion, that it is the symbol of feeling, and a special language of emotional communication, and a self-gratifying activity like play. Each account captures a significant insight yet claims to be an exclusive explanation. Reviewing some of the most prominent theories such as imitation, emotion, expression, communication, symbol, form, it appears that none of these can satisfy as an exclusive explanation, yet each identifies a significant aspect of aesthetic appreciation. However, most of these theories explain the experience by replacing it with a surrogate. What is needed is a descriptive account of aesthetic experience in its own terms, a truly empirical theory.

Notes

Chapter 1

1 Wolfgang Welsch has explored this more fully. See *Undoing Aesthetics* (London, Thousand Oaks, and New Delhi: Sage Publications, 1997) and his edited volume, *Die Aktualität Des Ästhetischen* (München: Wilhelm Fink Verlag, 1993).
2 It is important to recognize Dewey's pioneering work in recognizing the primacy of sensible experience. See, for example, "The Postulate of Immediate Experience," in *The Influence of Darwin on Philosophy*, ed. John Dewey (New York: Peter Smith, 1951), 226–41. "Immediate empiricism postulates that things . . . are what they are experienced as." (227).
3 See Eugene Hughes and Arnold Berleant, "Aesthetic Engagement as a Pathway to Mental Health and Wellbeing," in *Oxford Handbook of Mental Health and Contemporary Western Aesthetics* (Oxford University Press, 2023).

Chapter 2

1 See my early discussion of this issue in "Aesthetics and the Contemporary Arts," *The Journal of Aesthetics and Art Criticism* XXIX, no. 2 (Winter 1970): 155–68. Reprinted in *The Philosophy of the Visual Arts*, ed. Philip Alperson (New York: Oxford University Press, 1992).
2 Most of the ideas characteristic of traditional, "modern" aesthetics find their support in Immanuel Kant's *Critique of Judgment* (1790, 1793).
3 The literature here has become extensive. Some of the foundational works include R. W. Hepburn, "Contemporary Aesthetics and the Neglect of Natural Beauty," in *Wonder and Other Essays*, ed. Ann Loades (Edinburgh: The University Press, 1984); *The Reach of the Aesthetic* (Aldershot: Ashgate, 2001); Arnold Berleant, *The Aesthetics of Environment* (Philadelphia: Temple University Press, 1992); *Living in the Landscape: Toward an Aesthetics of Environment* (Lawrence: University Press of Kansas, 1997); *Aesthetics and Environment, Theme and Variations* (Aldershot: Ashgate, 2005); Allen Carlson, *Aesthetics and the Environment* (New York: Routledge, 2000); *Nature and Landscape: An Introduction to Environmental Aesthetics* (New York: Columbia University Press, 2009); Yrjö Sepänmaa, *The Beauty of Environment: A General Model for Environmental Aesthetics* (Denton, TX:

Environmental Ethics Books, P.O. Box 310980, 1993); Emily Brady, *Aesthetics of the Natural Environment* (Edinburgh: Edinburgh University Press, 2003).
4 See "Designing Outer Space," in *The Aesthetics of Environment*, ed. Arnold Berleant (Philadelphia: Temple University Press, 1992), 99–113.
5 Zeng Fanren, 《生态美学导论》 *An Introduction to Ecological Aesthetics, A Review of the Relationship between Eco-aesthetics and Environmental Aesthetics* (Beijing: The Commercial Press, 2010), in Chinese. "Eco-aesthetics" is the term Zeng and his followers use as a shortened form of "ecological aesthetics." See also Xiangzhan Cheng, "On the Four Keystones of Ecological Aesthetic Appreciation," *Tianjin Social Sciences* 5 (2012): 221–37 (in Chinese), *Asian Ecocriticism Reader*, ed. Simon C. Estok and Won-Chung Kim (in English).
6 The literature here is small but growing. See Arnold Berleant, *Sensibility and Sense: The Aesthetic Transformation of the Human World* (Exeter: Imprint Academic, 2010); *Aesthetics beyond the Arts* (Aldershot: Ashgate, 2012); Miyahara Kojiro and Fujisaka Shingo, *Invitation to Social Aesthetics; Exploration of Society through Sensibility* (Kyoto: Minerva Shobō, 2012) (in Japanese). An extended discussion of negative aesthetics occurs in *Sensibility and Sense*, 155–92.
7 Originated by the art critic Nicolas Bourriaud in his 1998 book, *Esthétique relationnelle* (*Relational Aesthetics*). Bourriaud later associated this idea to the effects of the internet on mental space.
8 *Relational Aesthetics*, 113, 13.
9 Jacques Rancière, *The Politics of Aesthetics: The Distribution of the Sensible,* trans. Gabriel Rockhill (London and New York: Continuum International, 2004).
10 Crispin Sartwell, *Political Aesthetics* (Ithaca: Cornell University Press, 2010).
11 Davide Panagia, *The Political Life of Sensation* (Durham: Duke University Press, 2009).
12 Berleant, *Sensibility and Sense*; *Aesthetics beyond the Arts*; Arnold Berleant, "The Co-optation of Sensibility and the Subversion of Beauty," *Filozofski vestnik* XXXVI, no. 1 (2015): 9–26 (Ljubljana). Special issue on everyday aesthetics. In Slovenian. Also in *Pragmatism Today* 6, no. 2 (Winter 2015): 38–47. http://dx.doi.org/10.17613/M6BC5X.
13 Consider, for example, this striking passage by the nineteenth century novelist George Eliot: "[U]nder his calm and somewhat self-repressed exterior there was a fervor which made him easily find poetry and romance among the events of everyday life. And perhaps poetry and romance are as plentiful as ever in the world except for those phlegmatic natures who I suspect would in any age have regarded them as a dull form of erroneous thinking. They exist very easily in the same room with the microscope and even in railway carriages: what banishes them is the vacuum in gentlemen and lady passengers. How should all the apparatus of heaven and earth, from the farthest firmament to the tender bosom of the mother who nourished us, make poetry for a mind that has no movements of awe and

tenderness, no sense of fellowship which thrills from the near to the distant, and back again from the distant to the near?" George Eliot, *Daniel Deronda* (1876) (New York: Knopf, 2000), 221.
14 John Dewey, *Art as Experience* (1934) (New York: G. P. Putnam's Sons, 1958).
15 Ibid., 19.
16 Ibid., 46.
17 David Novitz, *The Boundaries of Art* (Philadelphia: Temple University Press, 1992).
18 Arnold Berleant, *Art and Engagement* (Philadelphia: Temple University Press, 1992).
19 Berleant, "Aesthetics and the Contemporary Arts." Reprinted in *The Philosophy of the Visual Arts* and in part in *Esthetics Contemporary*, ed. Richard Kostelanetz, 1978.
20 Andrew Light and Jonathan M. Smith, eds., *Aesthetics of Everyday Life* (New York: Columbia University Press, 2005).
21 Katya Mandoki, *Everyday Aesthetics: Prosaics, the Play of Culture and Social Identities* (Aldershot: Ashgate, 2007).
22 Yuriko Saito, *Everyday Aesthetics* (Oxford: Oxford University Press, 2007). See also her more recent *Aesthetics of the Familiar: Everyday Life and World-Making* (Oxford: Oxford University Press, 2017).
23 Thomas Leddy, *The Extraordinary in the Ordinary: The Aesthetics of Everyday Life* (Peterborough: Broadview, 2012).
24 A further sign of the extension of the aesthetic may be seen in the annual French observance in Marseilles of a *Semaine de la Pop Philosophie*. See www.lesrencontresplacepublique.fr (accessed August 14, 2012).

Chapter 3

1 Sensibility is capable of being influenced and even manipulated by social forces and practices. I have explored such influence on aesthetic perception in what I call "the co-optation of sensibility" in Chapter 8.
2 Kant was the principal advocate of disinterested appreciation, part of a philosophical tradition that goes back to Aristotle's elevation of the highest form of knowledge as contemplative. Using disinterestedness as the criterion of aesthetic appreciation, Kant called the aesthetic value in practical objects "dependent" beauty, in contrast with the "pure" beauty found in disinterested contemplation. See Immanuel Kant, *Critique of Judgment* (1790).
3 Pierre Bourdieu, *Distinction: A Social Critique of the Judgement of Taste* (1979), translated by Richard Nice (Cambridge, MA: Harvard Univeristy Press, 1987).
4 Arnold Berleant, *The Aesthetic Field: A Phenomenology of Aesthetic Experience* (Springfield: C. C. Thomas, 1970). Second (electronic) edition, with a new Preface, 2000.

5   I articulated this view more fully in *The Aesthetic Field* and in later publications.
6   See my essay, "Getting Along Beautifully," in *Aesthetics in the Human Environment*, ed. Pauline von Bonsdorff and Arto Haapala (Lahti: International Institute of Applied Aesthetics, 1999), 12–29.
7   See "Art, Terrorism, and the Negative Sublime," Chapter 9. Originally published in *Contemporary Aesthetics* 7 (November 4, 2009). https://digitalcommons.risd.edu/cgi/viewcontent.cgi?article=1206&context=liberalarts_contempaesthetics.
8   See Shannon Spaulding, "On Direct Social Perception," *Consciousness and Cognition* 36, (November 2015): 472–82. https://doi.org/10.1016/j.concog.2015.01.003; and Martha Raile Alligood, "Empathy: The Importance of Recognizing Two Types," *Journal of Psychosocial Nursing and Mental Health Services* 30, no. 3 (1992): 13. https://doi.org/10.3928/0279-3695-19920301-06.
9   I explored this in an early study in social aesthetics, "Education as Aesthetic Process," *The Journal of Aesthetic Education* 5, no. 3 (July 1971): 139–47. Reprinted as "Education as Aesthetic," in *Living in the Landscape: Toward an Aesthetics of Environment*, ed. A. Berleant (Lawrence: University Press of Kansas, 1997).
10 See, for example, the Aesthetics in Mental Health Network (AiMH). http://valuesbasedpractice.org/what-do-we-do/networks/aesthetics-in-mental-health-network-aimh/.
11 Aristotle, *Nicomachean Ethics,* Book Eight, Chapter 3. *Nicomachean Ethics,* trans. Martin Ostwald (Indianapolis: Bobbs-Merrill, 1962), 219.
12 I have explored the makings of a social aesthetic in "On Getting Along Beautifully: Ideas for a Social Aesthetics," in *Aesthetics in the Human Environment*, ed. Pauline von Bonsdorff and Arto Haapala (Lahti: International Institute of Applied Aesthetics, 1999), 12–29. Reprinted in Arnold Berleant, *Aesthetics and Environment, Theme and Variations* (Farnham and Burlington, VT: Ashgate, 2005).
13 A study in social aesthetics through group singing has been documented in a master's thesis by Coelho, Cecília Maria V. T. at the University of Sao Paolo. The thesis is available online at http://www.teses.usp.br/teses/disponiveis/47/47134/tde-29052017-162107/pt-br.php.

Chapter 4

1   Arnold Berleant, "On the Circularity of the Cogito," *Philosophy and Phenomenological Research* XXVI, no. 3 (March 1966): 431 3. http://dx.doi.org/10.17613/M6JW1F.
2   Duchamp, as quoted in "Eleven Europeans in America," James Johnson Sweeney (ed.), *The Museum of Modern Art Bulletin* (New York) 13, no. 4/5 (1946): 20.

3. *Étant donné* is in the collection of the Philadelphia Museum of Art.
4. The choice of a snow shoveler to illustrate the claim of circularity in "On the Circularity of the Cogito" was a complete (and serendipitous) coincidence. See endnote 11.
5. James J. Gibson, *The Senses Considered as Perceptual Systems* (Boston: Houghton-Mifflin, 1966).
6. This account summarizes the analysis offered in Berleant, "On the Circularity of the Cogito."
7. Ibid., 432.

Chapter 5

1. See Justus Buchler, *The Metaphysics of Natural Complexes* (New York: Columbia University Press, 1966); 2nd ed. (New York: State University of New York Press, 1990).
2. Val Plumwood, *Environmental Culture: The Ecological Crisis of Reason* (London and New York: Routledge, 2002), develops the implications of ecological thinking for philosophic rationality and ethics. The same cultural and natural embeddedness that affects our understanding of environmental aesthetics influences profoundly our understanding of environmental justice.
3. See especially Arnold Berleant, *The Aesthetics of Environment* (Philadelphia: Temple University Press, 1992).
4. Cheng Xiangzhan offers an account of the influence of this understanding of environmental aesthetics on the development of ecological aesthetics in China. See Cheng Xiangzhan, "Environmental Aesthetics and Ecological Aesthetics: Arnold Berleant's Impact on Ecological Aesthetics in China," *Contemporary Aesthetics*, "Aesthetic Engagement and Sensibility: Reflections on Arnold Berleant's Work." Special Volume 9 (2021), edited by Bogna J. Gladden-Obidzinska. Originally published in *Sztuka i Filosofia* 37 (2011): 24–35 (in Polish).
5. Such work is widely scattered and is international in scope. Three environmental designers whose work combines ecological and aesthetic concerns are the American Patricia Johanson, the Brazilian Fernando Chacel, and the Chinese Yu Kongjian.
6. *Genesis* 1:28-29.
7. Plato, *The Republic* V, 475–80; VI–VII.
8. For example, the German *Umwelt*; the French *environs*.
9. The Orphic ideas have been traced to the fourth century BCE but are likely even older. Relevant here is its mythology in which Zeus designates his illegitimate child Dionysus as his heir. His wife, Hera, incites the Titans to murder and eat Dionysus, but Zeus, when he learns of this, incinerates the Titans with a thunderbolt.

Mankind is born from the ashes, which contain the bodies of the Titans and Dionysus, resulting in humans having a divine soul (Dionysus) and a body (the Titans) to which the soul is in bondage.

10 See especially Berleant, *The Aesthetics of Environment.*
11 Zeng Fanren, in particular, has developed the conception of an ecological environmental aesthetic. See Zeng Fanren, "A Conception of Ecological Aesthetics in the Perspective of Today's Ecological Civilization," *Literary Review* 4 (2005); "A Review on the Relationship between Ecological Aesthetics and Environmental Aesthetics," *Exploration and Free Views* 9 (2008): 61–3. See also Zeng Fanren, *Collected Articles on Aesthetics of Ecological Existence*, 2nd ed. (Changchun: Jilin People's Press, 2003), revised and enlarged in 2009.

Chapter 6

1 *Wikipedia* lists twenty-five in Europe alone.
2 A notable example is the *Encyclopedia of Aesthetics*, 2nd ed. (New York: Oxford University Press, 2015).
3 See especially the *Ion* but also the *Republic*. CHK *Phaedrus*.
4 *The Poetics*.
5 Marjorie Hope Nicolson, *Mountain Gloom and Mountain Glory* (New York: Norton, 1963, c1957).
6 While our perceptual experience is never pure sensation since it is shaped into complexity by previous experience, education, and cultural conventions, aesthetic appreciation nonetheless centers around perceptual experience.
7 Immanuel Kant, *Critique of Judgment* (1790).
8 An important mid-twentieth century study of the contribution of science to aesthetics was Thomas Munro's *Toward Science in Aesthetics* (New York: Liberal Arts Press,1956), which ranges over psychology, sociology, and art history within a naturalistic philosophical framework.
9 See Denis Dutton, *The Art Instinct: Beauty, Pleasure, and Human Evolution* (New York: Bloomsbury, 2009); Stephen Davies, *The Artful Species: Aesthetics, Art and Evolution* (Oxford: Oxford University Press, 2012).
10 Allen Carlson is especially notable for his insistence, but Holmes Ralston III and Glenn Parsons should also be mentioned.
11 Jusuck Koh, Zeng Fanren, and Xiangzhan Cheng are especially prominent in this effort.
12 Jusuck Koh, "Ecological Design: A Post-Modern Design Paradigm of Holistic Philosophy and Evolutionary Ethic," *Landscape Journal* 1, no. 1 (Fall, 1982): 76–84, Madison: University of Wisconsin Press. Specific references are to this paper. Jusuck

Koh, "An Ecological Aesthetic," *Landscape Journal* 7 (1988): 177–91; "Ecological Aesthetics," *Landscape Journal* (Fall, 1988): 77–191 (first written in 1985); "An Ecological Theory of Form, Evolutionary Principles of Design," Proceedings of the 71st Annual Meeting of the Association of Collegial Schools of Architecture, 1983; "Seeking an Integrative Aesthetics," *Gimme Shelter: Global Discourses in Aesthetics,* 2009. International Association of Aesthetics, International Yearbook of Aesthetics, Vol. 15 (2011).

13 Arnold Berleant, *The Aesthetic Field: A Phenomenology of Aesthetic Experience* (Springfield, IL: Charles Thomas, 1970); Roger Barker, *Ecological Psychology: Concepts and Methods of Studying the Environment of Human Behavior* (Stanford: Stanford University Press, 1968); J. J. Gibson, *The Ecological Approach to Visual Perception* (Boston: Houghton-Mifflin, 1979).

14 "Ecological Aesthetics," Conclusion.

15 Cheng Xiangzhan, "On the Four Key Points of Ecological Appreciation," in *Ecological Aesthetics and Ecological Assessment and Planning,* ed. X. Cheng, A. Berleant, P. Gobster, X. Wang (Henan, China: Henan People's Press, 2013).

16 Cheng Xiangzhan, "Environmental Aesthetics and Ecological Aesthetics: Connections and Differences," Ch. 1 in *Ecological Aesthetics and Ecological Assessment and Planning,* ed. Cheng et al., 29.

17 Xiangzhan, "On the Four Keystones of Ecological Aesthetic Appreciation," Ch. 3 in *Ecological Aesthetics and Ecological Assessment and Planning,* ed. Cheng et al., 85–104.

18 Ibid., 89.

19 Kant, *Critique of Judgment,* § 8.

20 Aldo Leopold, *A Sand County Almanac, and Sketches Here and There* (Oxford: Oxford University Press, 1949).

21 Ibid., 99. The reference is to B. Callicott, *Companion to A Sand County Almanac: Interpretive and Critical Essays* (Wisconsin: The University of Wisconsin Press, 1987).

22 "On the Four Keystones of Ecological Aesthetic Appreciation," 102.

23 "Ecological Design," II, 1, 2.

24 Ibid., III, 2.

25 Ibid.

26 Ibid., 96.

27 Ibid., 91.

28 Ibid., 98.

29 Ibid., 99.

30 Ibid., 99; Ch. 4, esp. 145.

31 Normative contradictions are, unfortunately, far more common. These include a festering, organically productive bog, whose rich effluents create a repugnant stench, the proposal to fill in a coastal wetland that provides a buffer for storm

surges and a haven for migrating waterfowl I order to provide a site for vacation houses with a scenic vista, a plush, silk oriental rug whose thousands of knots were tied by children's fingers, and the most obvious instance of all, the Pyramids, an architectural and engineering marvel built by slave labor.
32 See references in endnote 13.

Chapter 7

1   This is a modified version of an essay that appears in *Theme Parks and Themed Places*, ed. M. J. King (Popular Press). It owes much to Margaret J. King. I am also grateful to my colleagues José Reissig, David Sprintzen, and Michael Shodell for their valuable insights. The assistance of my wife, Riva Berleant-Schiller, has, as always, been incalculable.
2   Jean Baudrillard, *Simulacra and Simulation*, trans. Sheila Faria Glaser (Ann Arbor: University of Michigan Press, 1981 [1994]).
3   J. F. Lyotard, *The Postmodern Condition* (Minneapolis: University of Minnesota Press, 1984), 81.
4   Umberto Eco, "Travels in Hyperreality," in *Travels in Hyperreality*, ed. John Radziewicz (New York: Harcourt Brace Jovanovich, 1986), 43. Stefan Morawski, "On the Subject of and in Post-Modernism," *British Journal of Aesthetics* 32, no. 1 (January 1992): 57.
5   Bob Shacochis, "In Deepest Gringolandia," *Harpers* 279, no. 1670 (July 1989): 42–50; Alun Howkens, "Peace of the Country," *New Statesman and Society* 2, no. 61 (August 4, 1989): 12–13; Alice Thomas Ellis, "Crumbling Urns," *Spectator* 261, no. 8350 (July 23, 1988): 34–5. In "The Influence of a Multi-Theme Park on Cultural Beliefs as a Function of Schema Salience: Promoting and Undermining the Myth of the Old West," Donna Morganstern and Jeff Greenberg show how theme park visits can influence beliefs about the past. *Journal of Applied Social Psychology* 18 (June 1988): 584–96.
6   Eco, "Travels in Hyperreality," 43.
7   See Christopher Frayling, "Themes Like Old Times," *Punch* 298, no. 7774 (January 26, 1990): 30–3.
8   Quoted in Eco, "Travels in Hyperreality," 43.
9   Lyotard, *The Postmodern Condition*, 81.
10 John Stuart Mill, *Utilitarianism* (Indianapolis: Bobbs-Merrill, 1957), 14 (Ch. II).
11 John Dewey, *The Quest for Certainty: A Study of the Relation of Knowledge and Action* (New York: Minton, Balch & Co., 1929).
12 Maurice Merleau-Ponty, *The Visible and the Invisible* (Evanston: Northwestern University Press, 1968), 91, 94.

Chapter 8

1 Katya Mandoki, *Everyday Aesthetics: Prosaics, the Play of Culture and Social Identities* (Aldershot: Ashgate, 2007).
2 Arnold Berleant, *Sensibility and Sense: The Aesthetic Transformation of the Human World* (Charlottesville: Imprint Academic, 2010), 156.
3 *Cf.* A. Berleant, "What Is Aesthetic Engagement?" *Contemporary Aesthetics* 11 (2013). http://www.contempaesthetics.org/newvolume/pages/article.php?articleID=684.
4 Thomas Leddy, *The Extraordinary in the Ordinary: The Aesthetics of Everyday Life* (Peterborough, Ont: Broadview, 2012).
5 See Arnold Berleant, "The Negative Aesthetics of Everyday Life," in *Sensibility and Sense: The Aesthetic Transformation of the Human World* (Charlottesville: Imprint Academic, 2010), 155–74 and Arnold Berleant, "Art, Terrorism, and the Negative Sublime." in *Sensibility and Sense: The Aesthetic Transformation of the Human World* (Charlottesville: Imprint Academic, 2010), 175–92.
6 See Crispin Sartwell, *Political Aesthetics* (Ithaca: Cornell University Press, 2010); Davide Panagia, *The Political Life of Sensation* (Durham: Duke University Press, 2009); Arnold Berleant, *Sensibility and Sense,* Part Three: Social Aesthetics; Arnold Berleant, *Aesthetics beyond the Arts* (Burlington, Farnham: Ashgate, 2012), ch.16, "The Aesthetic Politics of Environment," 181–94.
7 Pauliina Rautio, "On Hanging Laundry: The Place of Beauty in Managing Everyday Life," *Contemporary Aesthetics* 7 (2009). https://digitalcommons.risd.edu/cgi/viewcontent.cgi?article=1209&context=liberalarts_contempaesthetics.
8 Yuriko Saito, "Future Directions for Environmental Aesthetics," in *Environmental Aesthetics: Crossing Divides and Breaking Ground*, ed. Martin Drenthen and Jozef Keulartz (New York: Fordham University Press, 2014), 26.
9 The literature on everyday aesthetics is already substantial and growing. While it is a recent trend, it has long been recognized. See, for example, John Dewey, *Art as Experience* (New York: Minton, Balch, and Co., 1934); and Melvin Rader and Bertram Jessup, *Art and Human Values* (Englewood Cliffs: Prentice-Hall, 1976), especially chapter 5. Important contributions to the resurgence of interest in everyday aesthetics are *Aesthetics of Everyday Life*, ed. Andrew Light and Jonathan M. Smith (New York: Columbia University Press, 2005); Mandoki, *Everyday Aesthetics*; Yuriko Saito, *Everyday Aesthetics* (Oxford: Oxford University Press, 2007); Leddy, *The Extraordinary in the Ordinary*; *Aesthetics of Everyday Life*; *East and West*, ed. Liu Yuedi and Curtis L. Carter (Newcastle upon Tyne: Cambridge Scholars Publ., 2014).
10 Recently discovered internal sugar industry documents provide compelling evidence that the sugar industry had initiated research expressly intended to exonerate sugar as a major risk factor for coronary heart disease. The documents show that a trade group called the Sugar Research Foundation, known today as the Sugar Association, paid three Harvard scientists the equivalent of about $50,000 in

today's dollars to publish a 1967 review of research on sugar, fat, and heart disease. The studies used in the review were handpicked by the sugar group. Anahad O'Connor, "Sugar Backers Paid to Shift Blame to Fat," *The New York Times,* New York edition, September 13, 2016, A1.

11 Selected critique of "soft" drinks: Coca-Cola Company, PepsiCo Inc, Nestlé SA. Except for bottled water, these drinks tend to be overloaded with sugar, which is addictive and harmful.

    The high consumption of sugar is linked to cardiovascular disease, metabolic syndrome (increases risk for heart disease, stroke, diabetes), and type 2 diabetes. Coca-Cola (addictive: narcotic, sugar). A typical 12 oz (355 mL) can contains 38 g of sugar (usually in the form of HFCS). In 2013, Coke products could be found in over 200 countries worldwide, with consumers downing more than 1.8 billion company beverage servings each day. Coca-Cola contains 34 mg of caffeine per 12 fluid ounces (9.8 mg per 100 mL). Kola nuts act as a flavoring agent and the source of caffeine in Coca-Cola. Now cocaine free. Remains high in sugar and caffeine.

12 The "Big Mac," for example, is a hamburger consisting of two high-fat patties topped by a slice of American cheese, with dressing, lettuce, pickles, and onions on a sesame bun, all of which contains as much or more fat than protein. In the United States, a Big Mac contains 29 grams of fat to 25 grams of protein, with similar proportions in the many other countries where McDonald's restaurants are found. Japan has the highest proportion of fat: 30.5 grams to 25.5 grams of protein. See the article and references on "Big Mac" in *Wikipedia* (accessed November 11, 2014).

13 French fries are a striking example, where the fat-saturated outer crust often penetrates and displaces any soft potato core. In addition, cream or cheese sauces are ladled over many dishes, preceded by cream soup and accompanied by a lavish supply of rolls and butter, not to mention the rich dessert offerings. (I speak here obviously of Western, especially American cuisine.) Please note that I am not condemning the appeal of such foods but rather the encouragement of patterns of exaggerated taste and overconsumption that underlie their use. Taste is heavily influenced by learning, and the omnipresence of advertising encourages the acquisition of such inflated desires.

14 Techniques of persuasion span the range of rationality.

    1. Direct techniques to which people consciously respond and deliberately accept:
        a. Information
        b. Logical proof
        c. Debate

    2. Indirect forms of persuasion by which people are enticed or inadvertently slip into accepting:
        a. Ritual

  b. Rhetoric
  c. Propaganda
  d. Advertising
  e. Salesmanship

15 *Cf.* the work of Theodor Adorno and Herbert Marcuse.

16 See the *Stanford Encyclopedia of Philosophy* entry on Marcuse.

17 See his *Simulacra and Simulation* (Ann Arbor: The University of Michigan Press, 1994). Baudrillard was a prolific writer and the literature by and about him is large.

  There is a pressing need for thorough and comprehensive studies of the original and critical literature on postmodernism, critical theory, simulacra and hyperreality, and forms of co-optation that are powerful and almost irresistible determinants of the structures and content of human perceptions of reality.

18 Spinoza may have been prescient: "[A]l] those things which bring us pleasure are good. But seeing that things do not work with the object of giving us pleasure, and that their power of action is not tempered to suit our advantage, and, lastly, that pleasure is generally referred to one part of the body more than to the other parts; therefore most emotions of pleasure (unless reason and watchfulness be at hand), and consequently the desires arising therefrom, may become excessive. Moreover we may add that emotion leads us to pay most regard to what is agreeable in the present, nor can we estimate what is future with emotions equally vivid." *The Ethics*, Part IV, Prop. XXX, 242.

  "We may thus readily conceive the power which clear and distinct knowledge, and especially that . . . founded on the actual knowledge of God [i.e. Nature] possesses over the emotions: if it does not absolutely destroy them, in so far as they are passions . . .; at any rate, it causes them to occupy a very small part of the mind." *The Ethics*, Part V, Prop. XX, Note V, 256.

19 Earlier versions of this essay were presented at the Emancipation Conference, Fordham University, New York, February 28, 2015, and at the University of Maine, April 14, 2016, and published as "The Co-optation of Sensibility and the Subversion of Beauty," in *Filozofski vestnik* XXXVI, no. 1 (2015) (Lljubljana) special issue on everyday aesthetics in Slovenian and English, and in *Pragmatism Today* VI, no. 2 (Winter 2015): 37–47.

  I am indebted to Riva Berleant-Schiller, Aleš Erjavec, Kevin Melchionne, Larry Shiner, and Yuriko Saito for their valuable information and suggestions.

Chapter 9

1 Recent work includes Katya Mandoki, *Everyday Aesthetics: Prosaics, the Play of Culture and Social Identities* (Aldershot: Ashgate, 2007); Yuriko Saito, *Everyday*

Aesthetics (Oxford: Oxford University Press, 2007); *The Aesthetics of Everyday Life*, ed. Andrew Light and Jonathan M. Smith (New York: Columbia University Press, 2005).
2   Arnold Berleant, *Art and Engagement* (Philadelphia: Temple, 1992), 40.
3   Immanuel Kant, *Critique of Judgment*, ed. J. H. Bernard (New York: Hafner, 1951) §4. See A. Berleant, "Aesthetics and the Contemporary Arts," *The Journal of Aesthetics and Art Criticism* XXIX, no. 2 (Winter l970): l55–68. Reprinted in Arnold Berleant, *Re-thinking Aesthetics, Rogue Essays on Aesthetics and the Arts* (Aldershot: Ashgate, 2004), ch. 4.
4   *The Republic* Bk. II, 377A-382; Bk. III, 376E-403B.
5   Immanuel Kant, *Critique of Judgment*, First Book, §2–5.
6   Developing such an aesthetic has been the incentive of most of my previous work. See especially Berleant, *Re-thinking Aesthetics, Rogue Essays on Aesthetics and the Arts*; Arnold Berleant, *Art and Engagement* (Philadelphia: Temple University Press, 1991); and *The Aesthetic Field: A Phenomenology of Aesthetic Experience* (Springfield, IL: C. C. Thomas l970). Second (electronic) edition, with a new Preface, 2000.
7   Stockhausen, cited in Emmanouil Aretoulakis, "Aesthetic Appreciation, Ethics, and 9/11," *Contemporary Aesthetics* 6 (2008): sect. 1. Hirst, a British artist, called the September 11 terrorist attacks "a visually stunning artwork." Aretoulakis argues that "there is a need for aesthetic appreciation when contemplating a violent event such as the 9/11 terrorist attacks. What is more, appreciation of the beautiful, even in case of a 9/11, seems necessary because it is a key to establishing an ethical stance towards terror, life, and art. It should be stressed that independent aesthetic experience is not important in itself but as a means to cultivating an authentic moral and ethical judgment." My discussion of terrorism was stimulated by Aretoulakis's thoughtful and balanced consideration of the aesthetic significance of the 9/11 attacks.
8   See Walter Reich (ed.), *Origins of Terrorism: Psychologies, Ideologies, Theologies, States of Mind* (Washington, DC: Woodrow Wilson Center Press, 1998).
9   Alain Badiou, *The Meaning of Sarkozy* (London and New York: Verso, 2008), 92.
10 One is reminded of Hobbes's characterization of the nature of war as not actual fighting but, "in the known disposition thereto," a description that applies not only to what has been called a "cold war" but equally to a society in a state of continual fear and thus easily moved to violence. See Thomas Hobbes, *Leviathan* (1660), ch.13.
11 This is a problem that stands apart from the aesthetic questions I am dealing with here and clearly requires its own separate treatment. As a version of the means-end problem, it has long history of philosophical debate.
12 Mandoki, *Everyday Aesthetics*.
13 Both Burke and Kant noted the impossibility of experiencing the sublime when one's safety is at risk. Cf. Kant, *Critique of Judgment*, §28.

14 Edmund Burke, *Philosophical Inquiry into the Origin of our Ideas of the Sublime and Beautiful* (1757) (Oxford: Oxford University Press, 1990). Burke did not originate the concept; a treatise *On the Sublime* is attributed to Longinus, in the third century CE, although its authorship and date of composition have been contested.

15 Burke, *Philosophical Inquiry into the Origin of Our Ideas of the Sublime and Beautiful*, Part One, Section VII; Part Two, Sections I and II; Part IV, Section III; 36, 53–4, 119.

16 Ibid., Part Two, Section II, 54.

17 *Critique of Judgment*, §28.

18 Ibid., §27.

19 Ibid., §28. "War itself, if it is carried on with order and with a sacred respect for the rights of citizens, has something sublime in it, and makes the disposition of the people who carry it on thus only the more sublime, the more numerous are the dangers to which they are exposed and in respect of which they behave with courage" (102).

20 There is a resemblance here to Lyotard's characterization of the sublime as making 'the unpresentable perceptible. "The art object no longer bends itself to models, but tries to present the fact that there is an unpresentable . . ." Cf. Jean-François Lyotard, *The Postmodern Condition: A Report on Knowledge* (1979) (Minneapolis: University of Minnesota Press, 1984), 81; "The Sublime and the Avant-Garde," in *The Lyotard Reader*, ed. Andrew Benjamin (Cambridge, MA: Blackwell, 1989), 207.

21 "A Refusal to Mourn the Death, by Fire, of a Child in London," in *The Collected Poems of Dylan Thomas* (New York: New Directions, 1957), 112. https://poets.org/poem/refusal-mourn-death-fire-child-london (accessed January 24, 2023).

22 "far from articulating the need of personal expression on the artistic level, art becomes fully politicized as an agency that acts on its own in the social sphere, thus enabling itself to interact with and affect the world directly." Aretoulakis, "Aesthetic Appreciation, Ethics, and 9/11," sect. 4. Again, "If we do not merely settle into thinking of art as personal expression within the canonically bounded domain of the aesthetic, and we ascribe to art an active involvement . . . then we better be ready to come to terms with art as a realm in which humanity exercises its utmost creative/destructive potential, and not in the so-called (since Hegel) world of the spirit but in the world itself." Stathis Gourgouris, "Transformation, Not Transcendence," *Boundary 2* 31, no. 2 (2004): 55–79. Quoted in Aretoulakis, "Aesthetic Appreciation, Ethics, and 9/11."

23 Aretoulakis, "Aesthetic Appreciation, Ethics, and 9/11," sect. 5. Katya Mandoki saw it plainly: "What must be noted is that art and reality, like aesthetics and the everyday, are totally entwined, not because of the explicit will of the artist, but because there is nothing further, beneath or beyond reality. Even dreams are real, as dreams. The effort to unite art-reality is, therefore, unnecessary. Moreover, when art manifests itself as a mechanism for evasion or for emancipation . . . they are fatally

and irremediably immersed in reality, whether indexically pointing at it by the evasion itself (silence is very eloquent) or by assuming particular sides for criticism or emancipation." Mandoki, *Everyday Aesthetics*, 15–16.
24 I have called such a joining of the aesthetic and the ethical "humanistic function." See my essay, "Aesthetic Function," in *Living in the Landscape: Toward an Aesthetics of Environment*, ed. Arnold Berleant (Lawrence: University Press of Kansas, 1997).

Chapter 10

1 Negative aesthetics is a substantive domain of aesthetic value that is not identical with aesthetic failures, as in kitsch, insipid art, or thoroughly unsuccessful art. Identifying and recognizing negative aesthetics is a critical dimension of aesthetic appreciation. See Arnold Berleant, *Sensibility and Sense: The Aesthetic Transformation of the Human World* ((Exeter: Imprint Academic, 2010); *Aesthetics beyond the Arts: New and Recent Essays* (Farnham and Burlington, VT: Ashgate, 2012); Yuriko Saito, *Aesthetics of the Familiar* (Oxford: Oxford University Press, 2017), 169–70, 214–16.
2 The writings of the Marquis de Sade are an extreme case but hardly representative of the common phenomenon of aestheticizing violence.
3 https://en.wikipedia.org/wiki/The_Battle_of_San_Romano#/media/File:Uccello_Battle_of_San_Romano_Uffizi.jpg.
4 https://en.wikipedia.org/wiki/The_Battle_of_Trafalgar_(painting)#/media/File:Turner,_The_Battle_of_Trafalgar_(1822).jpg.
5 https://en.wikipedia.org/wiki/Guernica_(Picasso)#/media/File:PicassoGuernica.jpg.
6 https://commons.wikimedia.org/wiki/File:Peter_Paul_Rubens,_Crucifixion,_c.1618-1620.jpg.
7 https://en.wikipedia.org/wiki/Isenheim_Altarpiece#/media/File:Grunewald_Isenheim1.jpg.
8 Alfred, Lord Tennyson's narrative poem, "The Charge of the Light Brigade" (1854):
    Theirs not to reason why,
    Theirs but to do and die.
    Into the valley of Death
    Rode the six hundred.
9 One famous example is William James's essay, "The Moral Equivalent of War," which advocates disciplined social service as an alternative.
10 Giorgione, "Judith," 1504. http://www.dailyartmagazine.com/wp-content/uploads/2016/09/Giorgione_-_Judith_-_Eremitage-449x1024.jpg.
11 Jozef Kovalcik and Max Ryynänen, "The Art Scenes," *Contemporary Aesthetics* 16 (2018): §4.

12 I owe this quotation and some of the examples to William Pardue.
13 Henry A. Giroux, "Disturbing Pleasures: Murderous Images and the Aesthetics of Depravity," *Third Text* 26, no. 3 (May 2012): 259–73. Giroux quotes Susan Sontag, *Regarding the Pain of Others* (New York: Farrar, Straus and Giroux, 2003), 263.
14 Theodor Adorno, "Education after Auschwitz," in *Critical Models: Interventions and Catchwords*, trans. Henry W. Pickford (New York: Columbia University Press, 1998), 201.
15 Cf. Giroux, "Disturbing Pleasures," 263: "Walter Benjamin's claim is that in late modernity the mesmerising and seductive language of power underlies captivating spectacles that inextricably fuse aesthetics with a Fascist politics. To his credit Benjamin recognised the affective force of aesthetics and its at times perverse ability to 'privilege cultural forms over ethical norms' while mobilising emotions, desires and pleasures that delight in human suffering and become parasitic upon the pain of others. Benjamin's notion of the aesthetic and its relation to Fascism is important, in spite of appearing deterministic, because it highlights how fascist spectacles use the force of titillating sensations and serve to privilege the emotive and visceral at the expense of thoughtful engagement. In his analysis of Benjamin's notion of the aesthetic, Lutz Koepnick develops this point further by exploring how the fascist aesthetic 'mobilizes people's feelings primarily to neutralize their senses, massaging minds and emotions so that the individual succumbs to the charisma of vitalistic power.'"
16 The union of nature and the human is a central feature in the philosophy of the twentieth century French aesthetician, Mikel Dufrenne. See Maryvonne Saison, *La Nature Artiste. Mikel Dufrenne de l'esthétique au politique* (*Nature as Artist: Mikel Dufrenne, from aesthetics to politics*) (Paris: Editions de la Sorbonne, 2018). A brief summary can be found under Recent Publications in *Contemporary Aesthetics* 16 (2018).
17 Immanuel Kant, *Critique of Judgment*, trans. J. H. Bernard (New York: Hafner, 1951), §5, 4–5.
18 As Adorno famously observed, "Auschwitz begins wherever someone looks at a slaughterhouse and thinks: they're only animals."
19 In an interesting parallel, Joseph Kupfer associated the aesthetics of what he terms "ultra-violence" with objectifying its victims. See his *Experience as Art* (Albany: State University of New York Press, 1983), 54–5. He also found a social aesthetic implicit in the prevalence of violence. Cf. 61–5.
20 https://en.wikipedia.org/wiki/Isenheim_Altarpiece#/media/File:Grunewald_Isenheim1.jpg.
21 https://en.wikipedia.org/wiki/The_Triumph_of_Death#/media/File:Thetriumphofdeath.jpg.
22 The aesthetics of terrorism is the subject of "Art, Terrorism, and the Negative Sublime," first published in *Contemporary* Aesthetics 7 (2009). Reprinted in

Arts and Terror, ed. V. L. Marchenkov (Cambridge Scholars Publ., 2014), 1–15. Reprinted in *Artenol*, Winter 2016, 24–31. Originally published in Berleant, *Sensibility and Sense*, Ch. 10.
23 Other works consulted include Anna Mirzayan, "Creating Killing Machines: On the Relationship between Art and Predation in Surveillance Capitalism," *Evental Aesthetics* 7, no. 2 (2018): 7–31; Walter Benjamin, "Critique of Violence," in *Reflections: Essays, Aphorisms, Autobiographical Writings*, ed. Peter Demetz (New York: Schocken Books, 1986); Scott Nethersole, *Art and Violence in Early Renaissance Florence* (New Haven: Yale University Press, 2018).

I would like to express my appreciation to Prof. Yuriko Saito and Prof. Riva Berleant-Schiller for their valuable references and comments.

Chapter 11

1 Michel Foucault, *The Order of Thing, An Archaeology of the Human* Sciences (*Les mots et les choses*) (Paris: Éditions Gallimard, 1966).
2 Stefan Morawski, *The Troubles with Postmodernism* (London and New York: Routledge, 1996).
3 Ibid., 13–14.
4 Ibid., 14.
5 Ibid., 18–21.
6 Ibid., 34, 35, 48.
7 Jean-François Lyotard, *La Condition postmoderne: rapport sur le savoir* (Paris: Les Editions de Minuit, 1979).
8 Jean-François Lyotard, *The Postmodern Condition: A Report on Knowledge*, trans. G. Bennington and B. Massumi (Minneapolis: University of Minnesota Press, 1984), xxv.
9 Ibid., 77.
10 Ibid.
11 Ibid. Immanuel Kant, *Critique of Judgment* (1790) (New York: Hafner, 1951), §23.
12 Lyotard, *The Postmodern Condition*, 77–8.
13 Ibid., 78–9; Kant, *Critique of Judgment*, §29.
14 Lyotard, *The Postmodern Condition*, 81.
15 Ibid.
16 Morawski, *The Troubles with Postmodernism*, 51.
17 Ibid., 62, 81; Lyotard, *The Postmodern Condition*.
18 Morawski, *The Troubles with Postmodernism*, 63, 65, 95–7.
19 Ibid., 102.
20 Ibid.

21 I have elaborated the idea of a negative sublime in earlier publications. See *Sensibility and Sense: The Aesthetic Transformation of the Human World* (Exeter: Imprint Academic, 2010), ch. 10, "Art, Terrorism, and the Negative Sublime"; and "Reflections on the Aesthetics of Violence," *Contemporary Aesthetics*, Special Volume 7 (2019). http://dx.doi.org/10.17613/aph9-1969.
22 Kant, *Critique of Judgment*, §26, §28; Lyotard, *The Postmodern Condition.*, 77–9.
23 Kant, *Critique of Judgment*, §26.
24 Ibid., §28.
25 Edmund Burke, *A Philosophical Enquiry*, (1757). Part II, Section II. Kant, *Critique of Judgment*, §28, General Comment on the Exposition of Aesthetic Reflective Judgments.
26 Morawski, *The Troubles with Postmodernism*, 88–97.
27 E.g., Lawrence Durrell's four novels constituting *The Alexandria Quartet*.

Chapter 12

1 "On the Aesthetic Education of Man, 27th letter," *Schiller's Complete Works*, Vol. II, ed. and trans. Charles J. Hempel (Philadelphia: Kohler, 1861), 539–40.
2 Alexander Gottlieb Baumgarten, *Aesthetica*, Vol. I (Frankfurt a. O., 1750).
3 See my *Art and Engagement* (Philadelphia: Temple University Press, 1991).
4 Immanuel Kant, *Critique of Judgment* (1790), §10.
5 Baumgarten, *Aesthetica*.
6 Hegel follows Plato's restriction of the sensuous aspect of art to the "aesthetic" (theoretical) senses of sight and hearing, since the work of art is halfway between the directly perceived material object (and thus retains sensuousness) and the ideal universal of pure thought. The aesthetic senses should have no direct physical relation to (connection with) the object. G. W. F. Hegel, "The Philosophy of Fine Art," in *Philosophies of Art and Beauty*, ed. A. Hofstadter and R. Kuhns (New York: The Modern Library, 1964), 409. See also A. Berleant, "The Sensuous and the Sensual in Aesthetics," in *Re-thinking Aesthetics, Rogue Essays on Aesthetics and the Arts* (Aldershot: Ashgate Publishing Ltd, 2004), ch. V, 73–82.
7 See, for example, Maurice Merleau-Ponty, *Phenomenology of Perception*, trans. Colin Smith (London: Routledge & Kegan Paul, 1962), 233–4.
8 Wolfgang Welsch, "Aesthetics beyond Aesthetics: Toward a New Form of the Discipline," *Literature and Aesthetics*, October 1997, 17ff.
9 The interrelatedness of the factors in the aesthetic occasion is the central theme of my book, *The Aesthetic Field: A Phenomenology of Aesthetic Experience* (Springfield, IL: C. C. Thomas l970). Second edition, with a new Preface (2000) (http://cybereditions.com/spis/runisa/dll?SV:cyTheBooksTmp.), and is applied in much of my later work.

10 See *The Aesthetic Field,* ch. 1, "Surrogate Theories of Art," is also a critique of partial theories.
11 See my *The Aesthetics of Environment* (Philadelphia: Temple University Press, 1992), esp. chs. 1 and 3. My essay, "The Aesthetics of Community," in *Living in the Landscape: Toward an Aesthetics of Environment* (Lawrence: University Press of Kansas, 1997), ch. 9 (135–55), complements the present one.
12 James F. Weiner, *The Empty Place: Poetry, Space, and Being among the Foi of Papua, New Guinea* (Bloomington: Indiana University Press, 1991), 8.
13 Aristotle, *Nicomachean Ethics,* Bk. VIII, chs. 4 (1157a) and 5 (1157b).
14 An important exception is Guy Sircello's rich exploration in *Love and Beauty* (Princeton: Princeton University Press, 1989). He and others have illuminated the subject from other perspectives than the one taken here.
15 Plato, *The Republic,* III. 400–3; X. 602–7.
16 Henry David Thoreau, *A Week on the Concord and Merrimac Rivers,* ed. Carl F. Hovde et al. (Princeton: Princeton University Press, 1980), 285.
17 "Human Personality," in *Simone Weil: An Anthology,* ed. Sian Miles (New York: Weidenfeld and Nicolson, 1986). I am indebted to Prof. Hilde Hein for this reference.
18 See note 12.
19 "Even with Tomas she was obliged to behave lovingly because she needed him. We can never establish with certainty what part of our relations with others is the result of our emotions—love, antipathy, charity, or malice—and what part is predetermined by the constant power play among individuals. True human goodness, in all its purity and freedom, can come to the fore only when its recipient has no power. Mankind's true moral test, its fundamental test (which lies deeply buried from view), consists of its attitude towards those who are at its mercy: animals. And in this respect mankind has suffered a fundamental debacle, a debacle so fundamental that all others stem from it." Milan Kundera, *The Unbearable Lightness of Being* (New York: Harper & Row, 1984), 289.
20 "To love everyone is a noble enterprise. Unfortunately it denies one a certain faculty of discrimination." Anita Brookner, *A Family Romance* (London: Jonathan Cape, 1993).
21 If this is true, then one-sided love is a misnomer, much as Fromm interprets self-love as selfishness. Narcissism and subjective self-indulgence fail in the same way. Erich Fromm, *Man for Himself, an Inquiry into the Psychology of Ethics* (New York: Holt, 1947), ch. IV, 1.
22 Empedocles, *On Nature,* in *Ancilla to the Pre-Socratic Philosophers,* ed. K. Freeman (Oxford: Blackwell, 1952), fragments 18–21.
23 Plato, *Symposium,* 210–12a.
24 Schiller, "On the Aesthetic Education of Man," para. 11.
25 Josef Chytry, in *The Aesthetic State* (Berkeley and Los Angeles: University of California Press, 1989), draws his title and much of his inspiration from Schiller.

For Chytry, the "'aesthetic state' . . . stand[s] for a social and political community that accords primacy . . . to the aesthetic dimension in human consciousness and activity."

26 "Environmental aesthetics does not concern buildings and places alone. It deals with the conditions under which people join as participants in an integrated situation. Because of the central place of the human factor, an aesthetics of environment profoundly affects our moral understanding of human relationships and our social ethics. An environmental aesthetics of engagement suggests deep political changes away from hierarchy and its exercise of power and toward community, where people freely engage in mutually fulfilling activities. It implies a humane family order that relinquishes authoritarian control and encourages cooperation and reciprocity. It leads toward acceptance, friendship, and love that abandon exploitation and possessiveness and promote sharing and mutual empowerment." Berleant, *The Aesthetics of Environment*, 12–13.

27 See ch. 13, "Aesthetics and Community," note 12.

Chapter 13

1 Justus Buchler, *Metaphysics of Natural Complexes*, 2nd ed. (Albany: State University of New York Press, 1999).
2 B. F. Skinner's, *Beyond Freedom and Dignity* (New York: Bantam, 1984), is a notable example of the latter.
3 It is important here to acknowledge the highly original contribution to our understanding of care in an aesthetic context that is presented in the recent book by Yuriko Saito, *Aesthetics of Care: Practice in Everyday Life* (London: Bloomsbury, 2022).
4 John Dewey, *Human Nature and Conduct* (New York: Modern Library, 1922).
5 Erich Fromm, *Man for Himself, An Inquiry into the Psychology of Ethics* (New York: Holt, 1947).
6 My book, Arnold Berleant, *The Aesthetics of Environment* (Philadelphia: Temple University Press, 1992), expands and applies this idea.
7 See William James, *Pluralistic Universe*, Lectures 2 and 9, ed. Fredson Bowers (Cambridge, MA: Harvard University Press, 1909).
8 *The Aesthetics of Environment*, ch. 2 and *passim*.
9 Aristotle, *Nicomachaean Ethics*, (350 B.C.E.) Bk. VIII, chs. 4, 13. http://classics.mit.edu/Aristotle/nicomachaen.8.viii.html.
10 See my book, *The Aesthetic Field* (Springfield: C. C. Thomas, 1970).
11 John Locke, *Second Treatise of Government* (London, England, 1689); Friedrich Nietzsche, *The Birth of Tragedy* (Germany: E.W. Fritzsch, 1872); Edmund Husserl, *Cartesian Meditations*, Fifth Meditation (Netherlands: Springer, 1977); Edmund

Husserl, *The Crisis of European Science and Transcendental Phenomenology* (Cambridge: Cambridge University Press, 2012).
12 See Berleant, *The Aesthetic Field*. See also Arnold Berleant, *Art and Engagement* (Philadelphia: Temple University Press, 1991).
13 Martin Buber, *I and Thou*, 2nd ed. (New York: Scribners, 1958), 6–10.
14 "Environmental aesthetics does not concern buildings and places alone. It deals with the conditions under which people join as participants in an integrated situation. Because of the central place of the human factor, an aesthetics of environment profoundly affects our moral understanding of human relationships and our social ethics. An environmental aesthetics of engagement suggests deep political changes away from hierarchy and its exercise of power and toward community, where people freely engage in mutually fulfilling activities. It implies a humane family order that relinquishes authoritarian control and encourages cooperation and reciprocity. It leads toward acceptance, friendship, and love that abandon exploitation and possessiveness and promote sharing and mutual empowerment." Berleant, *The Aesthetics of Environment*, 12–13.

Bibliography

Adorno, Theodor. "Education After Auschwitz." In *Critical Models: Interventions and Catchwords*, translated by Henry W. Pickford, 1–10. New York: Columbia University Press, 1998.

Aretoulakis, Emmanouil. "Aesthetic Appreciation, Ethics, and 9/11." *Contemporary Aesthetics* 6 (2008). https://digitalcommons.risd.edu/cgi/viewcontent.cgi?article=1137&context=liberalarts_contempaesthetics.

Aristotle. *Nicomachean Ethics*. Translated by Martin Ostwald. Indianapolis: Bobbs-Merrill, 1962.

Aristotle. *The Poetics*. Translated by Malcolm Heath. New York: Penguin Classics, 1997.

Badiou, Alain. *The Meaning of Sarkozy*. London and New York: Verso, 2008.

Barker, Roger. *Ecological Psychology: Concepts and Methods of Studying the Environment of Human Behavior*. Stanford: Stanford University Press, 1968.

Baumgarten, Alexander Gottlieb. *Aesthetica*. Frankfurt a. O., 1750.

Benjamin, Andrew, ed. *The Lyotard Reader*. Cambridge: Blackwell, 1989.

Benjamin, Walter. "Critique of Violence." In *Reflections: Essays, Aphorisms, Autobiographical Writings*, edited by Peter Demetz, 277–300. New York: Schocken Books, 1986.

Berleant, Arnold. "Aesthetic Engagement as a Pathway to Mental Health and Wellbeing." In *Oxford Handbook of Mental Health and Contemporary Western Aesthetics*, edited by Arnold Berleant and Eugene Hughes. Oxford University Press, 2023.

Berleant, Arnold. *The Aesthetic Field: A Phenomenology of Aesthetic Experience*. Springfield: Charles Thomas, 1970.

Berleant, Arnold. *Aesthetics Beyond the Arts*. Aldershot: Ashgate, 2012.

Berleant, Arnold. "Aesthetics and the Contemporary Arts." [1970]. In *The Philosophy of the Visual Arts*, edited by Phil Alperson, 155–68. New York: Oxford University Press, 1992.

Berleant, Arnold. *The Aesthetics of Environment*. Philadelphia: Temple University Press, 1992.

Berleant, Arnold. *Art and Engagement*. Philadelphia: Temple University Press, 1991.

Berleant, Arnold. *Living in the Landscape: Toward an Aesthetics of Environment*. Lawrence: University Press of Kansas, 1997.

Berleant, Arnold. "On the Circularity of the Cogito." *Philosophy and Phenomenological Research* XXVI, no. 3 (March 1966): 431–3.

Berleant, Arnold. *Re-thinking Aesthetics, Rogue Essays on Aesthetics and the Arts*. Aldershot: Ashgate, 2004.

Berleant, Arnold. *Sensibility and Sense: The Aesthetic Transformation of the Human World*. Exeter: Imprint Academic, 2010.

Berleant, Arnold. "What Is Aesthetic Engagement?" *Contemporary Aesthetics* 11 (2013). https://digitalcommons.risd.edu/cgi/viewcontent.cgi?article=1269&context=liberalarts_contempaesthetics.

Berleant, Arnold and Allen Carlson, eds. *Aesthetics and Environment, Theme and Variations*. Aldershot: Ashgate Publishing Ltd., 2005.

Bourdieu, Pierre. *Distinction: A Social Critique of the Judgement of Taste*, [1979]. Translated by Richard Nice. Cambridge, MA: Harvard Univeristy Press, 1987.

Bourriaud, Nicolas. *Esthétique Relationnelle (Relational Aesthetics)*. Dijon, France: Les Presses du Reél, 1998.

Brady, Emily. *Aesthetics of the Natural Environment*. Edinburgh: Edinburgh University Press, 2003.

Buber, Martin. *I and Thou*, 2nd ed. New York: Scribners, 1958.

Buchler, Justus. *The Metaphysics of Natural Complexes*, [1966]. New York: State University of New York Press, 1990.

Burke, Edmund. *Philosophical Inquiry into the Origin of our Ideas of the Sublime and Beautiful*, [(1757)]. Oxford: Oxford University Press, 1990.

Callicott, B. *Companion to A Sand County Almanac: Interpretive and Critical Essays*. Wisconsin: The University of Wisconsin Press, 1987.

Carlson, Allen. *Aesthetics and the Environment*. New York: Routledge, 2000.

Carlson, Allen. *Nature and Landscape: An Introduction to Environmental Aesthetics*. New York: Columbia University Press, 2009.

Cheng, Xiangzhan. "Environmental Aesthetics and Ecological Aesthetics: Arnold Berleant's Impact on Ecological Aesthetics in China." *Sztuka i Filosofia* 37 (2011): 24–35. In Polish.

Cheng, Xiangzhan, Arnold Berleant, Paul Gobster, and X. Wang, eds. *Ecological Aesthetics and Ecological Assessment and Planning*. Henan, China: Henan People's Press, 2013.

Chytry, Josef. *The Aesthetic State*. Berkeley and Los Angeles: University of California Press, 1989.

Coelho, Cecília Maria V. T. "A experiência estética tecida pelo canto no processo Social: Sensibilidade, tempo e pertencimento." PhD diss., University of Sao Paolo, 2017.

Daily Art Magazine. "Judith." *Giorgione*. 1504. Accessed April 20, 2022. http://www.dailyartmagazine.com/wp-content/uploads/2016/09/Giorgione_-_Judith_-_Eremitage-449x1024.jpg .

Dewey, John. *Art as Experience*, [1934]. New York: G. P. Putnam's Sons, 1958.

Dewey, John. *Human Nature and Conduct*. New York: Modern Library, 1922.

Dewey, John. *The Quest for Certainty: A Study of the Relation of Knowledge and Action*. New York: Minton, Balch & Co., 1929.

Eco, Umberto. "Travels in Hyperreality." In *Travels in Hyperreality*, edited by John Radziewicz. New York: Harcourt Brace Jovanovich, 1986.

Eliot, George. *Daniel Deronda*, [1876]. New York: Knopf, 2000.

Ellis, Alice Thomas. "Crumbling Urns." *Spectator* 261, no. 8350 (July 23 1988): 34–5.

Empedocles. *On Nature*. In *Ancilla to the Pre-Socratic Philosophers*. Edited by Kathleen Freeman. London: Forgotten Books, 1948.

Estok, Simon C. and Won-Chung Kim, eds. *Asian Ecocriticism Reader*. New York: Palgrave Macmillan, 2013.

Foucault, Michel. *The Order of Thing, An Archaeology of the Human Sciences [Les mots et les choses]*. Paris: Éditions Gallimard, 1966.

Frayling, Christopher. "Themes Like Old Times." *Punch* 298, no. 7774 (January 26, 1990): 30–3.

Fromm, Erich. *Man for Himself, An Inquiry into the Psychology of Ethics*. New York: Holt, 1947. *Genesis* 1:28–29.

Gibson, James J. *The Ecological Approach to Visual Perception*. Boston: Houghton-Mifflin, 1979.

Gibson, James J. *The Senses Considered as Perceptual Systems*. Boston: Houghton-Mifflin, 1966.

Giroux, Henry A. "Disturbing Pleasures: Murderous Images and the Aesthetics of Depravity." *Third Text* 26, no. 3 (May 2012): 259–73.

Hegel, G. W. F. *The Philosophy of Fine Art*. In *Philosophies of Art and Beauty*. Edited by A. Hofstadter and R. Kuhns. New York: The Modern Library, 1964.

Hepburn, Ronald. "Contemporary Aesthetics and the Neglect of Natural Beauty." In *Wonder and Other Essays*, edited by Ann Loades, 113–26. Edinburgh: The University Press, 1984.

Hepburn, Ronald. *The Reach of the Aesthetic*. Aldershot: Ashgate, 2001.

Hobbes, Thomas. *Leviathan*. 1660.

Howkens, Alun. "Peace of the Country." *New Statesman and Society* 2, no. 61 (August 4, 1989): 12–13.

Husserl, Edmund. *Cartesian Meditations*. Fifth Meditation. Netherlands: Springer, 1977.

James, William. *Pluralistic Universe*, [1909], Lectures 2 and 9. Edited by Fredson Bowers. Cambridge, MA: Harvard University Press, 1909.

Kant, Immanuel. *Critique of Judgment*, [1790]. Translated by J. H. Bernard. New York: Hafner, 1951.

Kelley, Caffyn. *Art and Survival. Patricia Johanson's Environmental Projects*. Salt Spring Island, BC: Islands Institute of Interdisciplinary Studies, 2006.

Kelly, Michael, ed. *Encyclopedia of Aesthetics*, 2nd ed. New York: Oxford, 2015.

Koh, Jusuck. "An Ecological Aesthetic." *Landscape Journal* 7 (1988): 177–91.

Koh, Jusuck. "An Ecological Theory of Form, Evolutionary Principles of Design." *Proceedings of the 71st Annual Meeting of the Association of Collegial Schools of Architecture*, 1983.

Koh, Jusuck. "Ecological Design: A Post-Modern Design Paradigm of Holistic Philosophy and Evolutionary Ethic." *Landscape Journal* 1, no. 1 (Fall 1982): 76–84.

Koh, Jusuck. "Seeking an Integrative Aesthetics." Paper presented at Gimme Shelter: Global discources in aesthetics, Amsterdam, The Netherlands, 2009. https://edepot.wur.nl/137411.
Kojiro, Miyahara and Fujisaka Shingo. *Invitation to Social Aesthetics; Exploration of Society Through Sensibility*. Kyoto: Minerva Shobō, 2012. In Japanese.
Kovalcik, Jozef and Max Ryynänen. "The Art Scenes." *Contemporary Aesthetics* 16 (2018): §4.
Kundera, Milan. *The Unbearable Lightness of Being*. New York: Harper & Row, 1984.
Kupfer, Joseph. *Experience as Art*. Albany: State University of New York Press, 1983.
Leddy, Thomas. *The Extraordinary in the Ordinary: The Aesthetics of Everyday Life*. Peterborough, ON: Broadview, 2012.
Leopold, Aldo. *A Sand County Almanac, and Sketches Here and There*. Oxford: Oxford University Press, 1949.
Light, Andrew and Jonathan M. Smith, eds. *Aesthetics of Everyday Life*. New York: Columbia University Press, 2005.
Locke, John. *Second Treatise of Government*. 1700.
Lord Tennyson, Alfred. *The Charge of the Light Brigade*. 1854.
Lyotard, Jean-François. *La Condition Postmoderne: Rapport sur le savoir*. Paris: Les Editions de Minuit, 1979.
Lyotard, Jean-François. *The Postmodern Condition: A Report on Knowledge*. Translated by G. Bennington and B. Massumi. Minneapolis: University of Minnesota Press, 1984.
Mandoki, Katya. *Everyday Aesthetics: Prosaics, the Play of Culture and Social Identities*. Aldershot: Ashgate, 2007.
Merleau-Ponty, Maurice. *Phenomenology of Perception*. Translated by Colin Smith. London: Routledge, 2002.
Merleau-Ponty, Maurice. *The Visible and the Invisible*. Evanston: Northwestern University Press, 1968.
Miles, Sian, ed. *Simone Weil: An Anthology*. London: Weidenfeld and Nicolson, 2001.
Mill, John Stuart. *Utilitarianism*. Indianapolis: Bobbs-Merrill, 1957.
Mirzayan, Anna. "Creating Killing Machines: On the Relationship Between Art and Predation in Surveillance Capitalism." *Evental Aesthetics* 7, no. 2 (2018): 6–31.
Morawski, Stefan. "On the Subject of and in Post-Modernism." *British Journal of Aesthetics* 32, no. 1 (January 1992): 57.
Morawski, Stefan. *The Troubles with Postmodernism*. London and New York: Routledge, 1996.
Morganstern, Donna and Jeff Greenberg. "The Influence of a Multi-Theme Park on Cultural Beliefs as a Function of Schema Salience: Promoting and Undermining the Myth of the Old West." *Journal of Applied Social Psychology* 18 (June 1988): 584–96.
Munro, Thomas. *Toward Science in Aesthetics*. New York: Liberal Arts Press, 1956.
Nethersole, Scott. *Art and Violence in Early Renaissance Florence*. New Haven: Yale University Press, 2018.

Nicolson, Marjorie Hope. *Mountain Gloom and Mountain Glory*. New York: Norton, 1963.

Nietzsche, Friedrich. *The Birth of Tragedy*. Germany: E.W. Fritzsch, 1872.

Novitz, David. *The Boundaries of Art*. Philadelphia: Temple University Press, 1992.

O'Connor, Anahad. "Sugar Backers Paid to Shift Blame to Fat." *The New York Times*, September 13, 2016: A1.

Panagia, Davide. *The Political Life of Sensation*. Durham: Duke University Press, 2009.

Philadelphia Museum of Art. "Étant donné." *Marcel Duchamp*. Accessed December 29, 2021. https://www.philamuseum.org/image_bank/site_use/etant_donnes/clip_image002.jpg.

Philadelphia Museum of Art. "Étant donné." *Marcel Duchamp*. Accessed December 29, 2021. https://philamuseum.org/images/cad/mediaDecks/1969-41-1v1-pma-CX.jpg.

Plato. *Ion*.

Plato. *The Republic* V, 475–80; VI–VII.

Plato. *Symposium*, 210–12a.

Plumwood, Val. *Environmental Culture: The Ecological Crisis of Reason*. London and New York: Routledge, 2002.

Rader, Melvin and Bertram Jessup. *Art and Human Values*. Englewood Cliffs: Prentice-Hall, 1976.

Rancière, Jacques. *The Politics of Aesthetics: The Distribution of the Sensible*. Translated by Gabriel Rockhill. London and New York: Continuum International, 2004.

Rautio, Pauliina. "On Hanging Laundry: The Place of Beauty in Managing Everyday Life." *Contemporary Aesthetics* 7 (2009). https://digitalcommons.risd.edu/cgi/viewcontent.cgi?article=1209&context=liberalarts_contempaesthetics.

Reich, Walter, ed. *Origins of Terrorism: Psychologies, Ideologies, Theologies, States of Mind*. Washington, DC: Woodrow Wilson Center Press, 1998.

Saison, Maryvonne. *La Nature artiste. Mikel Dufrenne de l'esthétique au politique [Nature as Artist: Mikel Dufrenne, from Aesthetics to Politics]*. Paris: Editions de la Sorbonne, 2018.

Saito, Yuriko. *Aesthetics of Care: Practice in Everyday Life*. London: Bloomsbury, 2022.

Saito, Yuriko. *Aesthetics of the Familiar: Everyday Life and World-Making*. Oxford: Oxford University Press, 2017.

Saito, Yuriko. *Everyday Aesthetics*. Oxford: Oxford University Press, 2007.

Saito, Yuriko. "Future Directions for Environmental Aesthetics." In *Environmental Aesthetics: Crossing Divides and Breaking Ground*, edited by Martin Drenthen and Jozef Keulartz, 373–91. New York: Fordham University Press, 2014.

Sartwell, Crispin. *Political Aesthetics*. Ithaca: Cornell University Press, 2010.

Schiller, Friedrich. *On the Aesthetic Education of Man*, [1967]. Edited and translated with introduction, commentary and glossary by Elizabeth M. Wilkinson and L. A. Willoughby. Oxford: Clarendon Press, 1983.

Sepänmaa, Yrjö. *The Beauty of Environment: A General Model for Environmental Aesthetics*. Texas: Environmental Ethics Books, 1993.

Shacochis, Bob. "In Deepest Gringolandia." *Harpers* 279, no. 1670 (July 1989): 42–50.
Sircello, Guy. *Love and Beauty*. Princeton: Princeton University Press, 1989.
Skinner, B.F. *Beyond Freedom and Dignity*. New York: Bantam, 1984.
Sontag, Susan. *Regarding the Pain of Others*. New York: Farrar, Straus and Giroux, 2003.
Spinoza, B. *The Ethics*.
Sweeney, James Johnson, ed. "Eleven Europeans in America." *The Museum of Modern Art Bulletin* 13, no. 4/5 (1946): 20.
Thomas, Dylan. *The Collected Poems of Dylan Thomas*. New York: New Directions, 1957.
Thoreau, Henry David. *A Week on the Concord and Merrimac Rivers*. Edited by Carl F. Hovde, William L. Howarth, and Elizabeth Hall Witherell. Princeton: Princeton University Press, 2004.
Weiner, James F. *The Empty Place: Poetry, Space, and Being among the Foi of Papua New Guinea*. Indianapolis: Indiana University Press, 1991.
Welsch, Wolfgang. "Aesthetics Beyond Aesthetics: Toward a New Form of the Discipline." *The Sydney Society of Literature and Aesthetics* 7 (1997): 7–24.
Wikipedia. "Altarpiece." *Grunewald Isenheim*. Accessed April 20, 2022. https://en.wikipedia.org/wiki/Isenheim_Altarpiece#/media/File:Grunewald_Isenheim1.jpg.
Wikipedia. "The Battle of San Romano." *Uffizi*. Accessed April 20, 2022. https://en.wikipedia.org/wiki/The_Battle_of_San_Romano#/media/File:Uccello_Battle_of_San_Romano_Uffizi.jpg.
Wikipedia. "The Battle of Trafalgar." *Turner*. Accessed April 20, 2022. https://en.wikipedia.org/wiki/The_Battle_of_Trafalgar_(painting)#/media/File:Turner,_The_Battle_of_Trafalgar_(1822).jpg.
Wikiart. "Bicycle Wheel." *Marcel Duchamp*. Accessed December 29, 2021. https://uploads4.wikiart.org/images/marcel-duchamp/bicycle-wheel-1913.jpg!Large.jpg.
Wikipedia. "Big Mac." Accessed April 20, 2022. https://en.wikipedia.org/wiki/Big_Mac.
Wikipedia. "Crucifixion." *Peter Paul Rubens*. Accessed April 20, 2022. https://commons.wikimedia.org/wiki/File:Peter_Paul_Rubens,_Crucifixion,_c.1618-1620.jpg.
Wikimedia. "The Fountain." *Marcel Duchamp*. Accessed December 29, 2021. https://upload.wikimedia.org/wikipedia/commons/thumb/d/dd/Marcel_Duchamp%2C_1917%2C_Fountain%2C_photograph_by_Alfred_Stieglitz.jpg/459px-Marcel_Duchamp%2C_1917%2C_Fountain%2C_photograph_by_Alfred_Stieglitz.jpg.
Wikipedia. "Guernica." *Picasso*, 1937. Accessed April 20, 2022. https://en.wikipedia.org/wiki/Guernica_(Picasso)#/media/File:PicassoGuernica.jpg.
Wikiart. "In Advance of a Broken Arm." *Marcel Duchamp*. Accessed December 29, 2021. https://uploads1.wikiart.org/images/marcel-duchamp/in-advance-of-the-broken-arm-1915.jpg!Large.jpg.
Wikimedia. "Nude Descending a Staircase." *Marcel Duchamp*. Accessed December 29, 2021. https://upload.wikimedia.org/wikipedia/en/c/c0/Duchamp_-_Nude_Descending_a_Staircase.jpg

Wikipedia. "The Triumph of Death." *Pieter Bruegel the Elder*. 1562. Accessed April 20, 2022. https://en.wikipedia.org/wiki/The_Triumph_of_Death#/media/File:Thetriumphofdeath.jpg

Yuedi, Liu and Curtis L. Carter, eds. *Aesthetics of Everyday Life, East and West*. Newcastle upon Tyne: Cambridge Scholars Publ., 2014.

Zeng, Fan-ren, "A Conception of Ecological Aesthetics in the Perspective of Today's Ecological Civilization." *Literary Review* 4 (2005).

Zeng, Fan-ren, "A Review on the Relationship Between Ecological Aesthetics and Environmental Aesthetics." *Exploration and Free Views* 9 (2008): 61–3.

Zeng, Fan-ren, 生态美学导论》 *An Introduction to Ecological Aesthetics, A Review of the Relationship Between Eco-aesthetics and Environmental Aesthetics*. Beijing: The Commercial Press, 2010. In Chinese.

Zeng, Fan-ren, *Collected Articles on Aesthetics of Ecological Existence*, [2003]. Changchun: Jilin People's Press, 2009.

Index

absolute permanence 49
Abstract Art 9
active participant 31
active participation 8, 11
Adventureland 72
Aeschylus 109
aesthetic
   activity 58
   appreciation 11–12, 14–16, 25, 26,
      28, 30–4, 57–9, 62–5, 67, 84, 86,
      95, 108, 110–11, 114–15, 132–5,
      169, 172, 175, 181, 183
   awareness 12, 85, 125, 134, 143
   community 143, 146, 157–60, 162
   connection 31
   critique 7, 85
   disinterestedness 11, 163
   education 30, 129
   encounter 41, 132
   engagement 6, 11–12, 16, 25, 27–32,
      57, 61, 66, 84, 108, 114, 135, 137,
      140–1, 143
   environment 13
   experience 5, 12–16, 24–5, 29, 32,
      47, 50, 57–60, 63–6, 83, 85, 95,
      103–4, 107–8, 114–15, 125,
      134–5, 137–8, 143, 159, 161,
      163–4, 166, 167, 169, 181
   feature 72, 139
   field 16, 25–33, 60, 125, 135–7, 160
   fulfillment 7
   gratification 6, 14, 114
   impact 33, 98, 101–2, 115
   inquiry 3–5, 7–8, 11–12, 84–5, 167
   interest 12, 16, 67
   judgment 11, 164
   negativity 13, 103
   objects 130–1
   perception 6–7, 28, 32, 108, 133–4,
      137, 172
   phenomena 58–9
   pleasure 12, 103, 109, 112, 114
   practice 59
   principle 61, 63
   questioning 4, 6
   satisfaction 85, 97, 112–14, 133, 165
   senses 133, 158–9, 186
   sensibility 13–14, 81, 86, 114, 138
   situation 12, 26, 130, 132, 134–7,
      139–42
   standard 4
   theory 11, 13, 15–16, 66, 87, 104,
      114–15, 130, 132, 135, 166
   value 5–7, 12, 16–17, 24–6, 57, 59,
      63, 65–6, 83–4, 86, 101–2, 107,
      109, 136, 166, 172, 183
   violence 83
Aesthetica 8, 57, 186
aesthetics
   of the arts 130
   of the everyday 95
   of everyday life 14, 84–5
   of experience 8
   of nature 59–60
   of objects 130
   and politics 12
   of sensibility 8
   of terrorism 101, 115, 184
   that questions 4
   of violence 110, 115
The Aesthetics of Everyday Life 15, 172,
   178, 181
affordances 27, 37
Affördungsqualitäten 27
Africa 56
agriculture 49, 60
aisthēsis 4, 24, 57, 84, 107, 133
Al Qaida 100
Americas 56
Anthropocene 126
anthropocentric 59, 61
appreciation
   appreciator 12, 16, 25–6, 38–9, 125,
      132, 134–6, 140, 159–60

beauty 25
    experience 11, 114, 125, 132, 136
the appreciative 16, 26, 30, 38, 95, 131, 164
appropriation 86, 90, 97, 108, 110, 115
Aristotle 31, 57, 83, 91, 122, 139, 145–6, 158, 168, 172–3, 187–8
art
    fine 8, 84
    movements 10
    object 10–12, 15–17, 97, 125, 130–2, 134–6, 138, 159, 161, 163, 182
    painting 26, 28–9, 31, 34–5, 40, 64, 109–10, 113–14, 130–1, 140, 183
    public 11, 16
    visual 9–10, 34, 45, 125
    work 11, 13–14, 17, 28, 31, 34, 96, 98, 131, 181
Art and Engagement 14, 172, 181, 186, 189
Art as Experience 14, 172, 178
artist 8, 26, 34–5, 98, 102, 113, 125, 131, 134–6, 138, 140, 159–60, 164, 167, 181–2
artistic imagination 10
artistic process 11, 163
Asia 56, 99
audience 10, 13, 29, 57, 73, 81, 88, 96, 103, 110–11, 113, 115, 125, 134, 164
Aum Shinrikyo 100
aura 15, 131, 159

beauty 16, 24, 47, 56–7, 61, 65, 83–6, 107, 112, 129–30, 133, 138–40, 142, 165–6, 168, 172
behavioral setting 60
behavior patterns 59
Being Given 35
Bicycle Wheel 37
binary types of relation 30
biodiversity 62, 64–5
biological model 60
biological sciences 59
bodily experience 11
body 11, 53, 73, 84, 89, 105, 111, 125, 138–9, 146, 154, 156, 158, 164, 167, 175, 180
body deformation 111

The Boundaries of Art 14, 172
Buddhism 81, 113, 126
built environment 12, 24, 61

Canada 45, 74
care 30, 86, 98, 150, 188
Cartesian Meditations 41, 188
causal determinism 59
censorship 57, 97, 160
center of art 9
China 45, 52, 74, 174, 176
Chinese 12, 47, 53, 63, 66, 107, 171, 174
    environmental aestheticians 12, 53
    researchers 47
    thinking 66
Christian iconology 109
city 50, 79
civilization 5, 8, 51–2, 55
Classical period 57
Coelho, Cecília 173
cogito 41, 42
cognitive 16, 25–6, 41, 58, 62, 64–6, 76, 82, 84, 90, 119, 121, 124, 134–5, 158, 161, 164
    aesthetics 65–6
    model 25–6, 58
cognitivism 59, 64
colonialism 77
community 6–7, 13, 60, 115, 144–7, 152–3, 155–60, 162, 188–9
conceptual art 9–10
condition of aesthetics 8
Confucius 161
constructed environment 72
consumer culture 77, 85–6, 120
consumerism 77, 120
contemporary arts 15–16, 75, 83
contextual experience 48
co-optation 79, 86–8, 90, 172, 180
corporate colonialism 77
corporate culture 91
countryside 50
creative 16, 29–32, 34, 60–1, 113, 134, 136, 138, 160–1, 164, 182
creative process 60, 138
creativity 6, 58, 63, 74
critical aesthetics 91
critique 3–8, 11, 25, 66–7, 80, 90–1, 108, 115, 119, 121, 123, 179, 187

Critique of Judgment 170, 172, 175–6, 181–2, 184–6
crucifixion 109
crying point 29
Cubism 9, 10, 34
cultural ecology 50
cultural pluralism 71, 86
culture 41, 52, 74, 76–81, 84, 86, 88, 91, 107, 110, 112, 119–23, 125–6, 129, 136–7, 139, 149, 168

Dada 9–11, 34
dance 113, 120, 124–5, 130, 140
Daoism 52
dependent beauty 11
Dionysus 174, 175
direct social perception (DSP) 28, 173
Discourse on Method 41
disinterested appreciation 108, 115, 172
disinterestedness 25, 32, 114, 163, 167, 172
Disney World 71–82
divine soul 175
doubt 41–2, 119
dualism 63, 114
dualistic 12, 52, 148
dubito 41
dynamical sublime 104–5, 123–4
dynamic balance 61, 63

Eastern cultures 51–2, 113, 126
Eastern thought 54
eco-aesthetics 12
ecological 12, 47–8, 50–3, 55, 59–67, 171, 174–5
  aesthetics 12, 48, 50–1, 53, 55, 60–3, 65–6, 171, 174
  cognitivism 64
  design 60
  ethics 48, 61–2, 65
  perspective 48
  theory 59
ecology 45–50, 52–3, 58–64, 66
economics 60, 83
ecosystem 48, 50, 60–5, 155
eidos 41
eighteenth century 3, 11, 25, 57, 104, 114, 163
emotional co-optation 86, 89

Empedocles 141, 187
engaged perceiver 26
engagement 5, 25–6, 28–9, 31, 62–3, 83, 95, 96, 113–14, 134–5, 139–41, 159–61, 163, 184, 188–9
enlightenment 52, 124, 126
environment 5–8, 12, 24, 26–7, 29–30, 36, 45–50, 52–4, 57, 60–3, 65–6, 71–2, 74, 77–8, 83–6, 88, 131, 136–7, 154, 158, 162, 168, 188–9
environmental
  aesthetics 8, 12, 15, 45–7, 50, 53, 55, 61, 84, 137, 174, 188–9
  artist 34, 51
  consumption 5
  depredation 5
  design 28, 51, 60, 174
  disturbances 46
  ethics 8
  experience 6, 12, 49, 66–7
environs 174
Epcot Center 72, 74–5, 79
Étant donné 34–7, 39, 174
ethical values 62, 64–5, 67
ethics 13, 31, 63, 110, 147–9, 151, 162, 165, 168, 174
ethnic identity 56
Euripides 109
Europe 56, 110, 119, 175
evaluative judgment 6
everyday 8, 10, 12, 14–15, 29, 79, 85, 95, 97–8, 106, 171, 178, 180, 182
everyday aesthetics 8, 12, 14, 171, 178, 180
evolution 59, 66, 111, 162, 168
evolutionary theory 58–9
experience 3–7, 10, 12–17, 24–9, 31–2, 34, 38, 45, 48–51, 53–9, 62–6, 72, 79, 81–6, 88, 91, 95, 101, 103, 107–10, 113–15, 124, 130, 132–8, 140, 142–3, 146–9, 157–62, 164–9, 175
  of the arts 15, 26
  of beauty 83, 86
experience-based art 10
experiencing art 11
expressionism 9–10

Faces of Death   111
fascist aesthetic   112, 184
Fauvism   9
film   24, 80, 89, 98, 109–11, 113, 120–1, 137
Finland   45
Foi   139, 143, 187
folk epics   56
found art   26, 39, 97–8
Fountain   34, 37, 39
Freudian psychological theory   58
Frontierland   72
fulfilling environment   6
Future World   72, 74, 76, 78
Futurism   9–11

Giorgione   183
Girl with Pearl Earring   21
Golden Age   52
Greek Orphism   52
Greeks   56, 57
Ground Zero   98
Guernica   109, 183
gustatory co-optation   87

Happening   96
Hebrew *Bible*   51, 161
Hera   174
hidden participant   41
history of experience   49
human   4–7, 13–14, 16–17, 24, 27–32, 42, 46–56, 60–3, 65, 73, 82, 85, 86, 89–91, 95–7, 102, 104–6, 110–14, 126, 129, 131–2, 136–41, 143, 145–7, 149–51, 154, 156–8, 161–2, 164–6, 168, 180, 184, 187–9
  cultures   16
  environment   5, 17, 27, 52, 131, 162, 166
  experience   16, 24, 47, 52, 53, 95, 113, 145, 165
  life   5, 6, 14, 16, 28, 31–2, 56, 85, 91
  life experience   6
  needs   49, 164
  perceiver   50
  presence   27, 42, 82, 132, 137, 165
  sciences   27, 60, 149, 164
  sociality   145
  values   32
  world   4, 27, 31–2, 49, 51, 53–4, 65, 95, 97, 162, 164
humanism   5, 63, 124, 126
hyperreality   71, 90, 180

Iliad   109
Impressionism   9, 10
In Advance of a Broken Arm   37, 38, 42
inclusive unity   60–1, 63
India   52
individualism   149, 151–2, 154, 155
inquiry   3–5, 7–8, 12–13, 15, 26, 41, 45–8, 53, 59, 67, 84–5, 113
intellectual landscape   59
intimacy   137, 141, 143, 159, 161
invitational qualities   27
Italian Renaissance   110

Japan   52, 74, 179
Japanese culture   15
Japanese printmakers   29
judgment   5, 24, 66, 72, 80, 82, 98, 101, 103, 114, 121, 130, 132, 134, 139, 141, 146, 148, 156, 181

Kantian ethics   148
Kantian sublime   105, 121, 123

landscape   6, 12, 15, 17, 24, 26, 36, 45, 54, 60–1, 63, 65, 71, 75, 82, 84, 113, 133, 140
  design   6, 45, 61
language   15, 48, 50, 54, 58, 74, 109, 119, 139, 144, 158–9, 168–9, 184
  of environment   48
  of experience   50
literature   15, 45, 60–1, 87, 109, 119, 121, 170–1, 178, 180
love   13, 62, 139–44, 151, 159, 187–9

Magic Kingdom   72, 74, 76
Marquis de Sade   183
Marxism   58
mass culture   77, 91, 120
mass entertainment   71
mathematical sublime   104, 123–4
meaning of environment   26, 48–50
medical situations   30

Meditations on First Philosophy   41
mental eye   64
method of doubt   33, 42
MGM Studios   72–4, 76, 80
Middle Ages   110
Middle East   99
mid-eighteenth century   24, 84
mid-nineteenth century   59–60
mid-twentieth century   14, 58, 175
mode of experience   50, 105
modern art   9–10, 101, 121
modern artist   10
Modernism   177
modes   6–7, 10, 12, 56, 79, 107, 133, 141, 149, 156–7, 160–1
  of awareness   133
  of community   156, 160
morality   11, 63, 83, 97, 129, 141, 148–51, 153, 155, 168
moral propriety   58
moral value   12, 28, 102, 105–6
museum   11, 83

natural   6, 8, 16, 24, 26–9, 46–7, 51–2, 56–7, 60–3, 84, 90, 98, 107, 111, 123, 135, 146, 159, 162, 164, 168, 174
  beauty   6, 8, 16, 24, 26, 135
  science   47, 60, 168
  world   27, 51, 162, 164
nature   3–4, 7–8, 12, 24, 26, 28, 32, 51–2, 54, 56–61, 63–4, 66, 73, 78, 83, 85, 95–6, 104, 107, 110, 113–15, 122, 124, 129–30, 133, 136–7, 141, 147–8, 158–9, 161–2, 164–5, 181, 184
negative
  aesthetic   13, 108, 114, 166, 171, 183
  negativity   13, 105–6, 108, 115, 123–4, 126
  sublime   105–6, 123, 186
  values   13
neuroaesthetics   58
neuroscience   58
nineteenth century   9, 47, 58, 171
normative experience   24, 26, 66, 147, 164
Nude Descending a Staircase   34–5, 40

the object   10, 15–16, 25–6, 63, 85, 95, 97, 125–6, 132, 134–6, 140, 148, 158, 160–1, 163, 180, 186
the objective   16, 136
Oklahoma City   99
Op Art   9–10
Oriental art   61
Orphic   174
Orphic ideas   174

pain   13, 79, 102–4, 107–8, 110, 112, 121–2, 184
Papua New Guinea   139
participant   10, 14, 27, 39, 42, 131, 159–60
participation   11, 16, 49, 84, 108, 111, 113, 138, 141, 143, 165
passive role   30
perceiver   8, 26, 33, 37, 66
perception   4, 6, 24, 42, 53–5, 57, 59, 61–6, 84, 86, 89–91, 107, 130, 133, 136, 138–9, 142, 146, 158–9, 167
perceptual engagement   15, 31, 113
perceptual experience   7, 13, 17, 24, 28, 30, 47, 50, 55–6, 58, 61, 64, 83–4, 86–7, 90–1, 103, 107, 109–10, 113–14, 130, 133, 165, 175
the performative   16, 30
performer   26, 29, 125, 134–5, 137–8, 159–60
permanence   49
persuasion   160, 179
philosophy   11, 31, 33–4, 42, 46, 52–3, 58, 60, 82, 85, 97, 120, 122, 129, 132, 139, 146–7, 149–53, 155, 161–2, 167–8, 184
phronesis   122
Plato   41, 51, 56–8, 83, 96–7, 133, 140, 142, 146, 174, 186–7
Platonic philosophy   51
pleasure   26, 57, 74, 77, 80, 85, 89, 114, 121–2, 130, 133, 148, 180
pluralism   81, 143
political   5, 8, 12–14, 32, 52, 54–5, 58, 85–6, 89–91, 97, 99–102, 110, 112, 122, 124, 126, 142–3, 145–9, 152–5, 160, 162–3, 168, 188–9
  constraints   58
politics   13–14, 60, 84, 122, 145, 167, 184

Pol Pot 102
Pop Art 9–10
popular culture 71, 81, 89, 109, 121
postmodernism 71, 75–6, 80–2, 119–23, 125–6, 180
 architecture 75, 76
 sublime 105, 121–4, 126
practical art 61
practical wisdom 122
pre-Socratics 48
propaganda 89, 91, 160, 166
psychological co-optation 86
psychology 45, 59–60, 133, 145, 153, 175
public places 71, 88–9
pure beauty 25
pure sensation 4, 6, 133, 175

qualitative equilibrium 61
qualitative experience 148, 160
quantitative judgment 148
questioning aesthetics 4–7

Readymades 34–5, 37–9
reciprocity 16, 42, 134, 139, 141, 143–4, 154, 157, 160–2, 188–9
relational aesthetics 12–13
relational art 13
relativity physics 59, 66
Rembrandt 22, 25
Renaissance 57, 185
The Republic 51, 97, 174, 181, 187
ritual 109, 111, 139
Roman Coliseum 112

science 49, 52–3, 56–60, 62, 77–9, 82, 84, 119, 126, 133, 145–6, 161–2, 175
 in aesthetics 59
scientific
 cognition 59
 cognitivism 59
 knowledge 58, 65–7
 method 58
sculpture 34, 124–5, 131, 135, 138
seasonal changes 46
self 14, 25, 28, 41–2, 46, 75, 77, 89, 97, 99–100, 102, 111, 122, 125, 136, 141, 149–60, 169, 171, 187
self-portrait 22
sensation 13–14, 24, 130

sense
 awareness 84, 107, 130, 133
 engagement 47, 83
 experience 4, 6, 7, 24, 47, 49, 51, 84–6, 91, 97, 107, 133, 166, 170
 imagination 83
 perception 4, 6–7, 32, 47, 57, 101, 166
 qualities 11
seventeenth century 41, 57
situation 11–14, 25–6, 28–31, 33, 42, 45, 65–6, 72, 77, 85, 98, 102, 105, 131–2, 135–41, 150, 157, 159–60, 164, 188–9
social
 aesthetics 12–13, 32, 84, 129, 131–2, 137, 142, 162, 173
 behavior 110
 character 129
 critique 11, 13
 environment 29, 131
 ethics 6–7, 142, 149, 151, 188–9
 experience 13, 24, 147, 152
 order 103, 143–4, 147, 152, 154, 168
 practices 5, 7
 psychology 112, 133
 relationship 14, 31
the social 6–7, 12–13, 24–5, 47, 52, 55, 58, 60, 90, 99–101, 103, 106, 119, 129–32, 136–8, 142–3, 146, 150–2, 156, 161–3, 167–8, 182
Socrates 81, 142, 161
The Socratic tradition 81
somatic 4, 6, 26, 40, 84
 engagement 84
 experience 40
 memory 4, 6
Sophocles 109
The Sopranos 111
spectator 10, 110, 113–14
Stoics 81, 142
sublime 14, 80, 83, 103–5, 121–6, 181–2
sub specie aeternitatis 49
suburban 50
Surrealism 9–10
sustainability 5

Taoism 113

taste   25, 54, 62, 84, 87, 89, 97, 112, 114, 120, 122, 138, 142, 168, 179
technological co-optation   86, 89
technology   72, 76–7, 79, 87, 119, 124, 154
television   109, 137
terrorism   96, 98–103, 105, 115, 181
terrorist attack   98, 104–5, 108, 181
theater   24, 71, 98, 102, 105, 109, 112–13, 125, 136–7, 139–40
theme park   71, 78–81, 177
theocentric   59
theological doctrine   58
theory of catharsis   57
Titans   174, 175
Tomorrowland   72
traditional   8, 10, 12–16, 54, 60, 63, 66, 74–5, 84, 96–7, 101, 103, 113, 124, 126, 130–2, 135, 149–50, 168, 170
  aesthetics   131, 135, 167
  art   12, 16, 74, 96
  paradigms   8, 10
  sublime   126
  theory   16, 131, 167
tragic drama   57, 83
transcendent experience   57
truth   41, 51, 53, 82, 96, 126
twentieth century   33–4, 39, 41, 80–1, 84, 96, 119, 122, 132, 184

Umwelt   174
United Kingdom   45, 74
United States   45, 74, 78, 86, 90, 179
unity of form   63
urban
  aesthetics   8
  life   13
  urban   8, 13, 50, 78
utility   16, 25

Viennese actionist   111
viewer participation   10
violence   83, 95–6, 98–101, 104, 108–15, 144, 181, 183–4

ways of seeing   10
weakness   151, 154
weather   15, 46–7, 49
  events   46
  patterns   49
Western
  aesthetics   57, 60, 62, 84
  culture   41, 51–2, 54, 114, 138
  philosophy   3, 12, 41, 58
  thought   41, 57, 146
World Showcase   72, 74, 76, 78–9

Zen   126
Zeus   174